D0088927

belief

belief

readings on the reason for faith

Francis S. Collins

An Imprint of HarperCollinsPublishers

HarperOne

List of credits/permissions can be found on page 325 and constitutes as a continuation of this copyright page.

HarperCollins books may be purchased for educational, business, or sales promotional use. For information please write: Special Markets Department, HarperCollins Publishers, 10 East 53rd Street, New York, NY 10022.

HarperCollins Web site: http://www.harpercollins.com

FIRST EDITION

Library of Congress Cataloging-in-Publication Data
Collins, Francis S.
Belief : readings on the reason for faith / by Francis Collins. — 1st ed.
p. cm.
ISBN 978-0-06-178734-8
1. Faith. I. Title.
BT771.3.C64 2010
202'.2—dc22 2009041653

10 11 12 13 14 RRD(H) 10 9 8 7 6 5 4 3 2 1

CONTENTS

With All Your Mind

FRANCIS S. COLLINS

AT THE TOP of my stairway, positioned so that I pass it several times a day, is a verse from the Bible that has been elegantly rendered and decorated by my daughter. "If any man lacks wisdom," says the quote from the book of James, "let him ask of God, who gives to all willingly and without reproach, and it will be given to him." The verse powerfully points to the connection between faith and reason. But it also presumes the seeker of wisdom already has some sense of the Divine, and knows where to go for help. A more fundamental question is whether God exists at all.

"Is there a God?" has to be the most central and profound question we humans ask. Perhaps you have heard some say that this query cannot really be approached by reason. "You just have to have faith" is often the response an earnest seeker receives. But many people down through the ages have found that answer unsatisfying. Sure, they admit, you can't prove God's existence, or we would all be committed believers in lockstep to some universal faith—but how interesting would that be?

Very well . . . so absolute proof of God's existence is not going to be available in this life. But that doesn't mean deeply rational arguments for faith are not available for inspection and debate by interested believers, seekers, and skeptics. In fact, there is a fascinating range of literature available to assist the curious mind, some of it extending back many centuries.

This anthology on the subject of belief aims to provide a sampler of that rich intellectual tradition. If a potential adventure into these deep but refreshing waters intrigues you, then this collection is for you. Within these pages you will find the reflections of many of the world's greatest thinkers, from Plato to Pascal to Plantinga, and many others in between. Some of the excerpts will require more than one reading to digest. Others will resonate immediately with your experience, perhaps clarifying truths that you already sensed but never quite articulated. Some entries will be heartrending in their honesty about the tragic imperfections of the human condition, and the deep longing for something better. A few essays will make you smile, or even laugh out loud.

By picking up this book, you are displaying a welcome curiosity. But you are also countering several current trends. The increasingly secular Western world seems to be losing touch with the long history of intellectual arguments supporting a rational basis for faith. Our postmodern culture questions whether there is such a thing as absolute truth, and our philosophers cast doubt on the foundations of morality. We increasingly hear from those who borrow the latest findings from science to argue that humans are purely naturalistic beings. While these arguments may hold sway in academic circles, they generally fail to resonate with the general public.

All is not well in the church either. In the United States, 85 percent of Americans profess belief in God. But the percentage of believers is declining, and a sense of restlessness can be found in many faith communities. Many factors are contributing to this malaise—the sense that the church is out of touch with modern life, the stories of church leaders caught in acts of hypocrisy, the unfortunate linkage of large components of the U.S. Christian church to political agendas that project a narrow-minded and unloving image, the aggressive attacks by vociferous members of the "New Atheist" community, and the fear of the consequences of religious fundamentalism in the wake of 9/11. But for many young seekers and believers hungry for an understanding of the basis of faith, the absence of a vibrant intellectual component, particularly in the evangelical Christian church, is another significant factor that makes faith relatively unappealing. Perhaps the most scathing indictment of this situation was put forward by Mark Noll in 1994. "The scandal of the evangelical mind," he wrote in a book by that same name, "is that there is not much of an evangelical mind." Speaking recently with Professor Noll, I gather that there hasn't been much reason since then for him to change his point of view. Among other goals, this book is a modest effort to help change that.

~

A Brief History of the Relationship of Faith and Reason

Deliberations about faith and reason stretch back many centuries. Leaders of the world's great religions—from Moses to the Buddha to Confucius, Jesus, Augustine, Mohamed, Aquinas, and Maimonides—used rational arguments with great effectiveness to promote truths about faith and humankind. After a period of relative stagnation during the Middle Ages, the Renaissance brought scientific and theological explorations together in novel and highly productive ways. Theology was then called the "Queen of the Sciences"; Kepler, Copernicus, and Galileo were all men of strong religious faith, even as they upset the prevailing geocentric applecart. And Isaac Newton produced more written materials on biblical interpretation than all of his groundbreaking contributions to physics and mathematics combined. "Gravity," he wrote, "explains the motions of the planets, but it cannot explain who set the planets in motion. God governs all things and knows all that is or can be done."

The harmony of faith and reason began to show serious cracks in Europe, however, as the Enlightenment and the associated rise of materialism took hold in the late eighteenth century. The primary basis for a rejection of religion at that time actually rested not so much on logical arguments, but on resistance to the oppressive authority of the church. Expressing the views of many at the onset of the French Revolution, Voltaire wrote, "Is it any wonder that there are atheists in the world, when the church behaves so abominably?" As resistance to religious perspectives continued to grow in the nineteenth century, Darwin's theory of evolution upset the long-standing argument from design that had been a secure linchpin for the need for a Creator by theologians over the centuries. Philosophers joined the fray: Feuerbach proposed that God was nothing more than a human projection, and Freud adopted this same perspective in his influential writings about God as a delusion based on father-figure wish fulfillment.

Meanwhile, the initial strength of a strongly rational form of Christianity in the United States, buttressed by contributions from church leaders such as Jonathan Edwards, encountered a progressive dilution by naturalistic worldviews in the late nineteenth century—originally in the universities, but subsequently across many different social strata. Responding to the threat, the rise of fundamentalism in the Christian church gained momentum and refocused attention on the basic principles of the faith, but did so in a way that emphasized supernaturalism, the imminent second coming of Christ, and, consequentially, a downgrading of the importance of the life of the mind. Again from Mark Noll: "The treatment of fundamentalism may be said to have succeeded; the patient survived. But at least for the life of the mind, what survived was a patient horribly disfigured by the cure itself."

The Need for Re-engagement

And what about now? It is fair to say that public discussions of faith and reason in the early twenty-first century are more often than not abrasive and contentious, and tend to be dominated by extreme voices. There's not a lot of listening going on. On one side, angry atheist manifestos from authors such as Richard Dawkins, Christopher Hitchens, Daniel Dennett, and Sam Harris argue that religion is not only irrational, but that it is the source of most of the evil in the world. On the other side, certain ultraconservative Christian, Jewish, and Muslim leaders claim that solid conclusions from science, like the age of the universe, are not to be trusted, because of a disagreement with their personal readings of ancient sacred texts. There is now a camp for kids in the United Kingdom that aims to indoctrinate them with atheism, and a Creation Museum in Kentucky that shows humans romping with dinosaurs. Both of these extreme positions represent a closing of the mind to further debate, and a manifestation of hardened fundamentalism. Most people don't fully identify with either extreme, but aren't entirely sure how to respond. The battle of worldviews is having many real casualties.

This collection of essays is an attempt to provide a modest antidote to the cacophony of extreme voices dominating the microphones, bookshelves, and airways. Faith and reason are not, as many seem to be arguing today, mutually exclusive. They never have been. The letter to the Hebrews in the New Testament defines faith as "the substance of things hoped for, the evidence of things not seen." Evidence! Down through the centuries, humanity's greatest minds have developed interesting and compelling arguments about faith, based on moral philosophy, observations about nature, and examination of sacred texts. But outside of limited academic circles, these deeper perspectives are not heard from much these days. The goal of this anthology is to present some of these points of view, to spur on a more nuanced and intellectually rich discussion of the most profound questions that humanity asks: Is there a God? If so, what is God like? Does God care about me? And what, if anything, is the meaning of life?

My Own Perspective on Faith and Reason

I am an unlikely editor for this collection. I am not a philosopher or a theologian. Raised with only superficial exposure to religious perspectives as a child, I became an agnostic and later an atheist. Studying quantum mechanics in a PhD program at Yale, I saw no reason to believe in anything outside of the mathematical equations that described the behavior of matter and energy. I had never heard any arguments that connected faith in God with reason, and I assumed that believers must have to check their brains at the church door in order to enter.

But my own scientific and humanitarian interests subsequently led me to pursue a different path, and I enrolled in medical school. There the questions of life and death that had been purely hypothetical became wrenchingly real. As I sat at the bedside of good, honorable people who were facing the end of their life, and for whom faith in God remained a source of peace when medicine had failed them, I tried to imagine myself in the same position. And I had to admit, if asked to trade places, I would not be peaceful—I would be angry and terrified. Though I had previously assumed that any such comfort from faith was just a delusion, I had to confess that I didn't really understand why so many people around me—including some of my professors—were believers. I didn't know about "Pascal's Wager"—that there is much more to be lost by denying God's existence than by accepting it—but it began to dawn on me that I had ignored the seriousness of getting an answer to the God question. If there was any actual evidence to support belief, if faith really rested on a foundation in reason, then I'd better find out about it.

Thus began a personal exploration, in my midtwenties, of the rational basis for faith. Never having taken a course in philosophy or theology, this was all brand new. Initially, I tried to read some of the foundational texts of the monotheistic religions, and found much of their language inscrutable. Thankfully, a kind pastor in my neighborhood, aware of my confusion and the need for something more accessible, pointed me to C. S. Lewis's marvelous synthesis of the reasons for faith, *Mere Christianity*. I was stunned at the force of the logic from this Oxford scholar that filled every paragraph of this little book. As I absorbed the arguments, the door to the possibility of God began to open, and as it did, I began to see that the signposts had been around me all along.

Some of the evidence derived from nature itself. As a scientist, I was then and am now deeply invested in the idea that nature is ordered, and that science can discover it. But it never occurred to me to ask why order exists. Going even deeper, I had never really considered the most profound philosophical question of all—why is there something instead of nothing? And if there are realities called matter and energy that behave in certain ways, what about those mathematical equations I had been so in love with as a student of quantum mechanics—why should they work at all? What, to use Nobel Laureate Wigner's classic phrase, accounts for the "unreasonable effectiveness of mathematics"? Could this be a pointer toward a mathematical mind behind the universe?

And then there was the Big Bang. From observations about the red shift of retreating galaxies in the far-flung universe, and the measurement of background microwave radiation that reflects an echo of a massive explosion 13.7 billion years ago, it is clear that  our universe had a beginning, in an unimaginable cosmological singularity. The laws of physics break down there. If the universe had a beginning, how was it created? Nature has not been observed to create itself. To postulate a creator that is also part of nature provides no solution. Instead, one seems obligated to yield to the logic of the cosmological argument (called *Kalam* by Islamic scholars) that there was a First Cause, a supernatural Creator outside of the laws of nature, and outside of time and space.

Further strengthening the arguments for design in the universe, I learned about fine-tuning, the infinitely interesting observations often encapsulated in the somewhat confusing term "The Anthropic Principle." Basically, the simple mathematical laws that describe the behavior of matter and energy involve constants whose value cannot be derived; they must be determined by experiment. Gravity, for instance, follows a simple inverse square law as worked out by Isaac Newton:

$$F = G\frac{m_1 m_2}{r^2}$$

where m_1 and m_2 are the masses of two objects, r is the distance between them, and F is the gravitational force of attraction. G, the gravitational constant, was inferred to exist by Newton, but its value (6.673×10^{-11} N m^2 kg^{-2}) was only accurately determined by experiment many years later. The speed of light, the mass of the electron, and the strong and weak nuclear forces are other examples of physical constants that have a profound effect on nature. Over the past half century, mathematical physicists have investigated the consequences of slight variations in these constants. The conclusion is astounding: if any of these were to vary by even the tiniest degree, a universe capable of sustaining any imaginable form of life would be impossible. Thus, our universe cannot be considered just a lucky coincidence—the odds are way too small. Instead, one is forced to choose between three alternatives: 1) there may be as yet undiscovered laws of nature that demand that these constants only have these specific values; 2) there must be an almost infinite series of unobservable parallel universes with different values of these constants, but we can only exist in the one where everything turned out just right (the "Goldilocks Enigma" in the title of Paul Davies's recent book); or 3) there must be some intelligence behind our universe that has established these constants in a way that permits stability, complexity, life, and consciousness. Few physicists believe that option #1 is correct. And choosing *either* option #2 or #3 has to be considered a leap of faith.

These arguments from the observed order of the universe are compelling, but they say little about whether such a "creator" God would be interested in human beings. To be sure, the fine-tuning arguments, including the precise resonance of the masses of helium and beryllium that makes carbon-based life a possibility, encourage the notion that God must have been interested in something more than a sterile and boring universe. But what evidence might we have that God cares about each one of us? Do rational arguments for faith stop at deism (a "watchmaker" God who made the universe and wound it up, but is not interested in humans), or can they extend to theism as well?

This brings us to one of philosophy and theology's longest and deepest conversations, the existence of the Moral Law. One of the most notable and unique characteristics of humanity, across centuries, cultures, and geographic locations, is this universal human grasp of the concept of right and wrong, and an inner voice that calls us to do the right thing. We may not always agree on what behaviors are right (since those are heavily influenced by culture), but we generally agree that we should try to do good and avoid evil. When we break this Moral Law (which happens frequently, if we are honest), we make excuses, only further demonstrating that we feel bound by the law in our dealings with others. How can this be accounted for? If God actually exists, and has an interest in humans—a unique species with gifts of consciousness, intelligence, and free will—wouldn't the existence of this law, written on all of our hearts, be an interesting signpost toward a holy and personal God?

Many modern readers will be quick to object to this argument. Isn't this just a consequence of evolution? Before addressing that objection, let's be clear here: the central tenets of Darwin's theory—including gradual change over time, natural selection based on reproductive fitness, and descent from a common ancestor—have been convincingly shown to be correct (including for humans) by multiple lines of investigation, most powerfully from my own professional field of research on DNA. The "theory" of evolution is thus a theory in the same sense, and with the same relative strength of evidence, as the theory of gravitation. In the oft-quoted words of Theodosius Dobzhansky, a leading evolutionist and a believer in God, "Nothing in biology makes sense except in the light of evolution."

Though Darwin's publication of *The Origin of Species* in 1859

was widely embraced by many in the church as an insight into God's method of creation, more recently evolution has been perceived as a direct assault on belief in God. Philosopher Dan Dennett is fond of calling Darwin's theory a "universal acid" for any tendency toward religious thinking. But surely this claim is going beyond the evidence. If God has any real significance, God must be at least in part outside of nature (unless you are a pantheist, who believes that God and nature are the same thing). Science, including the science of evolution, is limited to exploring and understanding the natural world. Therefore, to apply scientific arguments to the question of God's existence, as if this were somehow a showstopper, is committing a category error. If God Almighty, unlimited by space or time, chose to use the mechanism of evolution to carry out a creative plan that led to a truly marvelous diversity of living things on a blue planet near the outer edge of a spiral galaxy, we would have to admit that this was a powerful and highly effective plan.

Now back to the Moral Law. Evolutionary arguments, which ultimately depend on reproductive fitness as the overarching goal, may explain some parts of this human urge toward moral behavior, especially if self-sacrificing altruistic acts are done on behalf of relatives or those from whom one might expect some future reciprocal benefit. But all evolutionary models lead to the requirement for reflexive hostility to outside groups, and we humans do not seem to have gotten that memo. Quite the opposite—we especially admire cases in which individuals make great sacrifices for strangers: think of Mother Teresa, or Oskar Schindler, or the Good Samaritan.

We should be somewhat skeptical of atheists who dismiss these acts of radical altruism as some sort of evolutionary misfiring. If these noble acts are frankly a scandal to reproductive fitness, might they instead point in a different direction, as argued by philosophers down through the ages—toward a holy, loving, and caring God, who instilled the Moral Law in each of us as a sign of our special nature and as a call to relationship with the Almighty?

Do not get me wrong. I am not arguing that the existence of the Moral Law somehow proves God's existence. Such proofs cannot be provided by the study of nature. And I freely admit that there is an inherent danger in arguing that the Moral Law points to some sort of supernatural intervention in the early days of human history;

this has the flavor of a "God of the gaps" argument. After all, much still remains to be understood about evolution's influence on human nature. But even if radically altruistic human acts can ultimately be explained on the basis of evolutionary mechanisms, this would do nothing to exclude God's hand. For if God chose the process of evolution in the beginning to create humans in *imago Dei* ("the image of God"), it would also be perfectly reasonable for God to use this same process to instill knowledge of the Moral Law.

A deeper question raised by this debate is the fundamental nature of good and evil. Does morality actually have any foundation? To be consistent, a committed atheist, who argues that evolution can fully account for all aspects of human nature, must also argue that the human urge toward altruism, including its most radical and self-sacrificial forms, is a purely evolutionary artifact. This forces the conclusion that the concepts of good and evil have no real foundation, and that we have been hoodwinked by evolution into thinking that morality provides meaningful standards of judgment. Few atheists seem willing to own up to this disturbing and depressing consequence of their worldview. On the contrary, the most aggressive of them seem quite comfortable pointing to the evil they see religion as having inspired. Isn't this rather inconsistent?

For myself, the arguments from the nature of the universe and the existence of the Moral Law led me, with considerable initial resistance, to a serious consideration of the possibility of a God who not only wound up the clock but who also has an enduring interest in a relationship with humans. In all honesty, that discovery wasn't the answer I expected or desired. But it became more and more compelling. And as it did, I realized that seeing all of humanity's nobler attributes through the constricted lens of atheism and materialism ultimately leads to philosophical impoverishment, and even to the

necessity of giving up concepts of benevolence and justice. I also found that a whole world of interesting questions opened up for me once I accepted the possibility of a spiritual aspect to humanity.

In further searching to discover the character of God, I sought greater understanding of the world's great religions. From this pursuit, at age twenty-seven, I became a committed Christian. I will not detail the reasons here that led to my specific decision to follow Christ, since I have written about that experience in *The Language of God: A Scientist Presents Evidence for Belief* (Free Press, 2006). And for a deeper exploration of the potential harmony of the scientific and spiritual worldviews, I would commend www.biologos.org, where my colleagues and I have embarked on an effort to provide responses to the questions about science and faith that are most frequently posed by believers, seekers, and skeptics.

Assembling an Anthology

Although I am generally considered a credible scientist, I am at best an amateur philosopher, and I have no credentials in theology at all. So being invited to curate a series of classic essays on faith and reason has been a challenging experience. I have been greatly aided by the hard work and significant contributions of my capable research assistant, Meg Saunders, who has served as a true intellectual colleague in this project.

Narrowing down a limited set of authors has been almost impossibly difficult. And with a limit on how many entries we could include in this book, it is virtually certain that anyone perusing the Table of Contents will generate their own list of serious omissions. Complaints are expected! Once having chosen a particular author for potential inclusion, it proved quite challenging to find the perfect essay that fit the theme of this book, as we sought a contribution that would be self-contained and brief enough to be read in a single sitting. Furthermore, as we hoped this collection would be a compendium for the reading pleasure of seekers, believers, and skeptics from all walks of life, the accessibility of the prose became a prime requirement for inclusion.

These realities led to a final set of choices that regrettably left out some historically important voices who proved to have difficult writing styles for the nonexpert (Aristotle and Immanuel Kant, for instance), but included others (like Madeleine L'Engle), who might surprise the reader who was expecting a lineup of the "usual suspects." The majority of the contributors write from a Christian perspective, however, Mahatma Gandhi and the Dalai Lama make appearances, as do two compelling Jewish voices, Elie Wiesel and

Viktor Frankl. A special effort was made to identify women authors, but, unfortunately, because of the scarce representation of women in the world's output of literature on faith and reason, this was a difficult goal to meet. There is no doubt that this skewed representation needs to be corrected in the future.

There proved to be no perfect way to organize these readings. One possibility would have been to present them chronologically, beginning with Plato and extending to the modern era. An even simpler approach would have been to present them alphabetically. But to assist the reader in diving in, the selections are organized around ten themes. The list of themes begins with classic arguments for faith and reason and progresses to other major issues, such as the meaning of truth, the existence of evil and suffering, and the possibility of miracles.

I would suggest starting with Bishop Tom Wright's compelling and intriguing summary of the modern case for faith and reason, and then heading off in whatever direction you find the most interesting—or the most vexing. If you encounter an essay that doesn't speak to you, move on to another one within the same theme. If you find a selection to be particularly helpful, seek out other works by that author—there is a wealth of material out there, and much of it can be downloaded from the Internet.

In Matthew 22.36–37, Jesus is asked by the disciples to name the greatest commandment in the Law. He responds, "Love the Lord your God with all your heart and all your soul and all your mind." I find it of great interest that Christ added "all your mind" to this exhortation (the original verse from Deuteronomy does not include this). But here in the twenty-first century, many seem to have concluded that the spiritual experience and the life of the mind ought to occupy separate domains, and that disruptions, conflicts, and disenchantments will result if the firewall comes down. Surely humanity's ongoing search for truth is not enriched by such limitations. In the words of Socrates (at least as imagined by Plato), the key to a fully mature and richly rewarding life, both for us as individuals and as a society, is to "follow the argument wherever it leads," unafraid of the consequences. If this collection of essays provides even a small encouragement in this direction for the seeker, the believer, or the skeptic, that will be gratifying indeed!

belief

Getting Started:

Stating the Modern Case

N. T. WRIGHT

Nicholas Thomas "Tom" Wright (1948–) is a British academic, theologian, and priest. Currently, he serves as the Bishop of Durham in the Church of England. A prolific writer and widely admired expert on the New Testament, he has published more than thirty books.

During his career Wright has been both a student and lecturer at Oxford University, where he discovered his principal intellectual enjoyment—the exchange produced by a formidable examination of the intersection between faith and reason. From this passion, he is able to engage his reader on topics that resonate deeply within them without making them feel preached to or marginalized. From the excerpt chosen, Wright takes us very deliberately into two distinct but related discussions: one on justice and the other on spirituality. Using imagery and prose harkening back to his forerunner at Oxford, C. S. Lewis, Wright challenges us to consider these age-old subjects in a new light, paying particular attention to how they relate to an often unarticulated longing deep within our souls. The following selection is from Simply Christian.

Putting the World to Rights

I HAD A dream the other night, a powerful and interesting dream. And the really frustrating thing about it is that I can't remember what it was about. I had a flash of it as I woke up, enough to make me think how extraordinary and meaningful it was; and then it was gone. And so, to misquote T. S. Eliot, I had the meaning but missed the experience.

Our passion for justice often seems like that. We dream the dream of justice. We glimpse, for a moment, a world at one, a world put to rights, a world where things work out, where societies function fairly and efficiently, where we not only know what we ought to do but actually do it. And then we wake up and come back to reality. But what are we hearing when we're dreaming that dream?

It's as though we can hear, not perhaps a voice itself, but the echo of a voice: a voice speaking with calm, healing authority, speaking about justice, about things being put to rights, about peace and hope and prosperity for all. The voice continues to echo in our imagination, our subconscious. We want to go back and listen to it again, but having woken up we can't get back into the dream. Other people sometimes tell us it was just a fantasy, and we're half-inclined to believe them, even though that condemns us to cynicism.

But the voice goes on, calling us, beckoning us, luring us to think that there might be such a thing as justice, as the world being put to rights, even though we find it so elusive. We're like moths trying to fly to the moon. We all know there's something called justice, but we can't quite get to it.

You can test this out easily. Go to any school or playgroup where the children are old enough to talk to each other. Listen to what they are saying. Pretty soon one child will say to another, or perhaps to a teacher: "That's not *fair!*"

You don't have to teach children about fairness and unfairness. A sense of justice comes with the kit of being human. We know about it, as we say, in our bones.

You fall off your bicycle and break your leg. You go to the hospital and they fix it. You stagger around on crutches for a while. Then, rather gingerly, you start to walk normally again. Pretty soon you've forgotten about the whole thing. You're back to normal. There *is* such a thing as putting something to rights, as fixing it, as getting it back on track. You can fix a broken leg, a broken toy, a broken television.

So why can't we fix injustice?

It isn't for want of trying. We have courts of law and magistrates and judges and lawyers in plenty. I used to live in a part of London where there was so much justice going on that it hurt—lawmakers, law enforcers, a Lord Chief Justice, a police headquarters, and, just a couple of miles away, enough barristers to run a battleship. (Though, since they would all be arguing with one another, the battleship might be going around in circles.) Other countries have similarly heavyweight organizations designed to make laws and implement them.

And yet we have a sense that justice itself slips through our fingers. Sometimes it works; often it doesn't. Innocent people get convicted; guilty people are let off. The bullies, and those who can bribe their way out of trouble, get away with wrongdoing—not always, but often enough for us to notice, and to wonder why.

People hurt others badly and walk away laughing. Victims don't always get compensated. Sometimes they spend the rest of their lives coping with sorrow, hurt, and bitterness.

The same thing is going on in the wider world. Countries invade other countries and get away with it. The rich use the power of their money to get even richer while the poor, who can't do anything about it, get even poorer. Most of us scratch our heads and wonder why, and then go out and buy another product whose profit goes to the rich company.

I don't want to be too despondent. There *is* such a thing as justice, and sometimes it comes out on top. Brutal tyrannies are overthrown. Apartheid was dismantled. Sometimes wise and creative leaders arise and people follow them into good and just actions. Serious criminals are sometimes caught, brought to trial, convicted, and punished. Things that are seriously wrong in society are sometimes put splendidly to rights. New projects give hope to the poor. Diplomats achieve solid and lasting peace. But just when you think it's safe to relax . . . it all goes wrong again.

And even though we can solve a few of the world's problems, at least temporarily, we know perfectly well that there are others we simply can't and won't.

Just after Christmas of 2004 an earthquake and tidal wave killed more than three times as many people in a single day as the total number of American soldiers who died in the entire Vietnam War. There are some things in our world, on our *planet,* which make us say, "That's not right!" even when there's nobody to blame. A tectonic plate's got to do what a tectonic plate's got to do. The earthquake wasn't caused by some wicked global capitalist, by a late-blossoming Marxist, or by a fundamentalist with a bomb. It just *happened.* And in that happening we see a world in pain, a world out of joint, a world where things occur that we seem powerless to make right.

The most telling examples are the ones closest to home. I have high moral standards. I have thought about them. I have preached about them. Good heavens, I have even written *books* about them.

And still I break them. The line between justice and injustice, between things being right and things not being right, can't be drawn between "us" and "them." It runs right down through the middle of each one of us. The ancient philosophers, not least Aristotle, saw this as a wrinkle in the system, a puzzle at several levels. We all know what we ought to do (give or take a few details); but we all manage, at least some of the time, not to do it.

Isn't this odd?

How does it happen that, on the one hand, we all share not just a sense that there is such a thing as justice, but a passion for it, a deep longing that things should be put to rights, a sense of out-of-jointness that goes on nagging and gnawing and sometimes screaming at us—and yet, on the other hand, after millennia of human struggle and searching and love and longing and hatred and hope and fussing and philosophizing, we still can't seem to get much closer to it than people did in the most ancient societies we can discover?

The Cry for Justice

Recent years have witnessed extravagant examples of human actions that have outraged our sense of justice. People sometimes talk as if the last fifty years have seen a decline in morality. But actually these have been some of the most morally sensitive, indeed moralistic, times in recorded history. People care, and care passionately, about the places where the world needs putting to rights.

Powerful generals sent millions to die in the trenches in the First World War, while they themselves lived in luxury behind the lines or back home. When we read the poets who found themselves caught up in that war, we sense behind their poignant puzzlement a smoldering anger at the folly and, yes, the injustice of it all. Why should it have happened? How can we put it to rights?

An explosive cocktail of ideologies sent millions to die in the gas chambers. Bits and pieces of religious prejudice, warped philosophies, fear of people who are "different," economic hardship, and the need for scapegoats were all mixed together by a brilliant demagogue who told people what at least some of them wanted to believe, and who demanded human sacrifices as the price of "progress." You only have to mention Hitler or the Holocaust to awaken the question: How did it happen? Where is justice? How can we get it? How can we put things right? And, in particular, How can we stop it from happening again?

But we can't, or so it seems. Nobody stopped the Turks from killing millions of Armenians from 1915 to 1917 (in fact, Hitler famously referred to this when he was encouraging his colleagues to kill Jews). Nobody stopped Tutsis and Hutus in Rwanda from killing each other in very large numbers in 1994. The world had said "Never again" after the Nazi Holocaust, but genocide *was* happening again, and we discovered to our horror that there was nothing we could do to stop it.

And then there was apartheid. Massive injustice was perpetrated against a very large population in South Africa for a very long time. Other countries, of course, had done similar things, but they had been more effective in squashing opposition. Think of the "reservations" for "Native Americans": I remember the shock when I saw an old "cowboys and Indians" movie and realized that when I was young, I—like most of my contemporaries—would have gone along unquestioningly with the assumption that cowboys were basically good and Indians basically bad. The world has woken up to the reality of racial prejudice since then; but getting rid of it is like squashing the air out of a balloon. You deal with one corner only to find it popping up somewhere else. The world got together over apartheid and said, "This won't do"; but at least some of the moral energy came from what the psychologists call *projection*—that is, condemning someone else for something we are doing ourselves. Rebuking someone on the other side of the world (while ignoring the same problems back home) is very convenient, and it provides a deep but spurious sense of moral satisfaction.

And now we have the new global evils: rampant, uncaring, and irresponsible materialism and capitalism on the one hand; raging, unthinking religious fundamentalism on the other. As one famous book puts it, we have "Jihad versus McWorld." (Whether there is such a thing as caring capitalism, or for that matter thoughtful fundamentalism, isn't the point at the moment.) This brings us back to where we were a few minutes ago. It doesn't take a PhD in macroeconomics to know that if the rich are getting richer by the minute, and the poor poorer, there is something badly wrong.

Meanwhile, we all want a happy and secure home life. Dr. Johnson, the eighteenth-century conversationalist, once remarked that the aim and goal of all human endeavor is "to be happy at home." But in the Western world, and many other parts as well, homes and families are tearing themselves apart. The gentle art of being gentle—of kindness and forgiveness, sensitivity and thoughtfulness, and generosity and humility and good old-fashioned love—have gone out of fashion. Ironically, everyone is demanding their "rights," and this demand is so shrill that it destroys one of the most basic "rights," if we can put it like that: the "right," or at least the longing and hope, to have a peaceful, stable, secure, and caring place to live, to be, to learn, and to flourish.

Once again people ask the question: Why is it like this? Does it *have* to be like this? Can things be put to rights and, if so, how? Can the world be rescued? Can *we* be rescued?

And once again we find ourselves asking: Isn't it odd that it should be like that? Isn't it strange that we should all want things to be put to rights but can't seem to do it? And isn't the oddest thing of all the fact that I, myself, know what I ought to do but often don't do it?

A Voice or a Dream?

There are three basic ways of explaining this sense of the echo of a voice, this call to justice, this dream of a world (and all of us within it) put to rights.

We can say, if we like, that it is indeed only a dream, a projection of childish fantasies, and that we have to get used to living in the world the way it is. Down that road we find Machiavelli and Nietzsche, the world of naked power and grabbing what you can get, the world where the only sin is to be caught.

Or we can say, if we like, that the dream is of a different world altogether, a world where we really belong, where everything is indeed put to rights, a world into which we can escape in our dreams in the present and hope to escape one day for good—but a world that has little purchase on the present world except that people who live in this one sometimes find themselves dreaming of that one. That approach leaves the unscrupulous bullies running this world, but it consoles us with the thought that things will be better somewhere, sometime, even if there's not much we can do about it here and now.

Or we can say, if we like, that the reason we have these dreams, the reason we have a sense of a memory of the echo of a voice, is that there is someone speaking to us, whispering in our inner ear—

someone who cares very much about this present world and our present selves, and who has made us and the world for a purpose that will indeed involve justice, things being put to rights, *ourselves* being put to rights, the world being rescued at last.

Three of the great religious traditions have taken this last option, and not surprisingly they are related; they are, as it were, second cousins. Judaism speaks of a God who made the world and built into it the passion for justice because it was his own passion. Christianity speaks of this same God having brought that passion into play (indeed, "passion plays" in various senses are a characteristic feature of Christianity) in the life and work of Jesus of Nazareth. Islam draws on some Jewish and some Christian stories and ideas and creates a new synthesis in which the revelation of God's will in the Qur'an is the ideal that would put the world to rights, if only it were obeyed. There are many differences among these three traditions, but on this point they are agreed, over against other philosophies and religions: the reason we think we have heard a voice is because we have. It wasn't a dream. There are ways of getting back in touch with that voice and making what it says come true. In real life. In *our* real lives.

The Hidden Spring

There was once a powerful dictator who ruled his country with an iron will. Every aspect of life was thought through and worked out according to a rational system. Nothing was left to chance.

The dictator noticed that the water sources around the country were erratic and in some cases dangerous. There were thousands of springs of water, often in the middle of towns and cities. They could be useful, but sometimes they caused floods, sometimes they got polluted, and often they burst out in new places and damaged roads, fields, and houses.

The dictator decided on a sensible, rational policy. The whole country, or at least every part where there was any suggestion of water, would be paved over with concrete so thick that no spring of water could ever penetrate it. The water that people needed would be brought to them by a complex system of pipes. Furthermore, the dictator decided, he would use the opportunity, while he was at it, to put into the water various chemicals that would make the people healthy. With the dictator controlling the supply, everyone would have what he decided they needed, and there wouldn't be any more nuisance from unregulated springs.

For many years the plan worked just fine. People got used to their water coming from the new system. It sometimes tasted a bit strange, and from time to time they would look back wistfully to the bubbling streams and fresh springs they used to enjoy. Some of the problems that people had formerly blamed on unregulated water hadn't gone away. It turned out that the air was just as polluted as the water had sometimes been, but the dictator couldn't, or didn't, do much about that. But mostly the new system seemed efficient. People praised the dictator for his forward-looking wisdom.

A generation passed. All seemed to be well. Then, without warning, the springs that had gone on bubbling and sparkling beneath the solid concrete could no longer be contained. In a sudden explosion—a cross between a volcano and an earthquake—they burst through the concrete that people had come to take for granted. Muddy, dirty water shot into the air and rushed through the streets and into houses, shops, and factories. Roads were torn up; whole cities were in chaos. Some people were delighted: at last they could get water again without depending on "The System." But the people who ran the official waterpipes were at a loss: suddenly everyone had more than enough water, but it wasn't pure and couldn't be controlled. . .

We in the Western world are the citizens of that country. The dictator is the philosophy that has shaped our world for the past two or more centuries, making most people materialists by default. And the water is what we today call "spirituality," the hidden spring that bubbles up within human hearts and human societies.

Many people today hear the very word "spirituality" like travelers in a desert hearing news of an oasis. This isn't surprising. The skepticism that we've been taught for the last two hundred years has paved our world with concrete, making people ashamed to admit that they have had profound and powerful "religious" experiences. Where before they would have gone to church, said their prayers, worshipped in this way or that, and understood what they were doing as part of the warp and woof of the rest of life, the mood of the Western world from roughly the 1780s through to the 1980s was very different. We will pipe you (said the prevailing philosophy) the water you need; we will arrange for "religion" to become a small subdepartment of ordinary life; it will be quite safe—harmless, in fact—with church life carefully separated off from everything else in the world, whether politics, art, sex, economics, or whatever. Those who want it can have enough to keep them going. Those who don't want their life, and their way of life, disrupted by anything "religious" can enjoy driving along concrete roads, visiting concrete-based shopping malls, living in concrete-floored houses. Live as if the rumor of God had never existed! We are, after all, in charge of our own fate! We are the captains of our own souls (whatever they may be)! That is the philosophy that has dominated our culture. From this point of view, spirituality is a private hobby, an upmarket version of daydreaming for those who like that kind of thing.

Millions in the Western world have enjoyed the temporary separation from "religious" interference that this philosophy has brought. Millions more, aware of the deep subterranean bubblings and yearnings of the water systems we call "spirituality," which can no more ultimately be denied than can endless springs of water under thick concrete, have done their best secretly to tap into it, using the official channels (the churches), but aware that there's more water available than most churches have let on. Many more again have been aware of an indefinable thirst, a longing for springs of living, refreshing water that they can bathe in, delight in, and drink to the full.

Now at last it has happened: the hidden springs have erupted, the concrete foundation has burst open, and life can never be the same again. The official guardians of the old water system (many of whom work in the media and in politics, and some of whom, naturally enough, work in the churches) are of course horrified to see the volcano of "spirituality" that has erupted in recent years. All this "New Age" mysticism, with tarot cards, crystals, horoscopes, and so on; all this fundamentalism, with militant Christians, militant Sikhs, militant Muslims, and many others bombing each other with God on their side. Surely, say the guardians of the official water system, all this is terribly unhealthy? Surely it will lead us back to superstition, to the old chaotic, polluted, and irrational water supply?

They have a point. But they must face a question in response: Does the fault not lie with those who wanted to pave over the springs with concrete in the first place? September 11, 2001, serves as a reminder of what happens when you try to organize a world on the assumption that religion and spirituality are merely private matters, and that what really matters is economics and politics instead. It wasn't just concrete floors, it was massive towers, that were smashed to pieces that day, by people driven by "religious" beliefs so powerful that the believers were ready to die for them. What should we say? That this merely shows how dangerous "religion" and "spirituality" really are? Or that we should have taken them into account all along?

Thirsty for Spirituality

The "hidden spring" of spirituality is the second feature of human life that, I suggest, functions as the echo of a voice; as a signpost pointing away from the bleak landscape of modern secularism and toward the possibility that we humans are made for more than this. There are many signs that, just as people in Eastern Europe are rediscovering freedom and democracy, people in Western Europe are rediscovering spirituality—even if some of the experiments in getting back on track are random, haphazard, or even downright dangerous.

This may seem to some a fairly Eurocentric point of view. In much (though not all) of North America, spirituality of one sort or another has never been out of fashion in the same way as it has in Europe. Things are, however, more complicated than that. It has been axiomatic in North America that religion and spirituality should stay in their proper place—in other words, well away from the rest of real life. Just because far more Americans go to church than Europeans, that doesn't mean that the same pressures to stifle the hidden spring have not been operating, or that the same questions haven't been surfacing.

When we look further afield, we quickly realize that, for most parts of the world, the project to pave everything with concrete has never really taken hold. If we think of Africa, the Middle East, the Far East, and for that matter Central and South America—in other words, the great majority of the human race—we find that something we could broadly describe as "spirituality" has been a constant factor in the life of families and villages, towns and cities, communities and societies. It takes different forms. It integrates in a thousand different ways with politics, with music, with art, with drama—in other words, with everyday life.

From our Western perspective this may appear odd. Anthropologists and other travelers sometimes comment on how quaint it is that people from otherwise sophisticated cultures (Japan, say) still cling to what from our perspective looks like a set of old superstitions. How strange that they still drink from the bubbling springs right at hand, when we've learned how much healthier it is to have our water piped and sanitized by a proper authority. But there are signs all around that we're no longer happy to think like this. We're ready to look again at the springs. Sometimes (from the Christian perspective this often seems funny) newspaper columnists report having visited a church or cathedral, *and having found it moving, and even enjoyable.* Surely, they imply, all right-thinking people had given up that kind of thing? They are usually quick to distance themselves from any suggestion of actually believing in the Christian message. But the sound of fresh bubbling water is hard to ignore. Fewer and fewer people, even in our materialistic world, are even trying to resist it.

This resurgence of interest in a different kind of life to that which can be put into a test tube and measured has taken many different forms. In 1969 the world-famous biologist Sir Alister Hardy founded the Religious Experience Research Unit. He broadcast an appeal for people to write in with stories of their own experience, intending to collect and classify the results in much the same way as nineteenth-century biologists and naturalists had collected and classified data about the myriad forms of life on our planet. The project has grown, and has collected over time a significant archive of material that can now be accessed via the Web (www.archiveshub.ac.uk/news/ahrerca.html). Anyone who supposes that religious experience is a minority interest, or that it has been steadily dying out as people in the modern world become more sophisticated, should look at the material and think again.

You would get a similar result if you went into a bookstore and looked at the section on spirituality. Actually, one of the signs of the times is that bookstores don't know what to call this category. Sometimes it's labeled "Spirituality" or "Mind, Body, and Spirit." Sometimes it's called "Religion"—though normally that leads you to leather-bound Bibles and prayer books designed to be given as presents, not to offer you springs of living water. Sometimes it's called "Self-Help," as though spirituality were some kind of do-it-yourself project, a weekend activity to make you feel better about yourself.

What you find in such sections is typically a rich mixture, depending on the manager and style of the bookstore. Sometimes there are some quite serious works of theology. Usually there are books to help you discover your "personality type" on one of the popular systems—the Myers-Briggs Type Indicator, for instance, or the Enneagram. Sometimes we are enticed further afield—into (for instance) exploring reincarnation: perhaps, if we discover who we were in a former life, we will understand why we think and feel the way we do now. Alternatively, many writers have urged us toward a kind of nature-mysticism in which we get in touch with the deep cycles and rhythms of the world around us, and indeed within us. Sometimes the movement is the other way, suggesting a quasi-Buddhist detachment from the world, a withdrawal into a spiritual world where the outward things of life cease to be so important. Sometimes a sudden fad sweeps across the Western world, whether for Kabbalah (originally a type of medieval Jewish mysticism, now subverted in some quarters into mere postmodern mumbo jumbo), for labyrinths (aids to prayer in some medieval cathedrals, notably Chartres, now more widely used in a blend of Christian spirituality and late-modern self-discovery), or for pilgrimage, where spiritual hunger rubs shoulders with globe-trotting curiosity.

In particular, and related especially to the part of the world where I now live—Great Britain—the last generation has seen a sudden upsurge of interest in all things Celtic. Indeed, the very word "Celtic" is enough, when attached to music, prayers, buildings, jewelry, T-shirts, and anything else that comes to hand, to win the attention, and often enough the money, of people in today's Western culture. It seems to speak of a haunting possibility of another world, a world in which God (whoever he may be) is more directly present, a world in which humans get along better with their natural environment, a world with roots far deeper, and a hidden music far richer, than the shrill and shallow world of modern technology, soap operas, and football managers. The world of the ancient Celts—Northumbria, Wales, Cornwall, Brittany, Ireland, and Scotland—seems a million miles from modern-day Christianity. That is, no doubt, why it is so attractive to people bored or even angry with official religion in Western churches.

But the real center of Celtic Christianity —the monastic life, with great stress on extreme bodily asceticism and energetic evangelism—is hardly what people are looking for today. St. Cuthbert, one of the greatest of the Celtic saints, used to pray standing up to his waist in the sea off the northeast coast of England. There's no evidence that the sea there was any less bitterly cold then than it is in our own day. Nor are there signs of today's cheerful Celtic enthusiasts embracing that kind of mortification of the flesh.

Rich and deep experiences of the type we call "spiritual" often—indeed, normally—engage the emotions in very profound ways. Sometimes such experiences produce such a deep sense of inner peace and happiness that people speak of having been for a while in what they can only call "heaven." Sometimes they even laugh out loud for sheer happiness. Sometimes the experience is of a sharing in the suffering of the world that is so painful and raw that the only possible response is to weep bitterly. I am not talking about the sense of well-being, or its opposite, that might come as a result of engaging in some deeply satisfying activity on the one hand, or in confronting some awful tragedy on the other. I am speaking of those widely reported times in which people have had the sense of living for a while in multiple dimensions not normally accessible to us, in one of which they experienced either such a wonderful resolution and joy, or such anguish and torment, as to make them react as though they were really undergoing those things for themselves. Such experiences, as every seasoned pastor or spiritual guide knows, can have a lasting and profound effect on one's life.

So what are we to make of "spirituality" as we listen for the echoes of a voice that might be addressing us?

What Makes Us So Thirsty?

The Christian explanation of the renewed interest in spirituality is quite straightforward. If anything like the Christian story is in fact true (in other words, if there is a God whom we can know most clearly in Jesus), this interest is exactly what we should expect; because in Jesus we glimpse a God who loves people and wants them to know and respond to that love. In fact, this is what we should expect if *any* of the stories told by religious people—that is, the great majority of people who have ever lived—are true: if there is any kind of divine force or being, it is at least thinkable that humans would find some kind of engagement with this being or power to be an attractive or at least interesting phenomenon.

This is precisely why there are such things as religions in the first place. When the astronomers see that a planet is behaving in a way they can't explain by reference to other already known planets, or to the sun itself, they postulate a further planet of a sort, size, and location that will explain the strange behavior. That's actually how the remoter planets were discovered. When physicists discover phenomena they can explain by no other means, they postulate new entities, not themselves capable of being directly observed, that explain them. That's how quarks and similar strange things have entered our language and understanding.

On the other hand, part of the Christian story (and for that matter, the Jewish and Muslim stories) is that human beings have been so seriously damaged by evil that what they need isn't simply better self-knowledge, or better social conditions, but help, and indeed rescue, from outside themselves. We should expect that in the quest for spiritual life many people will embrace options that are, to put it no more strongly for the moment, less than what would actually be best for them. People who have been starved of water for a long time will drink anything, even if it is polluted. People kept without food for long periods will eat anything they can find, from grass to uncooked meat. Thus, by itself "spirituality" may appear to be part of the problem as well as part of the solution.

There are, of course, other ways of explaining both the hunger for spirituality and the strange things people sometimes do to satisfy it. Many people at various stages of history, the last two hundred years in the Western world being one such time, have offered alternative accounts of this sense of a shared spiritual quest. "The fool says in his heart, 'There is no God'"—that was the verdict of an ancient Israelite poet (Psalm 14.1 and elsewhere)—yet there are many who have declared that it is the believer who is the fool. Spirituality is all the result of psychological forces, said Freud, such as projecting memories of a father figure onto a cosmic screen. It's all imagination or wishful thinking or both. The fact that people are hungry for spirituality doesn't *prove* anything. If the call to spirituality that we hear can be interpreted as the echo of a voice, it's one that is lost in the wind as quickly as it comes, leaving us to ask ourselves whether we imagined it or whether, if we really did hear something, it was simply the echo of our own voices.

But the question of why we yearn for spirituality is worth asking nonetheless. After all, if the contemporary quest for spirituality is based on the idea that there's someone or something "out there" with whom (or with which) we can be in contact, and if that idea is after all completely mistaken (so that we humans are in that sense alone in the cosmos), then spirituality might not be simply a harmless pursuit. It might actually be dangerous, if not to ourselves, then at least to those whose lives are affected by what we say and do. Some hard-nosed skeptics, seeing the damage done by (what they would call) religious fanatics—suicide bombers, apocalyptic fantasists, and the like—have declared that the sooner we recognize all this religion as a kind of neurosis, and either pay it no further attention or even try to have it banned outright or confined to the safety of consenting adults in private, the better. Every so often one hears on the radio, or reads in the newspaper, that some scientist has claimed to have found the neuron, or even the gene, that controls what seem (to the subject) to be "religious" experiences, with the result that such experiences are declared to be nothing more than internal mental or emotional events. Experiences like that, however powerful, would be no more of a signpost to an external reality than my toothache would be a sign that someone had punched me on the jaw. It is difficult to demonstrate, especially to a confirmed skeptic, that my spiritual experiences have any purchase on external reality.

Spirituality and Truth

One of the regular tactics the skeptic employs at this point is relativism. I vividly remember a school friend saying to me in exasperation, at the end of a conversation about Christian faith, "It's obviously true for you, but that doesn't mean it's true for anybody else." Many people today take exactly that line.

Saying "It's true for you" sounds fine and tolerant. But it only works because it's twisting the word "true" to mean, not "a true revelation of the way things are in the real world," but "something that is genuinely happening inside you." In fact, saying "It's true for you" in this sense is more or less equivalent to saying "It's *not* true for you," because the "it" in question—the spiritual sense or awareness or experience—is conveying, very powerfully, a message (that there is a loving God) that the challenger is reducing to something else (that you are having strong feelings that you misinterpret in that sense). This goes with several other pressures that have combined to make the notion of "truth" itself highly problematic within our world.

Once we see that the skeptic's retort is itself open to problems of this sort, we return to the possibility that the widespread hunger for spirituality, which has been reported in various ways across the whole of human experience, is a genuine signpost to something that remains just around the corner, out of sight. It may be the echo of a voice—a voice that is calling, not so loudly as to compel us to listen whether we choose to or not, but not so quietly as to be drowned out altogether by the noises going on in our heads and our world. If it were to join itself up with the passion for justice, some might conclude that it would at least be worth listening for further echoes of the same voice.

Classic Arguments for Faith and Reason

PLATO

Indisputably one of the greatest minds in world history, Plato (428/427–348/347 BC) lived more than three hundred years prior to Christ. Known and still admired throughout the Western world as a Greek thinker, philosopher, and mathematician, he was a student of Socrates and tutored Aristotle. Together these three intellectual titans are considered profound influencers on the modern approach to natural philosophy. Not content in just soaking in the learned culture of his time, Plato established the first center of higher education in Greece, the Academy in Athens.

Plato's famous pedagogical dialogues continue to gain far-reaching attention. Even today they are used to teach such subjects as philosophy, logic, rhetoric, and mathematics. From the perspective of the development of rational philosophy, Plato's thoughts and questions begin our quest in analyzing the compatibility of faith and reason. Implicit in his concept of reality is the existence of the supernatural, a spiritual domain outside human senses. The selections chosen are framed in a discussion on the existence of God. They encompass a wide range of issues: acknowledging the longing in our souls, asking meaningful questions about life, hypothesizing about divinity, exploring true knowledge, contemplating the idea of loving one's enemies, and critiquing atheism.

From *Plato and the Christians*

AN ATHENIAN: Tell me, you two, has God or a man been responsible for settling your laws for you?

CLEINIAS, A CRETAN: God, Sir, God, most decidedly.

DIVINITY NOT SUBJECT TO VARIATION

AN ATHENIAN: The stars and the whole system which they display always move on the same courses because this was determined of old a wonderful long time ago, and they do not alter their plan and waver, sometimes doing one thing and sometimes another, wandering about the sky or changing their circuits. This ought to have suggested to men that they are endowed with intelligence. But it suggested just the opposite to most of us. Because they do the same things and in the same way we thought they had no soul; and the multitude followed those who were mistaken in this and supposed that humanity was intelligent and alive, while the divine, because it continued to exhibit the same motions unaltered, was without mind. Whereas a man by putting himself in contact with what is more beautiful and better and in harmony with himself might come to apprehend that what always acts along the same lines and in the same way and for the same reasons is on that very account possessed of mind, and that the stars are of this nature, most beautiful to behold, satisfying the needs of all living creatures as they dance the most beautiful and magnificent of all dances and advance upon their courses. . . .

(EPINOMIS 983A): Let us then decide how such massive systems could revolve ceaselessly at the same rate as the stars now do, and what being could make them revolve. I assert that God must be the cause, and that it never could be possible any other way. For nothing could ever possess a soul by any means except God's agency, as we have shown. But when God is of a mind to do it, it is perfectly easy for him first of all to make the whole system into a living creature in spite of its bulk, then to set it in motion in whatever way he decides is best. So may we sum up all this in one true statement: heaven and earth and all the stars and the whole mass which they make up move precisely through an exact annual period of months and days, and all that occurs makes for our common good. Now this is impossible, unless a soul is conjoined to each and is in each separate part.

God Is Unchangeable
Socrates Debates with Adeimantus

Do you think God is a wizard so as purposely to make his appearance sometimes in one disguise and sometimes in another, on such occasions changing himself and transforming himself into many shapes, and on other occasions deceiving us and making us suppose he has done so; or do you think he is single, not multiple, and least of all abandons his own form?

At the moment I don't know how to answer, he said.

Well, what about this? If anything got detached from the form that properly belonged to it, the change must either be effected by itself or by something else, mustn't it?

Yes, it must.

Well, that which is in a very good state is the least likely to be altered and changed by something else? As for example the body by food and drink and work, or a plant by scorching heat and winds and such happenings—is not the healthiest and strongest least altered?

Of course.

And would not the soul that is bravest and wisest be least confused and altered by something it experienced from without?

Yes.

And again, I suppose that according to the same argument all manufactured articles and buildings and clothes are least altered by time and other agencies when they are well made and in good condition.

That is so.

Then a thing that is in proper condition either by nature or by art or by both is least subject to being changed by anything else.

It seems so.

But God and what belongs to him are in every way proper condition.

Of course.

Consequently, God least of all would suffer many alterations.

To be sure, least of all.

But would he then change and alter himself?

Obviously, he said, that is, if he does alter.

Well then, does he change himself to what is better and finer or to what is worse and less beautiful than himself?

It must be to the worse, if he does alter. For we shall not allow that God is at all deficient in beauty or goodness.

Quite right, said I. And that being so, do you think anyone, whether god or man, would willingly make himself worse in any way?

Impossible, he said.

Then, said I, it is impossible for a god to wish to alter himself, but it looks as if each of them being as fair and good as possible every abides in the single form that is his.

God Not the Cause of Evil

Socrates Debates with Adeimantus

Whatever God is, as such of course he must be represented in poetry, whenever the poet describes him in an epic or a lyric or a tragedy.

Yes, he must.

Now God is good and must be actually described as such, mustn't he?

And what then?

Nothing of what is good is harmful. Or is it?

No, I don't think it is.

Well then, does what is not harmful do harm?

Of course not.

But does what does not harm do any evil?

No, again.

But what does not do any evil would not be the cause of any evil, would it?

How could it be?

Again the good is advantageous.

Yes.

The cause of well-being?

Yes.

Then the good is not the cause of everything, but the cause of things that are good, and not the cause of evil things.

Exactly, he said.

Then, said I, God, since he is good, would not be the cause of everything, as most people say, but the cause of only a few of the things that happen to people. He would not be the cause of many things, because the good things that befall us are much fewer than the evil, and of the good things we must reckon none but God to be the cause, but of the evil we must seek some other causes and not God.

Atheists

An Athenian: Those who despise all these prods of the existence of the gods do not do it for a single sufficient reason, as anyone would say who had any sense. But that compels us to speak as we do, and how could anyone admonish these people with mild words when starting to teach them that gods exist? But we must try. It would never do for some of us to be furious from an excessive appetite for pleasure and the others from feeling angry at their being like that. So let some such unruffled speech as the following preface what we have to say to those who have their understanding corrupted, and let us suppress our feelings and speak mildly, as though in conversation with one of them:

> My child, you are young, and time as it passed will make you change many of the opinions you now hold and adopt the opposite. Wait till then therefore before becoming a judge of matters of great importance, and most important of all, though you now reckon it a mere nothing, the question of thinking rightly about the gods, and so having a good life or the reverse.

And first I could not possibly be thought to be deceiving you if I told you this one great fact about them, namely, that you and your friends are not the first and foremost to hold this opinion about the gods, but men are always appearing who suffer from the distemper, sometimes more and sometimes less in number. But I who have consorted with many of them would like to tell you, that no one who from childhood entertained the opinion that there were no gods ever continued till old age abiding in the same state of mind. But two other attitudes towards the gods do abide, not in many minds, but still in some. First there is the view that there are gods, but they take no interest in human affairs, and then the view that they do take interest, but are easily appeased with sacrifices and prayers. If you take my advice, you will wait for the clearest belief about them that can possibly arise in your mind, considering whether the matter stands thus or thus, and inquiring more particularly from the law-giver. And in the meantime do not venture on any want of piety to the gods.

The Creator's Purpose

Timaeus: Well, now let us say why the great Architect designed creation and this universe. He was good, and no jealousy about anything is ever found in the good. So being quite free from it he wished to make everything as far as possible good like himself. If one had this from wise men as the most authentic explanation of the origin of creation and the world one would be getting what is correct. He wished that all things should be good, and that as far as possible there should be nothing wrong with anything. He found the whole visible worlds not in a state of rest but moving at random and in no order. He brought it into order from disorder, thinking order in every way better than the opposite. It is not nor ever was allowable for him that is most good to do anything except what is most admirable. So as he considered the matter he began to find that in the whole of visible nature there was simply nothing without mind that was ever going to be superior to anything with mind, and also that it is impossible that anything should have mind without soul. On the strength of this consideration he began to contrive the universe by attaching mind to soul and soul to body, thus producing what is by nature most beautiful and good. So according to the most probable view one must say it is by the providence of God that this world is of a truth a living being with a soul and a mind.

Golden Rules

Socrates: In the course of such a long discussion, while other views have been refuted, this alone remains unshaken, namely, that doing wrong is to be avoided more carefully than being wronged, and more than anything a man must take trouble not to seem, but to be good, both in his private and his public life; and whoever becomes bad in any respect, he must be corrected. And the second best thing after being virtuous is to be made so by being corrected and paying the penalty. All complacency about oneself or about others whether few or many is to be avoided. On these lines advocacy is to be used on all occasions to promote justice, and so is every other accomplishment also. Hearken to me then and follow this course, and, if you keep to it you will come to be happy in life and death, as the argument shows. Let people despise and jeer at you for a fool if they like. Yes, yes, cheerfully let them knock you about. For no disaster can happen to you, if you practice virtue and are in fact a good man.

The Meat Which Endureth
Socrates Debates with Glauco

Look at it this way, I said. Are not hunger and thirst and such-like in a way a deficiency in the physical condition?

What then?

Are not ignorance and brainlessness likewise a deficiency in the condition of the soul?

Certainly.

Then he that has a portion of food and he who owns a mind would fill up these deficiencies?

How could it be otherwise?

But does the less real or the more real more truly fill up a deficiency?

Obviously the more real.

Which of the two kinds do you think has the greater share of pure reality, the kind that is concerned with food and drink and delicacies and nourishment in general, or the class that comprises truth and knowledge and mind and in a word all that is excellent? Sort it out like this. Ask yourself whether that which attaches itself to the truth and to what is always the same and knows no end, and is itself of that kind and exists in what is of that kind, seems to you to be more real, or does that seem more real which attaches itself to what is never the same and is subject to extinction, and is itself of that kind and exists in what is of that kind?

That which is always the same is much more real.

Then say now whether the reality of that which is always the same has more reality about it than it has knowledge.

Oh no!

Well then, more reality than it has truth?

No again.

Then if there is less truth, is there not less reality also?

There must be.

All things considered then the kind of thing that concerns the care of the body has a smaller share of truth and reality than the kind of things that concern the care of the soul?

Much smaller.

And don't you think the body stands in a similar relation to the soul?

I do.

Therefore that which is being filled with things that are more real and is in itself more real, is being more really filled than that which is being filled with things that are less real and is itself less real?

It certainly must be so.

VALUES

Socrates Debates with Protarchus

SOCRATES: Pleasure is not the foremost of possessions nor the second, but the first is somehow connected with measure and what is measurable and with timeliness and all things that one must reckon to be of that nature.

PROTARCHUS: It appears so from our present discussion.

SOCRATES: And the second is harmony, beauty, perfection, adequacy, and everything of that kind.

PROTARCHUS: It seems so anyway.

SOCRATES: For the third my guess is that you would not be far off the truth if you put mind and wisdom.

PROTARCHUS: Perhaps.

SOCRATES: Then would not the fourth be what is laid down as belonging to the soul, what we called knowledge and art and right opinion? They come naturally after the first three, being more akin to the Good than to pleasure.

PROTARCHUS: Maybe.

SOCRATES: The fifth would be what are defined as pleasures that bring no pain with them, meaning those pure pleasures of the soul, which proceed from knowledge and some from the senses.

PROTARCHUS: Perhaps.

SOCRATES: But "in the sixth generation," says Orpheus, "cease to deck the lay." And at the sixth choice our argument looks like having come to a full stop.

Love Your Enemies
Socrates Debates with Polemarchus

Can a just man justly harm anyone at all? I said.

Most certainly, he said. He *ought* to harm those who are both wicked and his enemies.

But when horses are harmed, do they become better or worse?

Worse.

Worse in the respect to the good qualities of a dog or of a horse?

Of a horse.

But if dogs are harmed, it is in respect to the good qualities of a dog and not of a horse, that they become worse.

Yes, naturally.

On the same lines, Polemarchus, are we not to say that when men are harmed they become worse in respect to the good qualities of man?

Of course.

But the good qualities of a man are comprised in justice, aren't they?

Yes, naturally.

And men who are harmed must naturally become worse?

It seems so.

Well, now, can musicians make people unmusical by their skill in music?

Impossible.

But perhaps men who are skilled in horsemanship can make people's horsemanship worse by their skill in horsemanship?

No.

But the just then—can they make people unjust by their justice? Or speaking generally can the good make people bad by virtue?

No, it is impossible.

And it is not the function of heart, but of its opposite, to make things cold?

Yes.

Not of dryness, but of its opposite, to make things wet?

Of course.

Not the function of the good, but of its opposite, to do harm?

Clearly.

But the just man is good?

Of course.

Then, Polemarchus, it is not the function of the just man to harm his friend or anybody else, but of his opposite, the unjust man.

You seem to me to be saying what is entirely true, Socrates.

Well then, if anyone says it is just to pay every man his due, but this in his mind means that from the just man harm is due to his enemies and benefit to his friends, the man who says it is not a wise man, and he has not spoken the truth. For we have seen that on no occasion is it just to harm anyone.

I agree, he said.

AUGUSTINE OF HIPPO

One of the most enduring fathers of Western (religious) Christian philosophy and thought, Augustine of Hippo (AD 354–430) was greatly influenced by Neoplatonists and writers such as Cicero. Through meticulous study of Plato's dialogues, Augustine learned the didactic style of presentation and argument as well as the foundation for the tenets of his thinking. After a dramatic conversion experience to Christianity, he began to study the Bible intensely. During one such study of the Gospel of John, Augustine articulated a central idea still held today: salvation comes by God's grace alone.

In a modern translation from one of his more analytical proofs, "Concerning the Freedom of the Will," Augustine argues for the existence of God from the examination of the idea of truth. In short, he posits that some truths cannot be disputed, like 2+2=4. They are absolute in nature because they are unchangeable. Therefore there must be, he concludes, an absolute mind—God. According to Augustine, each time a person confirms truth they are in essence affirming God's existence.

From "Concerning the Freedom of the Will"

II 3.7

AUGUSTINE. What clear evidence do we have that God exists? In order to answer this question, let me begin at a point which *is* clearly evident. Do you yourself exist? (Perhaps you are afraid to answer such a question because it sounds like a trick question. But you could not possibly be tricked by such a question if you did not exist.)

EUODIUS. Go on to the next point.

A. Since it is quite clearly evident that you do exist, and since this would not be so clearly evident to you if you were dead, it seems to be equally clear that you must be alive. Do you recognize that these two points must be absolutely true?

E. I understand that quite well.

A. Then my third point is also clearly evident. You do rationally understand things.

E. Evidently so!

A. In your opinion, which of these three (existence, life, or understanding) is the most important?

E. Understanding!

A. Why do you think that?

E. Because, of those three (existence, life, and understanding) it can be said that a stone exists and an animal lives. But I do not think that a stone lives or that an animal has rational understanding. However, a person who does not have rational understanding also exists and is alive. Therefore, without hesitation, I conclude that to have all three is better than to lack one or two. Whatever is alive certainly exists, but it is not true that a living being always has rational understanding. (Life without rationality is, in my opinion, what animal life is.) But it is certainly not correct to argue that whatever exists also has life and understanding. Surely a corpse exists, but no one says that a corpse is alive. Much less could anyone believe that something not alive could have rational understanding.

A. We agree then that two of these three are lacking in a corpse, one in an animal, and none in a human being.

E. That is right.

A. We also agree that understanding is the most important of the three, because someone who has understanding must also exist and be alive.

E. Indeed so!

II 3.8

A. Now tell me whether or not you know that you have the common bodily senses of sight, hearing, smell, taste, and touch?

E. I do.

A. What do you think is the nature of sight? That is, what do you think we perceive when we see?

E. Physical things.

A. Do we see hardness and softness?

E. No.

A. Then what is the proper function of the eyes? What do we see through them?

E. Color.

A. What is the proper function of the ears?

E. Sound.

A. Of smell?

E. Odor.

A. Of taste?

E. Flavor.

A. Of touch?

E. Soft or hard, smooth or rough, and many other similar qualities.

A. What about shape? Do we not perceive by both touch and sight that things are large or small, square or round, and so forth? Therefore, we cannot assign the perception of shape to sight or touch alone. It must be said to be a function of both sight and touch.

E. I understand that.

A. You understand then that while each of the senses uniquely relates to the perception of some particular properties of things, that some senses may perceive certain other properties in common.

E. Yes, I understand that also.

A. Which of these senses do we use to perceive what the proper function of each sense is and what properties are perceived by some or all of them in common?

E. None of them. We distinguish that by an inner sense.

A. Might not that inner sense be reason itself, the very thing that animals lack? It seems to me that it is by reason that we understand and come to know these things.

II 3.9

A. Reason itself distinguishes between its servants [the senses] and the perceptions they convey to it. In the same way, reason can also recognize the differences between itself and the bodily senses, and reason proves itself to be superior. But how does reason know itself unless it is by reason. In other words, it is only by reason that you know you have reason.

E. That is very true.

A. When we see a color, we do not through our sense of sight perceive our perception of color. Nor do we hear ourselves hearing a sound, or smell ourselves smelling a rose, or taste our tasting, or touch our touching. The five bodily senses perceive all bodily things, but the senses are not themselves perceived by any one of the senses.

E. That is manifestly correct.

II 4.10

A. . . . These points are clear: (1) physical things are perceived by a bodily sense; (2) this bodily sense cannot perceive itself; (3) there is an inner sense that can and does perceive the bodily sense and the fact that physical things are perceived by a bodily sense; (4) reason, thus, makes sense perceptions known, and it makes reason itself known, and together this is knowledge. Do you agree?

E. That is clearly right.

A. . . . I am really asking you to consider whether there is any thing in man's nature that is superior to reason.

E. I know of absolutely nothing that is superior to reason.

II 6.14

A. But what if we could find something that you could know without doubt both exists and is superior to reason? Would you hesitate to call it, whatever it may be, God?

E. If I were to find something to be superior to what is best in my nature, I would not necessarily call it God. I do not want to call something God simply because my reason happens to be inferior to it. God is that reality to which nothing else is superior.

A. Exactly! For God Himself gave your reason this reverent and true way of thinking about Him. But, if I may press the point, what if you find that there is nothing superior to our reason except the eternal and changeless reality? Would you hesitate to call that God? You know that physical reality is subject to change, and the life that animates physical bodies is subject to change. Reason itself changes, for sometimes reason strives for truth and sometimes it doesn't, sometimes it reaches truth and sometimes it doesn't. Surely if reason were to recognize (not through bodily senses such as touch, smell, taste, sight, or hearing but through itself alone) itself to be inferior to something that is eternal and unchangeable, then it must confess that this reality is God.

E. I will openly acknowledge that God is that reality to which there is nothing known to be superior.

A. That is good enough. Now all I have to do is show that such a being does exist. Either you will admit that this being is God or else, if there is something higher, you will admit that the higher reality is God. So whichever the case may be, if I can show, with God's help, that there is something higher than reason, then I will have demonstrated that God exists.

E. Then get on with the demonstration that you are promising.

II 8.20

A. Let me, then, have your close attention. Do you think that there is anything that can be found that all rational people, each with their own reason and mind, may perceive, some object that can be seen to be present to everyone (but not something like food or drink that undergoes change for the use of those to whom it is present), something that remains uncorrupted and whole whether it is actually seen by everyone or not? Or would you say that there is nothing like this?

E. Oh, no, I can think of many things like that. For example, mathematical truth is held in common by all rational people. Everyone who tries to solve a mathematical equation tries to grasp the solution by reason and understanding. One person may find the problem to be simple, another may find it difficult, still another may not be able to solve it at all. Nevertheless, the mathematical relationships are equally available to anyone who can grasp them. When someone perceives the truth involved, he does not thereby change it (in other words, he does not eat it up like food). Nor does that truth cease to be true just because someone makes an error in calculation; instead the error is no more and no less than the degree to which the truth is not properly perceived.

II 8.21

A. Quite right! I can see that you are familiar with these kinds of things for you found an answer quickly. But suppose I were to argue that the concept of number was not impressed on our minds by any inherent feature of numbers themselves but came rather from things that we perceive with the bodily senses so that number becomes, so to speak, a sensory image of visible things. What would you reply to such a view, or is that perhaps the view you hold?

E. No, I certainly do not hold that view. Even if I did perceive the meaning of numerals through one of the bodily senses, I would not grasp the meaning of addition or division through a bodily sense. It is by the light of my mind that I recognize whether someone has made an error in their addition or subtraction. When I perceive something with my bodily senses, whether it is the heavens or the earth or any physical thing they contain, I do not know how long they will last. But seven plus three are ten not only now but for evermore. There never was a time when seven plus three were not ten, and there never will be such a time. Therefore, as I see it, mathematical truths are incorruptible, and they are common to me and to all other rational persons.

II 8.22

A. I fully agree with your answer. It is absolutely correct. But you can easily see that even the meanings of the numerals themselves are not perceived directly by the bodily senses. If you think about it you will recognize that every number represents a given amount of units. For example, the number two represents twice as many units as the number one; three is one unit tripled; a number representing ten units is called ten. However many units any numeral contains is the name of that number. But a true notion of the "one" means cannot arise from the bodily senses. Anything perceived by the bodily senses is a physical thing and thus it is proved not to be "one." All physical bodies are made up of many parts. It is not necessary to discuss every small and almost undetectable particle, because no matter how small the tiny particle may be, it must have one part on the right, one on the left, one above and another below, one of the far side and another on the near side, parts at the ends and parts at the middle. No matter how small a thing is, it will be made up of such parts, and consequently we can regard no physical thing as truly and simply one. Yet it would be impossible to count those parts unless they could be differentiated into units.

Whenever I seek a simple unit (oneness) in a physical thing, even though I know that I will not find it, nevertheless I do know what I am looking for, and I know what it is that I do not find. Furthermore, I know that it cannot be found because it is not there at all. When I know that a physical object is not simply one, I know what oneness means. If I did not know what "one" meant, I would not be able to count "many" in a physical thing. Wherever my concept of oneness comes from, it does not come from the bodily senses, for by my senses I can only come to know physical things, which, as I have argued, are not truly and simply one. Moreover, if we have not perceived oneness through the bodily senses, then neither have we perceived any numbers through the bodily senses (none at least of those numbers that we understand by our reason), because all of those numbers are made up of combinations of one, and the bodily senses do not directly perceive the simple unit one.

Any small body can be divided in half, and each half can be divided into half. In other words, any physical thing has two halves, yet even they are not simply two. But the number two is exactly twice the number one and therefore has one for its half (that is, that which is truly and simply one), and simple oneness cannot be further divided into halves and thirds or any other fraction because oneness lacks parts and thus is truly one.

II 8.23

Furthermore, when we follow the accepted numerical order, we find that one is followed by two (which is the double of one). But the double of two is not the next number in the series. The double of two is four (which follows two after the interposition of three). This relational pattern runs through all the other numbers by a certain and unchangeable law . . .

What, then, is the source of our recognition of these mathematical relationships that we can clearly see run through all numbers in an absolutely regular way? No one of us has perceived all numbers with any bodily sense (numbers go on forever, they are innumerable). How then could we know that these mathematical relationships hold throughout all of them? By what idea or by what image do we see with such assurance that these mathematical relationships are an absolute law that holds throughout innumerable instances, unless we know these things through an inner light unknown to the bodily senses?

II 8.24

By these and many similar arguments, it must be clear to those to whom God has given rationality, and who are not blinded by obstinacy, (1) that the orderliness and the truth of mathematics are not perceived by the bodily senses, (2) that they are absolutely unchangeable and indestructible, and (3) that they are perceived by all rational people in common . . .

It is not without significance that in the Holy Scriptures number and wisdom are associated where it says: "I and my heart have longed [lit., "gone around"] to know and consider and seek after wisdom and number." [Eccl. 7.26, Septuagint]

II 9.25

A. But let me ask this: In your opinion, what do you think about wisdom itself? Does each person have an individual wisdom or is there one wisdom that we all share in common with each person becoming wiser the more fully he shares in it?

E. I cannot answer that unless I know what you mean by wisdom. Not everyone agrees on what actions or what words are wise. For example, those who go to war think they are acting wisely, while those who despise war and spend their time farming praise this way of life as the way of wisdom. Those who are shrewd businessmen think they are wise. Those who give up all temporal interests and devote themselves entirely to a search for truth through introspective meditation and theological study also believe this to be the path of wisdom. . . . There are literally countless other groups that believe that their ideas and theirs alone are truly wise.

Therefore, since the issue before us [concerning God's existence] is not a question of what we may happen to believe but rather what we may hold by clear understanding, I am not able to answer your question based on what I personally may believe wisdom to be unless I also come to know what wisdom is through contemplation or rational discernment.

II 9.26

A. Do you think that wisdom is ever found apart from truth that enables us to discern and know the supreme good? In the examples you have given of people seeking different goals, they all sought the good and shunned evil, but they sought different goals because they had different concepts of what the good is. Anyone who seeks what should not be sought is in error even though he would not seek it if he did not think that his aim was good. Someone who seeks nothing or who seeks that which ought to be sought is not in error. For instance, no one errs by seeking happiness. But one may err by choosing a pattern of life that does not lead to true happiness even though his motive for choosing that lifestyle may have been an honest search for happiness. We are in error whenever we choose to follow a path that does not lead us where we want to go. The more one errs in his way of life, the less wise he is, because his error leads him further away from the truth in which the supreme good is discerned and known. Only the supreme good will bring the real happiness that we all deserve. why?

Certainly we all wish to be happy. So in the same way we all wish to be wise, because no one is happy without wisdom. No one is happy without the supreme good that is discerned and known by wisdom. Therefore, just as the notion of happiness is in our minds before we ever actually experience happiness (for it is this prior notion of happiness that gives us the confidence to state without reservation that we desire to be happy), so in the same way we have the notion of wisdom in our minds even before we are wise. If anyone were to be asked whether he wants to be happy, it is this notion that enables him to confidently reply that he does.

II 9.27

A. Though you were unable to express it in words, it seems that we actually agree about the nature of wisdom. If you did not have a concept of wisdom in your mind, you could not know that you want to be wise or that you ought to be (which I am sure you will not deny). Therefore, tell me whether you think of wisdom as being a single reality equally available to all people in the same way mathematical truths are, or do you think (since each of us has his own mind and no one uses someone else's mind to perceive things) that there are as many wisdoms as there are people capable of becoming wise?

E. If the highest good is the same for all, then I suppose that the truth by which we discern and know that good, namely wisdom, must also be one and common to all.

A. Do you have any doubt about the supreme good, whatever it is, being the same for all people?

E. Yes, I really do, because it is quite obvious that different people enjoy different things.

A. I wish that no one had any doubts about the supreme good, just as no one doubts that if he achieved it (whatever it is) he would be happy. But this is an important question and we may need to discuss it at length. Let us take the extreme case and support that there are as many different supreme goods as there are different things sought by different people as their supreme good. It would not necessarily follow that wisdom itself is not a single reality known in common by all rational persons simply because the goods they choose to seek in the light of this common wisdom are varied. To argue that way would be like saying there must be as many suns since we see so many varied things in its light. . . . People do see many different things which they may freely choose to enjoy, but there is only one sun by whose light these different things are seen and chosen . . .

E. Well, of course it is possible that a single wisdom common to all could nevertheless allow individual choice of different goods, but what I want to know is whether or not this is the actual case. To grant that something is possible is not necessarily to agree that it is actually the case.

A. Nevertheless, we do agree that wisdom exists. But whether there is one common wisdom or whether there is a separate wisdom for each mind is a point that is still open for discussion.

E. That is correct.

II 10.28

A. Well, then, how do we know for sure that wisdom or wise men exist or that all men want to be happy? I have no doubt that you will agree that this is true. Do you know that this is true in the same way that you know your own thoughts (which, of course, are totally secret from me unless you tell me what you are thinking)? Or do you see this truth in such a way that you think it could be seen by me as well (even if you do not tell me)?

E. Undoubtedly you could also see it even against my will.

A. In other words, this is at least one truth that we have in common yet we both see it with our individual minds.

E. Yes, that is clearly the case.

A. You surely agree that we should earnestly seek after wisdom. This is also clearly true, is it not?

E. Certainly I agree with that.

A. Can we possibly deny that this truth is one and is commonly accepted by all who know it even though each individual must contemplate it in his own mind, not in my mind or yours or any other person's. This truth is surely present in common to all who think about it.

E. No, we could never deny that.

A. Is it not also absolutely true for all people that each person should seek to live justly, that the perfect is better than the imperfect, that equals should be treated as equals, that every man should be given what is due him?

E. Yes, it is.

A. Can you deny that an uncorrupted thing is better than a corrupted thing, or that the eternal is better than the temporal, or that something which cannot be injured is better than something that can be injured.

E. No one can deny that.

A. Then, can anyone say that this truth is private truth and that it is not available to any rational person who desires to think along these lines.

E. No one could claim that such truth belonged only to him since it is as available to all rational minds as it is true.

A. Or again, who could deny that we should turn ourselves away from corruption and turn in love toward that which is incorrupt? Or how can anyone recognize that something is true and then fail to understand that it is by nature absolute (unchangeable) and equally available to all who are able to see it?

E. What you say is certainly correct.

A. Well then, will anyone doubt that it is better to live by an unshakable moral conviction than to live by a code of ethics that changes with every difficulty of life?

E. Everyone would agree on that.

II 10.29

A. We need no more examples. It is enough that you and I agree on this point, and it is absolutely certain that such principles and insights into virtue are true and changeless and that individually or collectively they are able to be seen by any rational person with his own unaided mind. But what I want to know is whether you think that these things are related to wisdom. I believe that you consider a man to be wise if he has attained wisdom.

E. Yes, I do think that.

A. Could a man live righteously if he could not distinguish what were lower things so that he could subordinate them to the higher things, or if he could not recognize what things were equal, or what was due to each?

E. No, he could not.

A. Then you would agree that one who understands these things does so wisely?

E. Yes, of course. . . .

A. And the one who is not deterred by difficulties from the course he wisely chose also acts wisely, does he not?

E. He does.

A. It seems clear to me, then, that all those truths that we call principles and insights into virtue pertain to wisdom. The more someone uses these insights in his daily life, the more wisely does he live and act, and surely we cannot separate wise actions from wisdom itself.

E. Certainly not.

A. Therefore, just as there are mathematical truths that cannot be changed and that are available to the minds of any who can understand them, so, too, there are, as you have agreed in response to my questions, true and changeless principles of wisdom equally available to all to see who are capable of understanding them.

II 15.39

You said that if I could show that there was something superior to our minds that you would confess that it was God (provided that there was nothing still more excellent). I accepted those conditions and agreed that it would be enough for me to show that much. For if there is anything superior to truth then that would be God, but if there is nothing else superior to it, then Truth itself is God. Whichever is the case, you cannot deny that God exists, and this was the question we set out to discuss.

If you are still uneasy about our faith-assumption (received from the holy teaching of Christ) that there is a Father of Wisdom, remember that it is also a faith-assumption that the Wisdom begotten of the eternal Father is equal to Him. (It is not necessary to go into these matters further now for they must be firmly accepted by faith alone.)

God does exist. Indeed He exists truly and supremely. In my view we not only hold this as certain by our faith, but we also come to grasp it intellectually by a sure (though admittedly a tenuous) form of knowledge. . . . Do you have any further objections to raise?

ANSELM OF CANTERBURY

A disciple of Augustine, although they lived over six hundred years apart, Anselm of Canterbury (1033–1109) is recognized most for his interest in metaphysics, which includes his famous ontological argument for the existence of God. His idea went on to influence theologians and philosophers such as Descartes, Leibnitz, and Immanuel Kant (although Kant disagreed with him). Even the atheist Bertrand Russell admitted to being badly shaken when he first grasped this argument. Living in the medieval period, Anselm was a well-known Benedictine priest and philosopher; he eventually achieved the post of Archbishop of Canterbury.

As a devout follower of the Christian religion, Anselm was committed to the doctrines of his faith; but he was also interested in understanding the rational foundations of what he believed. In other words, reason was as important to him as faith. In a well-known quote he affirmed, "Neque enim quaero intelligere ut credam, sed credo ut intelligam. Nam et hoc credo, quia, nisi credidero, non intelligam." (Nor do I seek to understand that I may believe, but I believe that I may understand. For this, too, I believe, that, unless I first believe, I shall not understand.) In the following excerpt from Proslogium, *he lays out his classic rational argument for the existence of God.*

That God Truly Exists

WELL THEN, LORD, You who give understanding to faith, grant me that I may understand, as much as You see fit, that You exist as we believe You to exist, and that You are what we believe You to be. Now we believe that You are something than which nothing greater can be thought. Or can it be that a thing of such a nature does not exist, since "the Fool has said in his heart, there is no God" [Ps. 13.1; 52.1]? But surely, when this same Fool hears what I am speaking about, namely, "something-than-which-nothing-greater-can-be-thought," he understands what he hears, and what he understands is in his mind, even if he does not understand that it actually exists. Thus, when a painter plans beforehand what he is going to execute, he has [the picture] in his mind, but he does not yet think that it actually exists because he has not yet executed it. However, when he has actually painted it, then he both has it in his mind and understands that it exists because he has now made it. Even the Fool, then, is forced to agree that something-than-which-nothing-greater-can-be-thought exists in the mind, since he understands this when he hears it, and whatever is understood is in the mind. And surely that-than-which-a-greater-cannot-be-thought cannot exist in the mind alone. For if it exists solely in the mind, it can be thought to exist in reality also, which is greater. If then that-than-which-a-greater-cannot-be-thought exists in the mind alone, this same that-than-which-a-greater-*cannot*-be-thought is that-than-which-a-greater-*can*-be-thought. But this is obviously impossible. Therefore there is absolutely no doubt that something-than-which-a-greater-cannot-be-thought exists both in the mind and in reality.

That God Cannot Be Thought Not to Exist

And certainly this being so truly exists that it cannot be even thought not to exist. For something can be thought to exist that cannot be thought not to exist, and this is greater than that which can be thought not to exist. Hence, if that-than-which-a-greater-cannot-be-thought can be thought not to exist, then that-than-which-a-greater-cannot-be-thought is not the same as that-than-which-a-greater-cannot-be-thought, which is absurd. Something-than-which-a-greater-cannot-be-thought exists so truly then, that it cannot be even thought not to exist.

And You, Lord our God, are this being. You exist so truly, Lord my God, that You cannot even be thought not to exist. And this is as it should be, for if some intelligence could think of something better than You, the creature would be above its Creator and would judge its Creator—and that is completely absurd. In fact, everything else there is, except You alone, can be thought of as not existing. You alone, then, of all things most truly exist and therefore of all things possess existence to the highest degree; for anything else does not exist as truly, and so possesses existence to a lesser degree. Why then did "the Fool say in his heart, there is no God" [Ps. 13.1; 52.1] when it is so evident to any rational mind that You of all things exist to the highest degree? Why indeed, unless because he was stupid and a fool?

How "the Fool Said in His Heart" What Cannot Be Thought

How indeed has he "said in his heart" what he could not think; or how could he not think what he "said in his heart," since to "say in one's heart" and to "think" are the same? But if he really (indeed, since he really) both thought because he "said in his heart" and did not "say in his heart" because he could not think, there is not only one sense in which something is "said in one's heart" or thought. For in one sense a thing is thought when the word signifying it is thought; in another sense when the very object which the thing is is understood. In the first sense, then, God can be thought not to exist, but not at all in the second sense. No one, indeed, understanding what God is can think that God does not exist, even though he may say these words in his heart either without any [objective] signification or with some peculiar signification. For God is that-than-which-nothing-greater-can-be-thought. Whoever really understands this understands clearly that this same being so exists that not even in thought can it not exist. Thus whoever understands that God exists in such a way cannot think of Him as not existing.

I give thanks, good Lord, I give thanks to You, since what I believed before through Your free gift I now so understand through Your illumination, that if I did not want to *believe* that You existed, I should nevertheless be unable not to *understand* it.

THOMAS AQUINAS

A seminal work in medieval scholasticism, Summa Theologica *was produced by the quiet but physically imposing Italian theologian and philosopher Thomas Aquinas (1225–1274). Influenced by Aristotelian philosophy, Aquinas believed not only that knowledge is based on the perception of the senses but that faith is also a way to know truth. Since he was widely known by his contemporaries as someone who could cogently synthesize a line of argument for faith and reason, Aquinas embarked on producing a work that even a beginner could understand.*

Although never finished, Summa Theologica *is a persuasive structured summary of the basic theological teachings and doctrines of Aquinas's time. Among the variety of topics he addresses, two are included here: Aquinas's well-known five proofs for the existence of God, and what he calls the simplicity of God—an explanation describing the essence, or sum and substance of God.*

The Existence of God

THAT GOD EXISTS is in itself a self-evident truth; but it is not so to us who do not see the Essence of God; and it requires to be proved by those things that are more known as regards ourselves and less known in their nature, that is, by effects. Although we know God in a general way, we do not therefore know Him absolutely. It is possible to demonstrate the Existence of God by effects, which are more known to us than their causes, for effects being granted, a preexisting cause there must be; and we call this *demonstration quia*, not *propter quid*, for not even by effects do we know the Essence of God.

The existence of God may be shown by five proofs. The first is drawn from the principle of motion. It is evident to our senses that motion exists. Whatever is moved must be moved by some external agent. Nothing is moved unless it is in potentiality (*in poten-*

tial) to its term of motion. Motion is made accordingly as things are changed from the potential to the actual, and this requires some actual agent to move them from the potential state. Since it cannot be that anything should be both potential and actual as regards the same order, it follows that the mover and the moved cannot be identical. Thus, not to go on indefinitely, we must come at last to a First Cause immovable of motion; and there we find God.

The Second Proof consists in the order of Efficient Causes in sensible objects. Nothing can be its own efficient cause, for then it would exist before itself. In every order of being the first is the cause of the intermediate, and this latter the cause of the ultimate; so that if the cause be removed the effect ceases to be, and if the first is gone there can be neither the intermediate nor the ultimate. Hence, not to proceed indefinitely, there must be a First Efficient Cause; and there too we find God.

The Third Proof is taken from possible and necessary things. Some things may be or not be; they are possible, as they are subject to generation and decomposition; but everything could not be always thus, for what is not necessary at some time is not. If, therefore, all things may possibly not be, at some time there must have been nothing; and if this be true even now, there would be nothing, for what is not can only exist by that which is. All things, therefore, are not mere possibilities in their origin; there must exist some necessary thing. But whatever is necessary, either has cause for its necessity or it has not; and, not to proceed indefinitely, as regards necessary things with a cause for their being necessary, we are obliged to postulate something necessary in itself with no cause for its necessity, but itself the cause to other things of their necessity; and this is God.

The Fourth Proof proceeds from our finding some things better than others. A thing is said to be more or less as it approaches to that which is called most. There exists, therefore, something which is best and truest, the source to things of all goodness and truth and of all their other perfection; and this we call God.

The Fifth Proof is drawn from the idea of government. Some things are without understanding, yet they work for an end, because often or always they work in the same way to obtain the best end; hence it is evident that they attain the end not by chance, but by intention; and since they must act towards the end not by their own but by some one's knowledge, they reach the end because they are directed by an Intelligent Being. There must, therefore, be such an Intelligent Being Who directs all natural things to their end; and Him we call God.

The Simplicity of God

God is not corporeal; first, because movement is not possible to a body except by an external agent—God is the First Cause of motion, Himself being immovable, as was shown above; secondly, a body is a potentiality (*in potential*) because, as it is continuous, it is divisible indefinitely, whereas God is a Being in Act and Pure Act; thirdly, God is the noblest of all Beings in Act, and, therefore, cannot be corporeal, a body being either living or not living, and a living body is nobler than a not living body; but a living body does not live as such, otherwise every body would live, and so it must live by another, which is the soul. That which gives life to the body is nobler than the body. It is, therefore, impossible that God should be corporeal.

God is not composed of matter and form. Matter is of itself a potentiality. God is True Actuality, having no potentiality. Further, every created being is good and perfect by virtue of its form and by participation, as matter participates form; but as God is the first and highest Good, He is not Good by participation, but by His own Essence; therefore He is not composite. It is clear also, from His being the First Efficient Cause, and therefore, the First Cause and acting of Himself, and Form by His own Essence, why He is not composed of matter and form. God is identified with His Essence or Nature, whereas in single forms which are their own individuality the subject is the same as the nature; and, therefore, God is His own Deity and His own Life, and all else that can be predicated of Him. In things composed of matter and form nature differs from the subject, because the nature or essence comprehends in itself only what falls under the definition of Species, and so it does not comprehend the individualizing matter, and thereby it is distinguished from the subject. So God is not only His own Essence, but His own Existence; for whatever is in anything besides its own essence must be caused either by the essence or by some external agent; but it cannot be by the essence alone, for to be its own cause of being is beyond any being. If this is caused by an external agent, it must be as regards anything that has existence and essence distinct, that it should have a cause other than itself; but with God that cannot be, for He is, we have seen, the First Efficient Cause. Further, existence when distinct from essence is related to it as act to potentiality; but God is Pure Act with no potentiality, and, therefore, He is identified with His Essence; this is evident likewise from the fact that He is the First Being, and, therefore, must Be. If His Existence and Essence were not the same, He would Be by participation, and thus He would not be the First Being; which is absurd to say of God.

Neither is God, properly speaking, in any genus. Species is made of genus and difference; and that from which difference comes stands toward that which makes the genus as the actual to the potential (thus the rational may be compared to the sensitive, as the actual to the potential, and so on); but since in God the potential cannot be added to His Actuality, it cannot be that He should be as a species in a genus. Moreover, if God were in a genus, it must be that of Being, for genus signifies the essence of a thing, as when we predicate of a thing that it is such; but Being cannot be a genus, as Aristotle says, because every genus has differences external to its essence, whereas no difference can be external to simple being. Therefore, God is not  in a genus, for outside of Being there is only not-Being, which cannot be the difference among being. Besides, all the members of one genus have those things in common which constitute the genus in its essence (of which it may be predicated that it is such), but they differ in their being; thus the being of a man is not the same as that of a horse, nor is the being of one man the same as another's. There is a necessary difference, therefore, between being (or existence) and essence in things which are in a genus; whereas the contrary has been proved in God, and, therefore, He is not in a genus. Neither does He belong to a genus by reduction to first principles, for whatever belongs to a genus by reduction does not extend beyond it; whereas God is the First Principle of all Being, and hence He cannot be contained as the first principle in any particular genus.

Nor can there be any accident in God. The subject is to the accident as the potential is to the actual, and God being Pure Actuality, the potential has no place in Him. Then, as God is His own Existence, there can be nothing added to His Nature; just as heat has only heat, although a thing which is hot may have something external added to the heat, such as whiteness. Thirdly, whatever exists of itself is prior to that which is accidental. Hence, as God is the First Being, there cannot be in Him anything accidental.

God is, therefore, wholly Simple, for in Him there is no composition nor quantitative parts, neither is His Nature distinct from His Subject. He is wholly Simple likewise because what is composite comes after its component parts, and depends upon them; whereas God is the First Being. Moreover, a thing composite has a cause for its unity; but God has no cause, being Himself the First Efficient Cause. Also, in everything which is composite there is potentiality and actuality, which have no place in God. Finally, everything which is composite is a whole separate from its parts, whether like or unlike, which can in no way be said of God, Who is His own Form, or rather His own Being, and, therefore, is wholly Simple.

Neither does God enter into the composition of any other things, as some have erroneously thought and said that He was the soul of the first heavens, or the formal principle of all things, or primal matter (*material prima),* for God is the First Efficient Cause, and such cause is numerically distinct from the form of the effect, and can only agree with it in species, as in the case of man generating a man. Matter does not agree with its efficient cause either numerically or specifically, for it is *in potential,* and the latter is *in actu*. God, as the First Cause, is the highest, and acts by His own power; and so he is not a part of anything else. Nor can any part of a composite thing be the absolute first among beings, as God is; not matter nor form, which are the principles of anything composite; for matter, which is potentiality, is simply posterior to actuality, and form, which is part likewise, is participated form which comes after that which is Form by Essence. Therefore God does not enter into composition at all.

JOHN LOCKE

The British political theorist and philosopher John Locke (1632–1704) is highly regarded as one of the most influential minds of the seventeenth century. Known widely in America as having significantly influenced the writers of the Declaration of Independence, he is noted by many as a major contributor to modern thought and culture. He also had a considerable impact on many European philosophers, such as Voltaire and Rousseau, as well as many Scottish Enlightenment thinkers.

Less well known are his writings about faith. During Locke's day, religion and public thought did not divide on such sharp boundaries as they often do today. He wrote and lived during a time of heightened religious receptiveness. In the excerpt offered, taken from "Of Our Knowledge of the Existence of God," Locke provides cogent logical arguments for "an eternal, most powerful, and most knowing Being."

Of Our Knowledge of the Existence of a God

THOUGH GOD HAS given us no innate ideas of himself; though he has stamped no original characters on our minds, wherein we may read his being; yet having furnished us with those faculties our minds are endowed with, he hath not left himself without witness: since we have sense, perception, and reason, and cannot want a clear proof of him, as long as we carry *ourselves* about us. Nor can we justly complain of our ignorance in this great point; since he has so plentifully provided us with the means to discover and know him; so far as is necessary to the end of our being, and the great concernment of our happiness. But, though its evidence be (if I mistake not) equal to mathematical certainty: yet it requires thought and attention; and the mind must apply itself to a regular deduction of it from some part of our intuitive knowledge, or else we shall be as uncertain and ignorant of this as of other propositions, which are in themselves capable of clear demonstration. To show, therefore, that we are capable of *knowing,* i.e. *being certain* that there is a God, and *how we may come by* this certainty, I think we need go no further than *ourselves,* and that undoubted knowledge we have of our own existence.

I think that it is beyond question, that man has a clear idea of his own being; he knows certainly he exists, and that he is something. He that can doubt whether he be anything or no, I speak not to; no more than I would argue with pure nothing, or endeavor to convince nonentity that it were something. If any one pretends to be so skeptical as to deny his own existence (for really to doubt of it is manifestly impossible,) let him for me enjoy his beloved happiness of being nothing, until hunger or some other pain convinces him of the contrary. This, then, I think I may take for a truth, which every one's certain knowledge assures him of, beyond the liberty of doubting, viz. that he is *something that actually exists*.

In the next place, man knows, by an intuitive certainty, that bare *nothing can no more produce any real being, than it can be equal to two right angles*. If a man knows not that nonentity, or that absence of all being, cannot be equal to two right angles, it is impossible he should know any demonstration in Euclid. If, therefore, we know there is some real being, and that nonentity cannot produce any real being, it is an evident demonstration, that *from eternity there has been something*; since what was not from eternity had a beginning; and what had a beginning must be produced by something else.

Next, it is evident, that what had its being and beginning from another, must also have all that which is in and belongs to its being from another too. All the power it has must be owing to and received from the same source. This eternal source, then, of all being must also be the source and original of all power; and so *this eternal Being must be also the most powerful.*

Again, a man finds in *himself* perception and knowledge. We have then got one step further; and we are certain now that there is not only some being, but some knowing, intelligent being in the world. There was a time, then, when there was no knowing being, and when knowledge began to be; or else there has been also *a knowing being from eternity.* If it be said, there was a time when no being had any knowledge, when that eternal being was void of all understanding; I reply, that then it was impossible there should ever have been any knowledge: it being as impossible that things wholly void of knowledge, and operating blindly, and without any perception, should produce a knowing being, as it is impossible that a triangle should make itself three angles bigger than two right ones. For it is as repugnant to the idea of senseless matter, that it should put into itself sense, perception, and knowledge, as it is repugnant to the idea of a triangle, that it should put into itself greater angles than two right ones.

Thus, from the consideration of ourselves, and what we infallibly find in our own constitutions, our reason leads us to the knowledge of this certain and evident truth,—*That there is an eternal, most powerful, and most knowing Being*; which whether any one will please to call God, it matters not. The thing is evident; and from this idea duly considered, will easily be deduced all those other attributes, which we ought to ascribe to this eternal Being.

. . . From what has been said, it is plain to me we have a more certain knowledge of the existence of a God, than of anything our senses have not immediately discovered to us. Nay, I presume I may say, that we more certainly know that there is a God, than that there is anything else without us. When I say we *know,* I mean there is such a knowledge within our reach which we cannot miss, if we will but apply our minds to that, as we do to several other inquiries.

How far the *idea* of a most perfect being, which a man may frame in his mind, does or does not prove the *existence* of a God, I will not here examine. For in the different make of men's tempers and application of their thoughts, some arguments prevail more on one, and some on another, for the confirmation of the same truth. But yet, I think, this I may say, that it is an ill way of establishing this truth, and silencing atheists, to lay the whole stress of so important a point as this upon that sole foundation: and take some men's having that idea of God in their minds (for it is evident that some men have none, and some worse than none, and the most very different,) for the only proof of a Deity; and out of an over fondness of that darling invention, cashier, or at least endeavor to invalidate all other arguments; and forbid us to hearken to those proofs, as being weak or fallacious, which our own existence, and the sensible parts of the universe offer so clearly and cogently to our thoughts, that I deem it impossible for a considering man to withstand them. For I judge it as certain and clear a truth as can anywhere be delivered, that "the invisible things of God are clearly seen from the creation of the world, being understood by the things that are made, even his eternal power and Godhead." Though our own being furnishes us, as I have shown, with an evident and incontestable proof of a Deity; and I believe nobody can avoid the cogency of it, who will but as carefully attend to it, as to any other demonstration of so many parts: yet this being so fundamental a truth, and of that consequence, that all religion and genuine morality depend thereon, I doubt not but I shall be forgiven by my reader if I go over some parts of this argument again, and enlarge a little more upon them.

There is no truth more evident than that *something* must be *from eternity*. I never yet heard of any one so unreasonable, or that could suppose so manifest a contradiction, as a time wherein there was perfectly nothing. This being of all absurdities the greatest, to imagine that pure nothing, the perfect negation and absence of all being, should ever produce any real existence.

It being, then, unavoidable for all rational creatures to conclude, that *something* has existed from eternity; let us next see *what kind of thing* that must be.

There are but two sorts of beings in the world that man knows or conceives.

First, such as are purely material, without sense, perception, or thought, as the clippings of our beards, and parings of our nails.

Secondly, sensible, thinking, perceiving beings, such as we find ourselves to be. Which, if you please, we will hereafter call *cogitative* and *incogitative* beings; which to our present purpose, if for nothing else, are perhaps better terms than material and immaterial.

If, then, there must be something eternal, let us see what sort of being it must be. And to that it is very obvious to reason, that it must necessarily be a cogitative being. For it is impossible to conceive that ever bare incogitative matter should produce a thinking intelligent being, as that nothing should of itself produce matter. Let us suppose any parcel of matter eternal, great or small, we shall find it, in itself, able to produce nothing. For example: let us suppose the matter of the next pebble we meet with eternal, closely united, and the parts firmly at rest together; if there were no other being in the world, must it not eternally remain so, a dead inactive lump? Is it possible to conceive it can add motion to itself, being purely matter, or produce anything? Matter, then, by its own strength, cannot produce in itself so much as motion: the motion it has must also be from eternity, or else be produced, and added to matter by some other being more powerful than matter; matter, as is evident, having not power to produce motion in itself. But let us suppose motion eternal too: yet matter, *incogitative* matter and motion, whatever changes it might produce a figure of bulk, could never produce thought: knowledge will still be as far beyond the power of motion and matter to produce, as matter is beyond the power of nothing or nonentity to produce. And I appeal to every one's own thoughts, whether he cannot as easily conceive matter produced by *nothing*, as thought to be produced by pure matter, when, before, there was no such thing as thought or an intelligent being existing? Divide matter into as many parts as you will (which we are apt to imagine a sort of spiritualizing, or making a thinking thing of it,) vary the figure and motion of it as much as you please—a globe, cube, cone, prism, cylinder, &c., whose diameters are but 100,000th part of a *gry*,[1] will operate no otherwise upon other bodies of proportionable bulk, than those of an inch or foot diameter; and you may as rationally expect to produce sense, thought, and knowledge, by putting together, in a certain figure and motion, gross particles of matter, as by those that are the very minutest that do anywhere exist. They knock, impel, and resist one another, just as the greater do; and that is all they can do. So that, if we will suppose *nothing* first or eternal, matter can never begin to be: if we suppose bare matter without motion, eternal, motion can never begin to be: if we suppose only matter and motion first, or eternal, thought can never begin to be. [For it is impossible to conceive that matter, either with or without motion, could have, originally, in and from itself, sense, perception, and knowledge; as is evident from hence, that then sense, perception, and knowledge, must be a property eternally inseparable from matter and every particle of it. Not to add, that, though our generally or specific conception of matter makes us speak of it as one thing, yet really all matter is not one individual thing, neither is there any such thing existing as *one* material being, or *one* single body that we know or can conceive. And therefore, if matter were the eternal first cogitative being, there would not be one eternal, infinite, cogitative being, but an infinite number of eternal, finite, cogitative beings, independent one of another, of limited force, and distinct thoughts, which could never produce that order, harmony, and beauty that are to be found in nature. Since, therefore, whatsoever is the first eternal being must necessarily be cogitative; and] whatsoever is the first of all things must necessarily contain in it, and actually have, at least, all the perfections that can ever after exist; nor can it ever give to another any perfection that it hath not either actually in itself, or, at least, in a higher degree; [it necessarily follows, that the first eternal being cannot be matter].

If, therefore, it be evident, that something necessarily must exist from eternity, it is also as evident, that that something must necessarily be a cogitative being: for it is as impossible that incogitative matter should produce a cogitative being, as that nothing, or the negation of all being, should produce a positive being or matter.

BLAISE PASCAL

"Everything that is incomprehensible does not cease to exist."

Blaise Pascal (1623–1662), the brilliant French physicist, mathematician, philosopher, and theologian, was reluctant to embrace the popularized philosophical beliefs about God of his time. To do so, he thought, would jeopardize the idea of a personal God. He passionately opposed adopting Aristotle's idea that God, or the Unmoved Mover, was distant and detached from human life. He believed this view dwarfed and diminished the biblical revelation.

Pascal was afflicted by lifelong ill health. After an accident that nearly took his life, he began a work that was never completed, and which is known today as the Pensées *(*Thoughts*). Some examples from this collection of profound reflections are included here. They were found on scraps of paper after his death, but are now considered a classic. The final excerpt included here is known as "Pascal's Wager."*

Pascal was a passionate seeker of truth, which he believed could be achieved by incorporating reason and faith. He concluded that the God described in the Bible could be personally known. After his death a crinkled piece of paper was found sewn into his shirt. It read, "God of Abraham, God of Isaac, God of Jacob, not of philosophers and scholars, God of Jesus Christ, my God and your God. Your God shall be my God."

Foundations

WE KNOW THE truth not only through our reason but also through our heart. It is through the latter that we know first principles, and reason, which has nothing to do with it, tries in vain to refute them. The skeptics have no other object than that, and they work at it to no purpose. We know that we are not dreaming, but, however unable we may be to prove it rationally, our inability proves nothing but the weakness of our reason, and not the uncertainty of all our knowledge, as they maintain. For knowledge of first principles, like space, time, motion, number, is as solid as any derived through reason, and it is on such knowledge, coming from the heart and instinct, that reason has to depend and base all its argument. The heart feels that there are three spatial dimensions and that there is an infinite series of numbers, and reason goes on to demonstrate that there are no two square numbers of which one is double the other. Principles are felt, propositions proved, and both with certainty though by different means. It is just as pointless and absurd for reason to demand proof of first principles from the heart before agreeing to accept them as it would be absurd for the heart to demand an intuition of all the propositions demonstrated by reason before agreeing to accept them.

Our inability must therefore serve only to humble reason, which would like to be the judge of everything, but not to confute our certainty. As if reason were the only way we could learn! Would to God, on the contrary, that we never needed it and knew everything by instinct and feeling! But nature has refused us this blessing, and has instead given us only very little knowledge of this kind; all other knowledge can be acquired only by reasoning.

That is why those to whom God has given religious faith by moving their hearts are very fortunate, and feel quite legitimately convinced, but to those who do not have it we can only give such faith through reasoning, until God gives it by moving their heart, without which faith is only human and useless for salvation. . . .

. . . Let man then contemplate the whole of nature in her full and lofty majesty, let him turn his gaze away from the lowly objects around him; let him behold the dazzling light set like an eternal lamp to light up the universe, let him see the earth as a mere speck compared to the vast orbit described by this star, and let him marvel at finding this vast orbit itself to be no more than the tiniest point compared to that described by the stars revolving in the firmament. But if our eyes stop there, let our imagination proceed further; it will grow weary of conceiving things before nature tires of producing them. The whole visible world is only an imperceptible dot in nature's ample bosom. No idea comes near it; it is no good inflating our conceptions beyond imaginable space, we only bring forth atoms compared to the reality of things. Nature is an infinite sphere whose center is everywhere and circumference nowhere. In short it is the greatest perceptible mark of God's omnipotence that our imagination should lose itself in that thought.

Let man, returning to himself, consider what he is in comparison with what exists; let him regard himself as lost, and from this little dungeon, in which he finds himself lodged, I mean the universe, let him learn to take the earth, its realms, its cities, its houses and himself at their proper value.

What is a man in the infinite?

But, to offer him another prodigy equally astounding, let him look into the tiniest things he knows. Let a mite show him in its minute body incomparably more minute parts, legs with joints, veins in its legs, blood in the veins, humors in the blood, drops in the humors, vapors in the drops: let him divide these things still further until he has exhausted his powers of imagination, and let the last thing he comes down to now be the subject of our discourse. He will perhaps think that this is the ultimate of minuteness in nature.

I want to show him a new abyss. I want to depict to him not only the visible universe, but all the conceivable immensity of nature enclosed in this miniature atom. Let him see there an infinity of universes, each with its firmament, its planets, its earth, in the same proportions as in the visible world, and on that earth animals, and finally mites, in which he will find again the same results as in the first; and finding the same thing yet again in the others without end or respite, he will be lost in such wonders, as astounding in their minuteness as the others in their amplitude. For who will not marvel that our body, a moment ago imperceptible in a universe, itself imperceptible in the bosom of the whole, should now be a colossus, a world, or rather a whole, compared to the nothingness beyond our reach? Anyone who considers himself in this way will be terrified at himself, and, seeing his mass, as given him by nature, supporting him between these two abysses of infinity and nothingness, will tremble at these marvels. I believe that with his curiosity changing into wonder he will be more disposed to contemplate them in silence than investigate them with presumption.

For, after all, what is man in nature? A nothing compared to the infinite, a whole compared to the nothing, a middle point between all and nothing, infinitely remote from an understanding of the extremes; the end of things and their principles are unattainably hidden from him in impenetrable secrecy.

Equally incapable of seeing the nothingness from which he emerges and the infinity in which he is engulfed.

What else can he do, then, but perceive some semblance of the middle of things, eternally hopeless of knowing either their principles or their end? All things have come out of nothingness and are carried onwards to infinity. Who can follow these astonishing processes? The author of these wonders understands them: no one else can.

Because they failed to contemplate these infinities, men have rashly undertaken to probe into nature as if there were some proportion between themselves and her.

Strangely enough they wanted to know the principles of things and go on from there to know everything, inspired by a presumption as infinite as their object. For there can be no doubt that such a plan could not be conceived without infinite presumption or a capacity as infinite as that of nature.

When we know better, we understand that, since nature has engraved her own image and that of her author on all things, they almost all share her double infinity. Thus we see that all the sciences are infinite in the range of their researches, for who can doubt that mathematics, for instance, has an infinity of infinities of propositions to expound? They are infinite also in the multiplicity and subtlety of their principles, for anyone can see that those which are supposed to be ultimate do not stand by themselves, but depend on others, which depend on others again, and thus never allow of any finality.

But we treat as ultimate those which seem so to our reason, as in material things we call a point indivisible when our senses can perceive nothing beyond it, although by its nature it is infinitely divisible.

Of these two infinities of science, that of greatness is much more obvious, and that is why it has occurred to few people to claim that they know everything. "I am going to speak about everything," Democritus used to say.

But the infinitely small is much harder to see. The philosophers have much more readily claimed to have reached it, and that is where they have all tripped up. This is the origin of such familiar titles as *Of the principles of things, Of the principles of philosophy,*[1] and the like, which are really as pretentious, though they do not look it, as this blatant one: *Of all that can be known.*[2]

We naturally believe we are more capable of reaching the center of things than of embracing their circumference, and the visible extent of the world is visibly greater than we. But since we in our turn are greater than small things, we think we are more capable of mastering them, and yet it takes no less capacity to reach nothingness than the whole. In either case it takes an infinite capacity, and it seems to me that anyone who had understood the ultimate principles of things might also succeed in knowing infinity. One depends on the other, and one leads to the other. These extremes touch and join by going in opposite directions, and they meet in God and God alone.

Of the Need of Seeking Truth

Second Part.

That man without faith cannot know the true good, nor justice.

All men seek happiness. To this there is no exception, what different means soever they employ, all tend to this goal. The reason that some men go to the wars and others avoid them is but the same desire attended in each with different views. Our will makes no step but towards this object. This is the motive of every action of every man, even of him who hangs himself.

And yet after so many years, no one without faith has arrived at the point to which all eyes are turned. All complain, princes and subjects, nobles and commons, old and young, strong and weak, learned and ignorant, sound and sick, of all countries, all times, all ages, and all conditions.

A trial so long, so constant and so uniform, should surely convince us of our inability to arrive at good by our own strength, but example teaches us but little. No resemblance is so exact but that there is some slight difference, and hence we expect that our endeavor will not be foiled on this occasion as before. Thus while the present never satisfies, experience deceives us, and from misfortune to misfortune leads us on to death, eternal crown of sorrows.

This desire, and this weakness cry aloud to us that there was once in man a true happiness, of which there now remains to him but the mark and the empty trace, which he vainly tries to fill from all that surrounds him, seeking from things absent the succor he finds not in things present; and these are all inadequate, because this infinite void can only be filled by an infinite and immutable object, that is to say, only by God himself.

He only is our true good, and since we have left him, it is strange that there is nothing in nature which has not served to take his place; neither the stars, nor heaven, earth, the elements, plants, cabbages, leeks, animals, insects, calves, serpents, fever, pestilence, war, famine, vices, adultery, incest. And since he has lost the true good, all things can equally appear good to him, even his own destruction, though so contrary to God, to reason, and to the whole course of nature.

Some seek good in authority, others in research and knowledge, others in pleasure. Others, who indeed are nearer the truth, have considered it necessary that the universal good which all men desire should not consist in any of those particular matters which can only be possessed by one, and which if once shared, afflict their possessor more by the want of what he has not, than they gladden him by the joy of what he has. They have apprehended that the true good should be such as all may possess at once, without diminution, and without envy, and that which none can lose against his will. And their reason is that this desire being natural to man, since it exists necessarily in all, and that all must have it, they conclude from it. . .

Infinite, nothing.—The soul of man is cast into the body, in which it finds number, time, dimension; it reasons thereon, and calls this nature or necessity, and cannot believe aught else.

Unity joined to infinity increases it not, any more than a foot measure added to infinite space. The finite is annihilated in presence of the infinite and becomes simply nought. Thus our intellect before God, thus our justice before the divine justice. There is not so great a disproportion between our justice and that of God, as between unity and infinity.

The justice of God must be as vast as his mercy, but justice towards the reprobate is less vast, and should be less amazing than mercy towards the elect.

We know that there is an infinite, but are ignorant of its nature. As we know it to be false that numbers are finite, it must therefore be true that there is an infinity in number, but what this is we know not. It can neither be odd nor even, for the addition of a unit can make no change in the nature of number; yet it is a number, and every number is either odd or even, at least this is understood of every finite number.

Thus we may well know that there is a God, without knowing what he is.

We know then the existence and the nature of the finite, because we also are finite and have dimension.

We know the existence of the infinite, and are ignorant of its nature, because it has dimension like us, but not limits like us. But we know neither the existence nor the nature of God, because he has neither dimension nor limits.

But by faith we know his existence, by glory we shall know his nature. Now I have already shown that we can know well the existence of a thing without knowing its nature.

Let us now speak according to the light of nature.

If there be a God, he is infinitely incomprehensible, since having neither parts nor limits he has no relation to us. We are then incapable of knowing either what he is or if he is. This being so, who will dare to undertake the solution of the question? Not we, who have no relation to him.

Who then will blame Christians for not being able to give a reason for their faith; those who profess a religion for which they cannot give a reason? They declare in putting it forth to the world that it is a foolishness, *stultitiam,* and then you complain that they do not prove it. Were they to prove it they would not keep their word, it is in lacking proof that they are not lacking in sense.—Yes, but although this excuses those who offer it as such, and takes away from them the blame of putting it forth without reason, it does not excuse those who receive it.—Let us then examine this point, and say "God is, or he is not." But to which side shall we incline? Reason can determine nothing about it. There is an infinite gulf fixed between us. A game is playing at the extremity of this infinite distance in which heads or tails may turn up.

What will you wager? There is no reason for backing either one or the other, you cannot reasonably argue in favor of either.

Do not then accuse of error those who have already chosen, for you know nothing about it.—No, but I blame them for having made, not this choice, but *a* choice, for again both the man who calls "heads" and his adversary are equally to blame, they are both in the wrong; the true course is not to wager at all.—

Yes, but you must wager; this depends not on your will, you are embarked in the affair. Which will you choose? Let us see. Since you must choose, let us see which least interests you. You have two things to lose, truth and good, and two things to stake, your reason and your will, your knowledge and your happiness; and your nature has two things to avoid, error and misery. Since you must needs choose, your reason is no more wounded in choosing one than the other. Here is one point cleared up, but what of your happiness? Let us weigh the gain and the loss in choosing heads that God is. Let us weigh the two cases: if you gain, you gain all; if you lose, you lose nothing. Wager then unhesitatingly that he is.—You are right. Yes, I must wager, but I may stake too much.—Let us see. Since there is an equal chance of gain and loss, if you had only to gain two lives for one, you might still wager. But were there three of them to gain, you would have to play, since needs must that you play, and you would be imprudent, since you must play, not to chance your life to gain three at a game where the chances of loss or gain are even. But there is an eternity of life and happiness. And that being so, were there an infinity of chances of which one only would be for you, you would still be right to stake one to win two, and you would act foolishly, being obliged to play, did you refuse to stake one life against three at a game in which out of an infinity of chances there be one for you, if there were an infinity of an infinitely happy life to win. But there is here an infinity of an infinitely happy life to win, a chance of gain against a finite number of chances of loss, and what you stake is finite; that is decided. Wherever the infinite exists and there is not an infinity of chances of loss against that of gain, there is no room for hesitation, you must risk the whole. Thus when a man is forced to play he must renounce reason to keep life, rather than hazard it for infinite gain, which is as likely to happen as the loss of nothingness.

For it is of no avail to say it is uncertain that we gain, and certain that we risk, and that the infinite distance between the certainty of that which is staked and the uncertainty of what we shall gain, equals the finite good which is certainly staked against an uncertain infinite. This is not so. Every gambler stakes a certainty to gain an uncertainty, and yet he stakes a finite certainty against a finite uncertainty without acting unreasonably. It is false to say there is infinite distance between the certain stake and the uncertain gain. There is in truth an infinity between the certainty of gain and the certainty of loss. But the uncertainty of gain is proportioned to the certainty of the stake, according to the proportion of chances of gain and loss, and if therefore there are as many chances on one side as on the other, the game is even. And thus the certainty of the venture is equal to the uncertainty of the winnings, so far is it from the truth that there is infinite distance between them. So that our argument is of infinite force, if we stake the finite in a game where there are equal chances of gain and loss, and the infinite is the winnings. This is demonstrable, and if men are capable of any truths, this is one.

I confess and admit it. Yet is there no means of seeing the hands at the game?—Yes, the Scripture and the rest, etc.

—Well, but my hands are tied and my mouth is gagged: I am forced to wager and am not free, none can release me, but I am so made that I cannot believe. What then would you have me do?

True. But understand at least your incapacity to believe, since your reason leads you to belief and yet you cannot believe. Labor then to convince yourself, not by increase of the proofs of God, but by the diminution of your passions. You would fain arrive at faith, but know not the way; you would heal yourself of unbelief, and you ask remedies for it. Learn of those who have been bound as you are, but who now stake all that they possess; these are they who know the way you would follow, who are cured of a disease of which you would be cured. Follow the way by which they began, by making believe that they believed, taking the holy water, having masses said, etc. Thus you will naturally be brought to believe, and will lose your acuteness.—But that is just what I fear.—Why? what have you to lose?

But to show you that this is the right way, this it is that will lessen the passions, which are your great obstacles, etc.—

What you say comforts and delights me, etc.—If my words please you, and seem to you cogent, know that they are those of one who has thrown himself on his knees before and after to pray that Being, infinite, and without parts, to whom he submits all his own being, that you also would submit to him all yours, for your own good and for his glory, and that this strength may be in accord with this weakness.

The end of this argument.—Now what evil will happen to you in taking this side? You will be trustworthy, honorable, humble, grateful, generous, friendly, sincere, and true. In truth you will no longer have those poisoned pleasures, glory and luxury, but you will have other pleasures. I tell you that you will gain in this life, at each step you make in this path you will see so much certainty of gain, so much nothingness in what you stake, that you will know at last that you have wagered on a certainty, an infinity, for which you have risked nothing.

The Meaning of Truth

OS GUINNESS

Having written over twenty-five books, Os Guinness (1941–) is a well-respected academic and cultural critic conversant on a variety of topics, including truth. Born during World War II in China to medical missionaries, Guinness began his life confronted with the horrific consequences of dogmatic absolutism.

At the dawn of the twenty-first century, and in direct reaction to the rigid assertions made in the twentieth century, truth in our time is finding it difficult to survive. We feel cagey admitting to anything with passion and resolve, and yet, what about the necessity for it? Does truth, both objective and nonrelativistic, have a place in our world? These questions and others are explored by Guinness. He weaves historical stories and a philosophical critique in this excerpt, from Time for Truth, *examining how they have bred our current worldviews.*

Differences Make a Difference

PRISONER 174517 WAS thirsty. Seeing a fat icicle hanging just outside his hut in the Auschwitz extermination camp, he reached out of the window and broke it off to quench his thirst. But before he could get the icicle to his mouth, a guard snatched it out of his hands and dashed it to pieces on the filthy ground.

"*Warum?*" the prisoner burst out instinctively—"Why?"

"*Hier ist kein warum,*" the guard answered with brutal finality—"Here there is no why."

That for Primo Levi, the Italian Jewish scientist and writer, was the essence of the death camps—places not only of unchallengeable, arbitrary authority but of absolute evil that defied all explanation. In the face of such wickedness, explanations born of psychology, sociology, and economics were pathetic in their inadequacy. One could only shoulder the weight of such an experience and bear witness to the world. “Never again” was too confident an assertion. “You never know” was the needed refrain.

Yet despite the horror, Levi gave the impression that he had survived the poison of Auschwitz and had come to terms with his nightmarish experience. One of only three remaining survivors of the six hundred fifty Italian Jews transported to Poland in 1944, he eventually married, had children, wrote books, won literary prizes, and lived a full life. His core mission, however, was always to serve as a witness to the truth, a guardian of the memory.

Writing about his deportation to Poland, he stated: “Auschwitz left its mark on me, but it did not remove my desire to live. On the contrary, that experience increased my desire, it gave my life a purpose, to bear witness, so that such a thing should never occur again.” While other direct or indirect victims of the Nazis committed suicide, including Walter Benjamin, Stefan Zweig, and Bruno Bettelheim, Levi many times argued against that act.

Thus many people were shocked and saddened when on April 11, 1987, more than forty years after his release from Auschwitz, Primo Levi plunged to his death down the stairwell of his home in Torino, Italy. Feeling the burden of witnessing, the guilt of surviving, the horror of revisionist denials of the camps, the weariness of repeating the same things, and even the anxiety of seeing his own memories fade, he joined the long sad list of the victims of the Nazi hell who took their own lives.

Levi’s mounting depression in the last weeks of his life was known to his family and friends. Significantly, in his last interview he begged the questioning journalist not to consider him a prophet: “Prophets are the plague of today, and perhaps of all time, because it is impossible to tell a true prophet from a false one.” In the same vein he had said earlier, “All prophets are false. I don’t believe in prophets, even though I come from a heritage of prophets.”

Prophets the “plague of all time”? Levi’s dismissal is understandable, for he was an atheist who had been to hell on earth and back. But it is sad, for the strong line of Hebrew prophets is not only a defining feature of his people’s heritage but one of the richest Jewish gifts to the history of the world. Elijah, Elisha, Isaiah, Jeremiah, Amos, Hosea, and many others—each was a hero of the moral word whose “Thus says the Lord” shattered the status quo of his day.

They each opened up perspectives on God's truth, justice, and peace that restored the world, moved it forward through a transcendent point of leverage, or simply drew a line in the sand to mark off evil.

The prophetic calling, however, was closed to Levi because in his universe he acknowledged no caller. Unlike Søren Kierkegaard with his questing "knight of faith," Levi recognized no higher majesty to dub him knight.

The Weight of Witness

It is often said that to have a fulfilling life, three essentials are required: a clear sense of personal identity, a deep sense of faith and meaning, and a strong sense of purpose and mission. Levi, it turned out, had a critical deficiency of the second and third, and in ways that poignantly illustrate our contemporary crisis of truth.

To all appearances, Primo Levi had a clear sense of identity and a passionate sense of purpose. "It is very likely," he said, "that without Auschwitz I would never have written, and would have given only little weight to my Jewish identity." But following Auschwitz, "My only thought was to survive and tell." Because of his desperate desire to tell his story to everyone he met, he would compare himself to Coleridge's ancient mariner who pestered the wedding guests.

Levi's most telling testimony can be read at Auschwitz itself. In 1980 the Polish government restructured the design of the camp and asked Levi to introduce the Italian section. Of the eight paragraphs he submitted, only the last one stands there today:

> Visitor, observe the remains of this camp and consider: Whatever country you come from, you are not a stranger. Act so that your journey is not useless, and our deaths not useless. For you and your sons, the ashes of Auschwitz hold a message. Act so that the fruit of hatred, whose traces you have seen here, bears no more seed, either tomorrow or for ever after.

What was it that undid Levi's mission to witness? The first and more obvious reason was philosophical. Levi lacked any sense of faith and meaning with which to interpret and handle his harrowing experience. An atheist when he went to Auschwitz, he could never get around the extermination camp as the black hole of godlessness, the extreme situation of absolute evil to which no response could ever be adequate.

For a time in 1944 he was struck by words from Dante's *Inferno*, "Consider what you came from. . . . You were not born to live like mindless brutes," which hit him "like the blast of a trumpet, like the voice of God." Two years later, in freedom and on meeting his wife, he felt he had at last found a place in the universe where it no longer appeared "that the world was God's error."

But in the end, the dark combination of Auschwitz and atheism always closed back in on him. For instance, in 1946 Levi described his raging in silence at an old Jew who thanked God for having escaped selection to the gas chambers—"If I was God, I would spit at Kuhn's prayer." Or as he stated more bluntly in his first book, *If This Is a Man*, "If there is an Auschwitz, then there cannot be a God." Forty years later, only months before his suicide, he wrote after those words in pencil: "I find no solution to the riddle. I seek, but I do not find it."

The second and less obvious reason for Levi's crisis was practical. He gradually realized that his mission—however noble and necessary—was impossible. As Liliane Atlan wrote in *An Opera for Theresientstadt,* Auschwitz is "an experience both impossible to pass on, and impossible to forget."

Most of the reasons for this difficulty are straightforward. Memories are tricky and eventually fade. Revisionists who deny history are shocking but are neither driven nor answered by facts. Besides, most people would rather not be reminded of evil of such magnitude. Then too many generations pass and the new world of entertainments treats evil as fantasy.

Levi, for example, was amused but stunned when a ten-year-old schoolboy solemnly told him that he should have cut a guard's throat as he switched off the power to the electric fence, and then urged him not to forget this advice should he find himself in the same situation again.

But the weight of the witness was always heavier on Levi than the sum of the problems. "We felt the weight of centuries on our shoulders," he wrote. And the heaviest burden of all was the guilt of surviving—"the best had been murdered"—along with the awful knowledge that confession was impossible, and yet without genuine confession there could be no real confrontation with evil. In the words of Itzhak Schipper, one of the "murdered best" killed in Majdanek in 1943: "No one will want to believe us, because our disaster is the disaster of the entire civilized world."

Finally, there was the agony of realizing that the ranks of the witnesses were thinning. "We are many (but every year our numbers diminish) . . . ," Levi wrote. "If we die in silence as our enemies desire . . . the world will not learn what man could do and what he can still do."

In a sense, Levi wrote at the end of his life, the hopelessness he [was] experiencing was worse than Auschwitz. For he was no longer young. The task of repeating the story was getting harder and harder. The burden of the witness was impossible. The way forward was hopeless. There was no other way out.

In the Steps of Sisyphus

Obviously no suicide ever returns to speak of his or her death, and Levi left no note, so we must pause in respect. But it is almost impossible to read Levi's last interviews and writings without thinking of Albert Camus and the myth of Sisyphus. In classical legend, Sisyphus was condemned by Zeus to push a huge stone up the hill only to have it roll down again each time—a story that Camus used to picture human fate in a world without God and without meaning.

For those who find themselves without faith in God and who conclude that the world they desire does not fit the world they discover, life is fundamentally deaf to their aspirations. And in fact, it is literally *absurd*. All meaning—including for Levi, the establishment of truth—is up to them. They must live so as to be able to say, in Nietzsche's words, "Thus I have willed it." Or as Frank Sinatra put it simply, "I did it my way."

So Levi must roll his "truth" up the hill again and again. When the vast indifference of the public makes the gradient steeper, he must push harder. When he rests for a moment and the revisionists shove his stone back down, he must start again. When his companions drop out and his energy flags, he must summon his strength one more time. Numb, exhausted, aching, despairing, he must roll it and roll it until he can roll it no more. In an absurd world no success will ever crown his labors with significance. He can have only one satisfaction: the rebel's reward of rolling, rolling, rolling, without end.

But there is an alternative to the fate of Sisyphus—and Nietzsche, Camus, Sinatra, and Levi. It is that truth, like meaning as a whole, is not for us to create but for us to discover. Each of us may be small, our lives short, and our influence puny. But if truth is there—objective absolute, independent of minds that know it—then we may count on it and find it a source of strength.

Another victim of totalitarian evil stood on this solid ground beyond himself as he declared, "One word of truth outweighs the entire world." Solzhenitsyn with his statement had not suddenly outpowered the Soviets with some self-generated "truth." Rather, outpowered, outnumbered, and outgunned, he as one single person seized and wielded truth as a sword that could not be resisted, crying out, "Grant, O Lord, that I may not break as I strike."

Primo Levi and Aleksandr Solzhenitsyn were both witnesses to the horrors they experienced. They were both spurred on by their passion not to betray the dying wish of millions to be remembered. But whereas Levi's view of truth left him a weary Sisyphus with a hopeless task, Solzhenitsyn's made him a sword in God's hand and allowed him to raise a voice to rally the world. "It is infinitely difficult to begin," he wrote in *The Oak and the Calf*, "when mere words must remove a great block of inert matter. But there is no other way if none of the material strength is on your side. And a shout in the mountains has been known to start an avalanche."

What am I arguing? Let me underscore it again. I am not countering the postmodern view of truth on behalf of the modern. One is as bad as the other; the postmodern is the direct descendant of the modern and the mirror image of its deficiencies. It is the more dangerous today only because it is more current. Nor am I raising purely theoretical arguments against the postmodern view of truth, for few people outside universities follow the complexities of the higher academic debates.

Rather, I am deliberately underscoring the practical difficulties that grow out of the theoretical deficiencies of the new radical relativism. We can easily be cowed into submission by the force or fashionability of new ideas without realizing their disastrous practical consequences for ordinary life. When that happens, the full answer to the problem in question must always include the theoretical answer. But practical arguments are an important first step in confronting the crisis.

With the present crisis of truth, practical arguments are vital in addressing two particular groups of people. One is those who hold to traditional Jewish and Christian assumptions about truth but have grown careless or hesitant in defending it. The other is those who do not hold to those beliefs but who care deeply about the society in which they live and the quality of their own lives in it. For each group, there are two powerful arguments for the practical importance of objective, nonrelativist truth. As the contrast between Primo Levi and Aleksandr Solzhenitsyn shows, differences between views of truth—far from being purely theoretical and irrelevant—make an enormous difference.

Red-Blooded Truth

For those who hold to traditional biblical assumptions of truth but are uncertain whether they are worth defending, two arguments for the importance of a high view of truth stand out, one lesser and one greater.

The lesser argument is that without truth we cannot answer the fundamental objection that faith in God is simply a form of "bad faith" or "poor faith." The wilder accusation of "bad faith" comes from outside the Jewish and Christian communities and is one of the deepest and most damaging charges against these faiths in the last two centuries. Jews and Christians believe, critics say, not because of good reasons but because they are afraid not to believe. Without faith, they would be naked to the alternatives, such as the terror of meaninglessness or the nameless dread of unspecified guilt. Faith is therefore a handy shield to ward off the fear, a comforting tune to whistle in the darkness; it is, however, fundamentally untrue, irrational, and illegitimate—and therefore "inauthentic" and "bad faith."

In modern times the charge of "bad faith" was raised by the French existentialists but is more widely associated with Marxist and Freudian attacks on religion—religion for Marx was the "opium of the people" and for Freud a "projection." Needless to say, the germ of the charge is far older and wider. "Fear made the gods," wrote Lucretius as a first-century BC Roman. Or as Henrik Ibsen remarked as a nineteenth-century Norwegian, "Take away the life-lie from the average man and you take away his happiness."

Whatever the historical period, the dynamic of the accusation is the same. As Aldous Huxley set it out more patiently,

> Man inhabits, for his own convenience, a homemade universe within the greater alien world of external matter and his own irrationality. Out of the illimitable blackness of the world the light of his customary thinking scoops, as it were, a little illuminated cave—a tunnel of brightness, in which, from the brink of consciousness to its death, he lives, moves, and has his being. . . . We ignore the outer darkness; or if we cannot ignore it, if it presses too insistently upon us, we disapprove of being afraid.

There are several possible responses to this charge, such as those who wield it are rarely courageous enough to turn it on their own beliefs, the very charge is itself the biblical critique of idols, and so on. But at the end of the day, there is no answer without one: Those who put their faith in God do so for all sorts of good reasons, but the very best reason is that they are finally, utterly, and incontrovertibly convinced that the faith in which they put their confidence is *true*.

"What is truth?" someone will immediately ask. Let me answer straightforwardly. In the biblical view, truth is that which is ultimately, finally, and absolutely real, or the "way it is," and therefore is utterly trustworthy and dependable, being grounded and anchored in God's own reality and truthfulness. But this stress on the personal foundation of truth is not—as in postmodernism—at the expense of the propositional. Both accuracy and authenticity are important to truth.

If in our ordinary speech, telling the truth is "telling it like it is," we can say that *a statement, an idea, or a belief is true if what it is about is as it is presented in the statement*. Belief in something doesn't make it true; only truth makes a belief true. But without truth, a belief may be only speculation plus sincerity. Or perhaps, worse still, bad faith. A sardonic nineteenth-century wit once suggested that three words be carved in stone over all church doors: "Important if true." To which the Christian would reply, "Important *because* true."

The milder accusation, the parallel dismissal of faith as "poor faith," comes from inside the church and is less serious but more common. Whereas both the Bible and the best thinkers of Christian history invite seekers to put their faith in God because the message conveying that invitation is true, countless Christians today believe for various other reasons. For instance, they believe faith is true "because it works" (pragmatism), because they "feel it is true in their experience" (subjectivism), because they sincerely believe it is "true for them" (relativism), and so on.

For some of these Christians the deficiency comes from bad teaching. For others the motive is escape. Retreating into the fortress of personal experience, they can pull up the drawbridge of faith and feel impregnable to reason. But for all of them the outcome is a sickly faith deprived of the rude vigor of truth.

Tendencies toward this schizophrenic split between faith and reason have been evident since the Enlightenment, aided by such philosophers as Spinoza, who argued that "Revelation and Philosophy stand on totally different footings," each with its own separate province. Earlier still in the thirteenth century, the idea led to the disastrous medieval notion of "double truth," according to which there are two truths—one for the supernatural world and one for the natural. Each was separate and contradictory, but the doubleness meant that the church could be right in theology while wrong in philosophy or science. Faith, in other words, was true even if it was nonsense. Believers could believe with their theological minds while disbelieving with their scientific minds.

Biblical faith, by contrast with both medieval and modern deficiencies, has a robust view of life. All truth is God's truth and is true everywhere, for everyone, under all conditions. Truth is true in the sense that it is objective and independent of the mind of any human knower. Being true, it cannot contradict itself.

Human beliefs and truth-claims, in contrast, may be relative because we humans are finite. Therefore all beliefs are partial and provisional. But truth—guaranteed by God—is quite different. Created by God, not us, it is partly discovered and partly disclosed. It is singular ("truth"), not plural ("truths"); certain, not doubtful; absolute and unconditional, not relative; and grounded in God's infinite knowing, not in our tiny capacity to know anything. As Jean Paul

Sartre acknowledged, in words that faith is happy to reverse, "There can be no eternal truth if there is no eternal and perfect consciousness to think it."

With such a rocklike view of truth, the Christian faith is not true because it works; it works because it is true. It is not true because we experience it; we experience it—deeply and gloriously—because it is true. It is not simply "true for us"; it is true for any who seek in order to find, because truth is true even if nobody believes it and falsehood is false even if everybody believes it. That is why truth does not yield to opinion, fashion, numbers, office, or sincerity—it is simply true and that is the end of it. It is one of the Permanent Things. All that and a great deal more hangs on the issue of truth, even though this is only the lesser argument for truth.

The Final Reality

The greater argument for the importance of a high view of truth is that for both Jews and Christians, truth matters infinitely and ultimately because it is a question of the trustworthiness of God himself. In contrast, for Western secularists final reality is only matter—a product of time plus chance—and truth to them has a corresponding status on that level.

As Darwinism has underscored more and more openly, natural selection does not favor a predisposition toward truth. On the contrary, "truth-directedness" is a handicap, and a lack of it [. . .] is an evolutionary advantage. This bias against truth quickly becomes practical: How does one support, let alone explain, the importance of truth from the perspective of secularist thinking? If Darwinism is right, perhaps human truth-directedness is part of our alienation and therefore the entire project of the university and human truth-seeking is futile.

Secularists who choose to continue giving truth its higher status—as, for example, traditional journalists in opposition to the "personal reportage" of New Journalism—have bestowed that status, not discovered it. A similar problem holds for the Eastern family of faiths, including Hinduism and Buddhism. For both of these religions, the final reality is the undifferentiated impersonal. So "truth," accordingly, is part and parcel of the world of human ignorance, bondage, and illusion ("maya") separated from that final reality, which we must transcend.

Nothing could be a greater contrast to the high status of truth in the biblical view. Final reality for Jews and Christians is neither matter nor the undifferentiated impersonal but an infinite, personal God. Infinite and yet personal, personal and yet infinite, God may be trusted because he is the True One. He is true, he acts truly, and he speaks truly, for Christians, most clearly and fully in Jesus, his effective, spoken "Word." God's truthfulness is therefore foundational for his trustworthiness. His covenant rests on his character; his truth can be counted on.

Jews and Christians are therefore immune to Darwin's "horrid doubt." In the biblical view, we humans can think freely and passionately pursue the full range of human inquiry—from coffee-bar discussions to the strivings of the noblest art to the tireless search for the scientific secrets of the universe and knowledge in all fields. And all the while we know that our intellectual powers and our very disposition as truth-seekers are underwritten by the truthfulness of the Creator in the universe. As John Paul II writes in his encyclical on truth, this is all possible thanks to "the splendor of truth which shines forth deep within the human spirit." Truth transcends us as humans; as we follow it, it leads us on, back, and up to One who is true.

"In the beginning was the Word," John's Gospel begins—which means that in the end meaning itself has meaning, guaranteed by God himself and now spoken forth as an effective, liberating Word.

In other words, for both Jews and Christians, truth is not finally a matter of philosophy but of theology. Philosophical issues are critical and—at least for philosophers—fascinating, but the theological issue is primary. For all the fragile precariousness of our human existence on our tiny earth in the vastness of space, we may throw the whole weight of our existence on God, including our truth-seeking desires, because he is wholly true.

If Might Makes Right

What of those people who do not hold to traditional or biblical assumptions of truth but who care about their society and their place in it? The response here might be harder, and even in the view of some, impossible. But in fact there are two powerful arguments for the importance of a high view of truth, even for those who do not believe in it. The first of the two is negative in nature: *Without truth we are all vulnerable to manipulation.*

The promise of postmodernism at first sight is a brave new world of freedom. "Truth is dead; knowledge is power," the exuberant cheerleaders tell us. We must therefore debunk the knowledge-claims confronting us and reach for the prize—freedom from the dominations constraining us. What could be simpler and more appealing?

There is only one snag. What happens when we succeed in cutting away truth claims to expose the web of power games only to find we have less power than the players we face? If truth is dead, right and wrong are neither, and all that remains is the will to power, and the conclusion is simple: Might makes right. Logic is only a power conspiracy. Victory goes to the strong and the weak go to the wall.

We can take the result in an individualistic direction, as Herbert Spencer did; a collective direction, as Karl Marx did; or a broad evolutionary direction, as proponents of the "selfish gene" propose. But the result is the same. When everything is reduced to the will-to-power, manipulation is the name of the game and victory goes to the strong and the ruthless. "Law!" Cornelius Vanderbilt once snorted. "What do I care about the law? H'aint I got the power?"

The power can be subtle, too. One biographer wrote of John F. Kennedy's manipulation as a master of "using candor in lieu of truth." People would walk away "thinking they've been told the truth. But, in fact, they've really been told nothing of true importance. The small and candid moments set up the big lie."

In Lenin's formulation, there is always power and always manipulation. The question is forever, "Who? Whom?" Duke University Professor Stanley Fish makes no bones about the outcome from the postmodern perspective. In an article entitled "There's No Such Thing as Free Speech and It's a Good Thing Too," he answers several common objections: "Some form of speech is always being restricted. . . . We have always and already slid down the slippery slope; someone is always going to be restricted next, and it is your job to make sure that that someone is not you."

Those who embrace postmodern power-playing are as suicidal as Aesop's eagle that, at the moment of its death, recognizes its own feathers on the offending arrow's shaft. To warn us of such folly,

Solzhenitsyn and Havel stand as lone sentinels. Face-to-face with the force of a totalitarian propaganda and repression far worse than anything in the West, they took their stand on truth and could not be moved.

Fortunately for us, the test is not likely to come on such a cosmic stage. But the same principle holds true at humbler levels—the difficulty may be a controlling boss, a highly manipulative professor, or an emotional tyrant of a family member. Without truth we are all vulnerable to manipulation.

Pablo Picasso is a cautionary example. A genius as an artist, he was often a monster in his relationships—especially with women—because of his controlling, devouring personality. "When I die," Picasso predicted years before the filming of *Titanic,* "it will be a shipwreck, and as when a big ship sinks, many people all around will be sucked down with it."

When Picasso died in 1973, at the age of ninety-one, his prediction came true. Three of those closest to him committed suicide (his second wife, an early mistress, and a grandson), and several others had psychiatric breakdowns. "He amazes me," said his friend, sculptor Alberto Giacometti. "He amazes me as a monster would, and I think he knows as well as we do that he's a monster." Indeed, Picasso referred to himself as "the Minotaur," the mythic Cretan monster that devoured maidens.

One mistress, Marie Therese, described how Picasso set about painting: "He first raped the woman and then he worked." Another told him, "You've never loved anyone in your life. You don't know how to love." Picasso himself was brutally blunt, "Every time I change wives I should burn the last one. Then maybe I'd be rid of them. They wouldn't be around now to complicate my existence."

Picasso's destructiveness was rooted in his childhood but was reinforced by his early acquaintance with Nietzsche through friends in Barcelona. "Truth cannot exist . . . truth does not exist," he used to mutter. "I am God, I am God."

Significantly, only one of Picasso's wives and mistresses—Francoise Gilot—survived him with integrity intact. She was forty years younger but not naïve. "Picasso," she later wrote in *My Life with Picasso,* "was like a conqueror, marching through life, accumulating power, women, wealth, glory, but none of that was very satisfying anymore." He was like Nietzsche's loveless superman who must suppress all caring: "Love is the danger of the loneliest one."

How did Gilot survive, well aware that it was foolish to be sucked into his orbit and fatal to come under his domination? The only safeguard, she said, was truth. Every day she had to be "Joan of Arc, wearing one's armor from day till night."

Freedom For

The second, and positive, argument for the importance of truth pales at the first with comparison in the negative, but it is no less important. It is that *without truth there is no genuine freedom and fulfillment.* Isaiah Berlin, the great Oxford philosopher, used to remind students repeatedly that although freedom has two parts, many young people never experience the highest freedom because they appreciate the lower.

Freedom, Berlin stressed, is both negative and positive. Negative freedom, or "freedom from," has an obvious appeal in the modern world. Teenagers, for example, are famous for acting as if all freedom is freedom *from* parents, *from* teachers, and *from* supervision. Many adults make the same mistake.

Modern America has all the appearance of a nation-sized demonstration of the adolescent error writ large. Decisively parting company with the wisdom of their founders, Americans have exchanged the "moral republic" of the framers for the "procedural republic" of today. While the American framers wisely avoided the foolish opposition between authority and freedom of the European Enlightenment through their emphasis on "tempered freedom" and "ordered liberty," the present generation has overthrown their vision altogether. Whereas the framers believed that liberty requires virtue, virtue requires faith, and faith requires liberty (which in turn requires virtue, and so on), modern Americans believe only in "due process" and the clash of competing self-interests in the neutral public square.

Many Americans equate freedom with privacy; as St. Jean de Creveocoeur observed, "Nobody disturbs them," or as Justice Brandeis said, "the right to be left alone." They confuse unfettered freedom of choice with freedom of consciousness; as Cardinal

Newman put it, "Conscience has rights before it has duties." They lower freedom of speech to freedom to offend. They stress rights without responsibilities. And they mistake the lower and easier freedom, "freedom under the rule of law," with the higher and harder freedom, the freedom born of virtue that inspires "obedience to the unenforceable."

Yet negative freedom is always limited and incomplete without positive freedom. "Freedom from" requires the complement of "freedom for." That is why, long ago, the Roman poet Tactitus wrote, "The more corrupt the state, the more laws." That is what Benjamin Franklin meant when he wrote, "Only a virtuous people are capable of freedom." Or what historian Lord Acton taught in his magisterial writings on liberty: Freedom is "not the power of doing what we like but the fight of being able to do what we ought." Yet having thrown over authority for the sake of reason, and now reason for the sake of desire, Americans find that the limitation of negative freedom becomes obvious: Those who set out to do what they like usually end up not liking what they've done.

D. H. Lawrence came to the conclusion that stopping at negative freedom was a central problem of Americans—freedom was always left in declarations, the rage for rights, the undying restlessness to "move on." He wrote in his essay "The Spirit of Place": "Men are free when they are obeying some deep, inward voice of religious belief. Obeying from within, . . . not when they are escaping to some wild west. The most unfree souls go west and shout of freedom. . . . The shout is a rattling of chains. Liberty in America has meant so far breaking away from all dominion. The true liberty will only begin when Americans discover the deepest whole self of man."

No one expressed this point more often and more clearly than G. K. Chesterton in *Orthodoxy*:

> The moment you step into a world of facts, you step into a world of limits. You can free things from alien or accidental laws, but not from the laws of their own nature. You may, if you like, free a tiger from his bars, but do not free him from his stripes. Do not free a camel from the burden of his hump: you may be freeing him from being a camel.

In other words, we are never freer than when we become most ourselves, most human, most just, most excellent, and the like. Yet, if this is the case, freedom has a requirement: The true, the good, and the free have to be lined up together. To be ourselves, we need to know who we are. To be fully human, we need to know what humanness is. To aspire after virtue, justice, excellent, and beauty, we do not need to know the content of those ideals but we need to practice them. After all, as the Greeks pointed out, if abstract virtue were enough, we could be virtuous while asleep.

In short, today the crisis of truth, tomorrow the corruption of freedom. Truth without freedom is a manacle, but freedom without truth is a mirage. If freedom is not to be vacuous and stunted, it requires truth—lived truth. As Pope John Paul II declared flatly when he was still a Polish cardinal under the Soviet tyranny: "There is no freedom without truth."

Will such arguments prevail? Not just in private life but in the public square? To be sure, we need to make them boldly, with imagination and compassion as well as force. But their strength lies in their pragmatisms. If truth is truth, it reaches out a strong hand to men and women caught by the abusiveness of a thousand kinds. If truth is truth, it strikes a chord in hearts everywhere that are yearning for deeper freedom. Truth, in sum, is far more powerful than mere talk about the truth. Human beings are truth-seekers by nature, and truth persuades by the force of its own reality.

MADELEINE L'ENGLE

Characterized by a didactic and animated style, Madeleine L'Engle (1918–2007) creatively steers her audiences through a literary experience. Recognized particularly for her internationally acclaimed work A Wrinkle in Time, *she traveled and spoke on a wide variety of subjects. As a writer, L'Engle engaged her audience to think about the more profound issues of the experience of life, like knowledge and truth.*

In the following chapter, from The Rock That Is Higher Than I, *L'Engle facilitates a discussion on the idea of story by encouraging the reader to think about their own story. She provides a vivid guide, using the biblical narrative and her own experiences to disrupt our conventional thinking about the differences between knowledge and truth—both in how they inform our nascent beliefs from what we read and deem true, and in the way we conclude certain things about ourselves from outside experiences and influences.*

Story as the Search for Truth

TRUTH IS FRIGHTENING. Pontius Pilate knew that, and washed his hands of truth when he washed his hands of Jesus.

Truth is demanding. It won't let us sit comfortably. It knocks out our cozy smugness and casual condemnation. It makes us move. It? *It?* For truth we can read Jesus. Jesus *is* truth. If we accept that Jesus is truth, we accept an enormous demand: Jesus is wholly God, and Jesus is wholly human. Dare we believe that? If we believe in Jesus, we must. And immediately that takes truth out of the limited realm of literalism.

But a lot of the world, including the Christian world (sometimes I think especially the Christian world), is hung up on literalism, and therefore confuses truth and fact. Perhaps that's why someone caught reading a novel frequently looks embarrassed, and tries to hide the book, pretending that what he's really reading is a book on how to fix his lawn mower or take out his own appendix. Is this rather general fear of story not so much a fear that story is not true, as that it might actually be true? And what about the word *fiction?* For many people it means something that is made up, is not true.

Karl Barth wrote that he took the Bible far too seriously to take it literally. Why is that statement frightening to some people? There is no way that you can read the entire Bible seriously and take every word literally. Contradictions start in the first chapter of Genesis. There are two Creation stories, two stories of the making of Adam and Eve. And that is all right. The Bible is still true.

People have always told stories as they searched for Truth. As our ancient ancestors sat around the campfire in front of their caves, they told the stories of their day in order to try to understand what their day had meant, what the truth of the mammoth hunt was, or the roar of the cave lion, or the falling in love of two young people. Bards and troubadours throughout the centuries have sung stories in order to give meaning to the events of human life. We read novels, go to the movies, watch television, in order to find out more about the human endeavor. As a child I read avidly and in stories I found truths which were not available in history or geography or social studies.

There is a prevalent illusion that nonfiction is factual and objective, and that when we read history we can find out what really happened. Not so! My mother was a Southerner and my father was a damnyankee, and I got two totally different versions of "the wa-ah," as my mother called what my father referred to as the Civil War. It's two very different wars, depending on the point of view.

After the "wa-ah" all anybody in my mother's family had was story. They had lost husbands and sons and homes and all worldly goods. They did not have enough to eat. Their houses had been burned. I have some of the family silver because it was buried under a live oak tree, and I have some of the portraits because they were cut out of the frames and buried, too. On one of my walls is an indifferent oil painting on wood of a landscape with a windmill. It is fascinating to me because there is a slash across the top made by a Yankee saber, and on the back is a rude chess or checkers board painted by the invading soldiers.

And I have stories. My great-grandmother, the first Madeleine

L'Engle, had been her father's hostess when he was ambassador to Spain. After the war the young widow cut up her velvet and brocade ballgowns to make trousers for her little sons and dresses for her daughter; there was no material to buy, and no money to buy it with had there been. I have her Bible, with her markings, and occasional spots from tears, and they, too, tell the story of her long, full life, going from riches to rags, grieving for the death of her young husband. She is remembered with great affection by all who knew her, as a merry person, full of vitality, but my mother, who adored her, told me that after her husband was killed she never wore anything but black or white for the rest of her long life.

Would I want to do that? I miss my husband daily, but I live in a very different world from that of the first Madeleine L'Engle.

Her mother-in-law, my great-great-grandmother, was a storyteller, too. She wrote her memoirs for her descendants, a delightful treasure. One of my favorite stories is that of her friendship with an African princess. Greatie, as my mother called her great-grandmother, was the princess' only champion and friend. This African woman had been brought to Florida by a slave trader and set up in a house on Fort George Island, off Jacksonville, where she was isolated and desperately homesick. Greatie did what she believed to be right, whether it was considered proper or not. Once a week she had herself rowed down the river to spend the day with the princess, and they became intimate friends. It is from the stories of both Greatie and Madeleine L'Engle that I drew the background for my novel *The Other Side of the Sun*. Is the novel true? I believe that it is. Much of it is not factual; indeed, there are many facts I would have no way of knowing. It is indeed a work of fiction. But it is, for me, true.

"But what," asked Pilate of Jesus, "is truth?"

William Blake writes, "Self-evident truth is one thing, and Truth the result of reasoning is another thing. Rational truth is not the truth of Christ, but the truth of Pilate."

For much of our lives we do need rational truth, the truth of Pilate. But we don't give our lives for it. History would be very different if Pilate had been willing to give his life for truth. But he was not. It was Jesus who willingly gave his life for truth, the truth of Love, the truth that goes beyond reason, through reason, and out on the other side. Such truth does not deny reason, but reason alone is not enough.

If truth and reason appear to be in conflict, then both must be re-examined, and scientists are as reluctant to do this tough work as are theologians. When the theory of plate tectonics and continental drift was first put forward (and how reasonable it seems now), the scientists got as upset as the theologians did when planet earth was displaced as the center of the universe. And as for those seven days of creation, nothing whatsoever is said in Genesis about God creating in human time. Isn't it rather arrogant of us to think that God had to use our ordinary, daily, wristwatch time? Scripture does make it clear that God's time and our time are not the same. The old hymn "a thousand ages in thy sight are but a moment past" reprises this. So why get so upset about the idea that God might have created in divine time, not human? What kind of a fact is this that people get so upset about? Facts are static, even comfortable, even when they are wrong! Truth pushes us to look at these facts in a new way, and that is not comfortable so it usually meets with resistance.

And how reasonable are we, with all our best efforts, able to be? Read two straightforward histories of any war, and you'll get two different wars, with the protagonists and antagonists reversed. No matter how objective the historian tries to be, personal bias will slip in, willy-nilly.

The Bible is not objective. Its stories are passionate, searching for truth (rather than fact), and searching most deeply in story. The story of David is one of the most complex and fascinating in the Bible, with its many prefigurings of Jesus. In working on *Certain Women* I discovered many more contradictions than I had remembered—two different ways of bringing David himself into the story, two different versions of Saul's death, for instance. But what the biblical narrator is trying to do is tell us the truth about King David, and the truth is more important than facts.

One of the major discoveries of the post-Newtonian sciences is that objectivity is, in fact, impossible. To look at something is to change it and to be changed by it.

Nevertheless there is still the common misconception, the illusion, that fact and truth are the same thing. No! We do not need faith for facts; we do need faith for truth. In his letter to Titus Paul speaks of the mystery of faith, and in Hebrews 11.1 he writes, *Now faith is the substance of things hoped for, the evidence of things not seen* (KJV).

The Bible has always challenged my imagination. But there have been many other stories that have opened doors and windows for me. The Greek and Roman myths I read when I was a child deal with basic truths that help illuminate my own problems. The myth of Sisyphus, for instance: there are many days when I feel like Sisyphus pushing that heavy rock up the mountainside, panting, sweating, as I heave it up, up, get it almost to the top, only to have it slip out of my grasp and roll all the way back down the mountain so that I have to start over again. Such myths have lasted because they are true to our human condition.

And because when I read I read with my Christian bias, whether I want to or not, the myth of Sisyphus offers me another truth. Sisyphus had to push that rock up the mountain over and over again. Jesus had to carry the cross only once. When it was done, it was done.

Jesus, the storyteller, told of a man who had a plank of wood in his eye and yet criticized another man for having a speck of dust in his eye. "*You hypocrite*," he said, "*first take the plank out of your own eye, and then you will see clearly to remove the speck from your brother's eye.*" This parable, like most of Jesus's stories, is true. Why must it be factual? Are we supposed to think that a man actually had a large plank of wood in his eye? The parable is, instead, a true story about our unwillingness to see our own enormous faults, and our eagerness to point out much smaller faults in other people. However, it's a lot easier to see this story as factual rather than true. If we can make ourselves believe that the man had a beam of wood in his eye, literally, then we don't have to look at our own faults, be challenged by Jesus's story, or maybe even feel that we have to do something about our faults. Literalism is a terrible crippler, but it does tend to let us off the hook. Or do I mean the cross?

A Zen story which makes much the same point as the parable of the plank and the speck concerns two Buddhist monks returning from a pilgrimage. It is spring, and the rains have fallen, and they come to a river which is swollen and running swiftly, so that the stepping stones are covered with water. A young girl stands by the river, afraid to cross, and the senior monk simply picks her up, sloshes across, sets her down on the other side and continues on his way. About an hour later the younger monk speaks. "Forgive me, I know you are older and wiser than I, and have been longer in the religious life, but do you really think that it was right for you, a celibate monk, to pick up that young girl in your arms and carry her that way?" And the older monk replied, "Oh, my son, are you still carrying her?"

How easy it is for us to project our own weaknesses onto other people.

I was once criticized for telling this story because it is a Buddhist story and therefore had to contradict Christianity. But does it? Should we not learn from each other? Jesus lived in a small world with many nations, and in his stories there are not only Samaritans, but Syro-Phoenicians, Romans—and many others. The stories of all nations I read as a child helped me to understand—intuitively rather than consciously—my own development as a human being, a Christian human being. And perhaps I learned even more from the stories I wrote.

James Carroll, in *The Communion of Saints,* writes, "The very act of story-telling, of arranging memory and invention according to the structure of narrative, is by definition holy. . . . We tell stories because we can't help it. We tell stories because we love to entertain and hope to edify. We tell stories because they fill the silence death imposes. We tell stories because they save us."

My great-great-grandmother, great-grandmother, grandmother, mother are alive for me because they are part of my story. My children and grandchildren and I tell stories about Hugh, my husband. We laugh and we remember—*re-member.* I tell stories about my friend, the theologian Canon Tallis, who was far more than my spiritual director with whom I had one of those wonders, a spiritual friendship. I do not believe that these stories are their immortality—that is something quite different. But remembering their stories is the best way I know to have them remain part of my mortal life. And I need them to be part of me, while at the same time I am quite willing for them all to be doing whatever it is that God has in mind for them to do. Can those who are part of the great cloud of witnesses which has gone before us be in two places at once? I believe that they can, just as Jesus could, after the Resurrection.

Let me tell you a story. Early in January of 1990 I was on a small boat with my eldest daughter and her family. This was a wonderful and special treat for us, and we were having a glorious time. One night I went to bed, read for a while, turned out the light, and went to sleep. After a while I slid into wakefulness, and I was aware that Hugh, my husband, was in bed with me, and it seemed perfectly natural for him to be there. I was in that state of consciousness that is neither dream nor waking, and I was grateful for his presence, though I knew that I must move carefully and not touch him, because if I did, he would vanish.

At the time that I was having this sense of Hugh's presence, around midnight or a little later, a radio call for us came through on the loudspeaker, and Josephine and Alan heard it and went to the radio room. There they learned that our beloved Tallis had died. They did not wake me. Early the next morning while I was drinking coffee, Alan came to my cabin and told me.

Later that day I told my daughter of my experience of the night before. She is brilliant and mathematical and eminently reasonable, and I asked her rather tentatively, "Do you think your father was there to tell me about Tallis?"

And she replied, "Well, Mother, that thought had crossed my mind."

Certainly it is outside the realm of reason and provable fact, but for me it touches the hem of truth. And the important thing is that I don't need to know anything more than what, for me, happened. That's all. That's enough.

I wish the church would be brave enough to acknowledge that there are questions to which, during our mortal lives, we have no answers. Too many answers lead to judgmentalism and to human beings (rather than God) deciding who can and who cannot go to heaven. I have a young friend whose father was unable to speak or move for weeks before his death, and his young son was devastated because, as far as he knew, his father had not accepted Jesus Christ as his personal Savior. "Please don't underestimate the power of Christ's love," I implored. "You have no way of knowing what Christ was doing with your father during those weeks when he could not speak and tell you what was going on within him. If you believe that God is love . . ."

"I do."

"Then trust that Love with your father."

I trust the love.

Does this mean that I do not believe in heaven—or hell, as punishment for our sins?

No. But I do not believe in the medieval version of heaven and hell. Heaven, for one thing, sounds unutterably dull, and I do not believe that God is ever dull.

In Ellis Peter's *The Heretic's Apprentice,* the young heretic talks about his feelings over the eternal damnation of infants who have died before they were baptized. "A human father wouldn't throw his baby into the flames," he protests. "Why would God do such a thing?"

His heresy is a heresy of love as, indeed, are many heresies. Why do human beings seem to feel the need to have other human beings suffer the torments of hell fire in order to be happy in heaven? I share the young heretic's heresy, though I do not believe it to be heresy. And I do not believe that God's love will ever fail. I do not know what lessons of love my husband or my friend Tallis are learning right now, but I believe that they are learning, going from strength to strength in understanding the astounding love of God for Creation.

But again we are in the language of mystery, not finite fact.

And yet again, like jesting Pilate, we may continue to ask, "What is truth?" And unless we allow truth to be a widening light, we hamstring ourselves. Love, for instance, is beyond the realm of provable fact. Why did my heart open for this man, rather than another? Why does my instinct tell me to say yes, here, and no, there? Why does this piece of music move me to tears, and that leave me cold? Since Hugh's death there are certain hymns I cannot sing without my eyes filling. We sang "A Mighty Fortress Is Our God" at both my mother's and my husband's funerals, and yet I can sing that strong affirmation without heaving with emotion. But I cannot sing "I Am the Bread of Life" without tear-ing up.

When I was in high school and college I looked at some of my mother's friends (all good, Christian, churchgoing women) and thought, *If this is what it means to be grown-up, I don't want it.*

Not my mother herself: she was a remarkable Southern woman, who, long before I was born, had ridden across the Sahara on a camel, and up the Andes on a donkey. In North Africa, in those days before planes, there were often long waits at desolate railroad stations, and my parents, with a couple of my father's journalist colleagues, would spread a blanket out on the platform and would play Halma. Halma, which is to Chinese Checkers more or less what chess is to checkers, was originally an Arab game, and they would often be ringed by Arabs, betting on them. Predictably, they bet on the men. It was a mistake. My mother, who had a mathematical sharpness I have not inherited, almost always won. No, it was not my mother who made me reluctant to be grown-up, but some of the women around her who had closed in, shut down, lost interest in new ideas, went to church to be safe, not challenged, who had forgotten how to play, forgotten story, forgotten how to laugh.

If we limit ourselves to the possible and provable, as I saw these people doing, we render ourselves incapable of change and growth, and that is something that should never end. If we limit ourselves to the age that we are, and forget all the ages that we have been, we diminish our truth.

Perhaps it is the child within us who is able to recognize the truth of story—the mysterious, the numinous, the unexplainable—and the grown-up within us who accepts these qualities with joy but understands that we also have responsibilities, that a promise is to be kept, homework is to be done, that we owe other people courtesy and consideration, and that we need to help care for our planet because it's the only one we've got.

I never want to lose the story-loving child within me, or the adolescent, or the young woman, or the middle-aged one, because all together they help me to be fully alive on this journey, and show me that I must be willing to go where it takes me, even through the valley of the shadow.

For centuries there have been stories that have been part of the vocabulary of even the moderately educated person. The great stories from Scripture, the Greek and Roman myths, the Arthurian legends, for instance. Pat, my physician friend, sent me the following quotation from the *Journal of Occupational Medicine,* taken, in turn, from Allan Bloom's *The Closing of the American Mind:*

> When I first noticed the decline in reading during the late sixties, I began asking my large introductory classes and any other group of younger students to which I spoke what books really counted for them? Most were silent, puzzled by the question. The notion of books as companions was foreign to them. Justice Black with his tattered copy of the Constitution in his pocket at all times is not an example that would mean much to them. There was no printed word to which they looked for counsel, inspiration, or for joy.

I hope that that is too radical a response to what has happened to our reading habits. While it is to some extent true, I hope that it is not wholly true, and I think that it is not, because of the large number of readers who write to me recommending and often sending me books they think I would enjoy, or who tell me that they turn to my stories for courage and comfort when they are in need. And I am encouraged, too, by my granddaughters and their college friends, and by their groans of anguish and ecstasy when they tell about the large sums of money they have just spent on books, not all of which are for their college courses.

But there is, alas, no doubt that we are becoming a vocabulary-deprived nation—nay, planet. Words have been dropping off all through this century, but the loss increased radically in the sixties with the immorality of "limited vocabulary." How on earth is a child going to learn words if the vocabulary is limited to what some "average" child is expected to know at the age of five or six or seven? When I was a child and came across a word I did not know in a story, I just went on reading and by the time I had come across the word in two or three more books, I had absorbed what it meant. It was easier for me to read Shakespeare in high school than it is for students today, not because my contemporaries and I were any brighter, but because far more vocabulary was familiar and available to us than to comparable students today.

We can, of course, dump the blame on television, but I don't think it's television alone that stops people from reading. It is, I suspect, fear of story, fear of imagination, fear of the unexplainable. The less vocabulary we have, the more limited our words, the more frightening the imagination becomes.

Allan Bloom continues,

> Imagine such a young person walking through the Louvre or the Uffizi and you can immediately grasp the condition of his soul. In his ignorance of the stories of Biblical or Greek or Roman Antiquity, Raphael, Leonardo, Michelangelo, Rembrandt, and all the others, can say nothing to him.

It is ironic that my little grandsons are mad about Mutant Ninja Turtles, and their parents have had to explain to them that Leonardo and Raphael and Michelangelo were real artists who lived and painted and sculpted hundreds of years ago. My grandsons find it difficult to understand that they weren't turtles. At least they are learning about great artists as well as turtles.

Bloom points out that these artists expected their viewers to recognize their subjects, to know the stories, and to have been influenced by them intellectually and spiritually. When such potent recognition no longer exists, Bloom says, "the voice of civilization has been stilled. It is meaning itself that vanishes beyond the dissolving horizon."

Meaning that vanishes?

Truth that vanishes?

And can the two be separated?

And how do we come to meaning and truth except through story?

The story of Abraham and Sarah, of Gideon, of Miriam, of David and Abigail, and finally, the story of Jesus of Nazareth—these affirm and reaffirm meaning for us.

Story helps us with the questions that have no answers. I wish the Church (of all denominations) would be brave enough to acknowledge that there are questions which, during our mortal lives, are not going to be answered. There are no answers to the wonder of Creation, the marvel of the Incarnation, the glory of the Resurrection. Too many answers lead to smug self-righteousness and—even worse—to human beings, rather than God, deciding who is and who is not loved by the Maker. Can't we trust God?

DOROTHY L. SAYERS

An affable personality and formidable intellect, Dorothy L. Sayers (1893–1957) was one of the twentieth century's most prominent British writers. She had a wonderfully vast and varied career, not only as a writer but also as a lecturer and lay theologian. Besides her specialty of detective novels, she produced plays, essays, poems, translations such as Dante's Divine Comedy, *and important works on spiritual topics.*

Believing strongly in the use of imagination to generate thinking, Sayers's essays take readers into controversial ideas, but with the use of humor and whimsy to sustain interest and avoid cynicism or reactionary anger. Even though she was not shy to speak out on important issues such as spirituality, she did it with the intent to engage, not to alienate. In the following essay, from Christian Letters to a Post-Christian World, *Sayers leads the reader through an entertaining look at the connection between history and Scripture. Her entry concludes with a powerful poem about truth.*

A Vote of Thanks to Cyrus

I OWE A certain debt to Cyrus the Persian. I made his acquaintance fairly early, for he lived between the pages of a children's magazine, in a series entitled *Tales from Herodotus,* or something of that kind. There was a picture of him being brought up by the herdsman of King Astyages, dressed in a short tunic very like the garment worn by the young Theseus or Perseus in the illustrations to Kingsley's *Heroes.* He belonged quite definitely to "classical times"; did he not overcome Croesus, that rich king of whom Solon had said, "Call no man happy until he is dead"? The story was half fairy tale—"his mother dreamed," "the oracle spoke"—but half history too: he commanded his soldiers to divert the course of the Euphrates, so that they might march into Babylon along the riverbed; that sounded like practical warfare. Cyrus was pigeon-holed in my mind with the Greeks and the Romans.

So for a long time he remained. And then, one day, I realized with a shock as of sacrilege, that on that famous expedition he had marched clean of our Herodotus and slap into the Bible. *Mene, mene, tekel upharsin*—the palace wall had blazed with the exploits of Cyrus, and Belshazzar's feast had broken up in disorder under the stern and warning eye of the prophet Daniel.

But Daniel and Belshazzar did not live in "the classics" at all. They lived in Church, with Adam and Abraham and Elijah, and were dressed like Bible characters, especially Daniel. And here was God—not Zeus or Apollo or any of the Olympian crowd, but the fierce and disheveled old gentleman from Mount Sinai—bursting into Greek history in a most uncharacteristic way, and taking an interest in events and people that seemed altogether outside His province. It was disconcerting.

And there was Esther. She lived in a book called *Stories from the Old Testament,* and had done very well for God's Chosen People by her diplomatic approach to King Ahasuerus. A good Old Testament–sounding name, Ahasuerus, reminding one of Ahab and Ahaz and Ahaziah. I cannot remember in what out-of-the-way primer of general knowledge I came across the astonishing equation, thrown out casually in passing phrase, "Ahasuerus (or Xerxes)." Xerxes!—but one knew all about Xerxes. He was not just "classics," but real history; it was against Xerxes that the Greeks had made their desperate and heroic stand at Thermopylae. There was none of the fairy-tale atmosphere of Cyrus about *him*—no dreams, no oracles, no faithful herdsman—only the noise and dust of armies tramping through the hard outlines and clear colors of a Grecian landscape, where the sun always shone so much more vividly than it did in the Bible.

I think it was chiefly Cyrus and Ahasuerus who prodded me into the belated conviction that history was all of a piece, and that the Bible was part of it. One might have expected Jesus to provide the link between the two worlds—the Caesars were classical history all right. But Jesus was a special case. One used a particular tone of voice in speaking of Him, and He dressed neither like Bible nor like classics—He dressed like Jesus, in a fashion closely imitated (down to the halo) by His disciples. If He belonged anywhere, it was to

Rome, in spite of strenuous prophetic efforts to identify Him with the story of the Bible Jews. Indeed, the Jews themselves had undergone a mysterious change in the blank pages between the Testaments: in the Old, they were "good" people; in the New, they were "bad" people—it seemed doubtful whether they really were the same people. Nevertheless, Old or New, all these people lived in Church and were "Bible characters" —they were not real in the sense that King Alfred was a real person; still less could their conduct be judged by the standards that applied to one's own contemporaries.

Most children, I suppose, begin by keeping different bits of history in watertight compartments, of which "Bible" is the tightest and most impenetrable. But some people seem never to grow out of this habit—possibly because of never having really met Cyrus and Ahasuerus (or Xerxes). Bible critics in particular appear to be persons of very leisurely mental growth. Take, for example, the notorious dispute about the Gospel according to St. John.

Into the details of that dispute I do not propose to go. I only want to point out that the arguments used are such as no critic would ever dream of applying to a modern book of memoirs written by one real person about another. The defects imputed to St. John would be virtues in Mr. Jones, and the value and authenticity of Mr. Jones's contribution to literature would be proved by the same arguments that are used to undermine the authenticity of St. John.

Suppose, for example, Mr. Bernard Shaw were now to publish a volume of reminiscences about Mr. William Archer: would anybody object that the account must be received with suspicion because most of Archer's other contemporaries were dead, or because the style of G. B. S. was very unlike that of a *Times* obituary notice, or because the book contained a great many intimate conversations not recorded in previous memoirs, and left out a number of facts that could easily be ascertained by reference to the *Dictionary of National Biography?* Or if Mr. Shaw (being a less vigorous octogenarian than he happily is) had dictated part of his material to a respectable clergyman, who had himself added a special note to say that Shaw was the real author and that readers might rely on the accuracy of the memoirs since, after all, Shaw was a close friend of Archer and ought to know—should we feel that these two worthy men were thereby revealed as self-confessed liars, and dismiss their joint work as valueless fabrication? Probably not; but then Mr. Shaw is a real person, and lives, not in the Bible, but in Westminster. The time has not come to doubt him. He is already a legend, but not yet a myth; two thousand years hence, perhaps—.

Let us pretend for a moment that Jesus is a "real" person who died within living memory, and that John is a "real" author, producing a "real" book; what sort of announcement shall we look for in the literary page of an ordinary newspaper? Let us put together a brief review, altering some of the names a little, to prevent that "Bible" feeling.

MEMOIRS OF JESUS CHRIST

By John Bar-Zebedee; edited by the Rev. John Elder, Vicar of St. Faith's, Ephesus (Kirk. 7s. 6d)

The general public has had to wait a long time for the intimate personal impressions of a great preacher, though the substance of them has for many years been familiarly known in Church circles. The friends of Mr. Bar-Zebedee have frequently urged the octogenarian divine to commit his early memories to paper; this he has now done, with the assistance and under the careful editorship of the Vicar of St. Faith's. The book fulfills a long-felt want.

Very little has actually been put in print about the striking personality who exercised so great an influence upon the last generation. The little anonymous collection of "Sayings" by "Q" is now, of course, out of print and unobtainable. This is the less regrettable in that the greater part of it has been embodied in Mr. J. Mark's brief obituary study and in the subsequent biographies of Mr. Matthews and Mr. Lucas (who, unhappily, was unable to complete his companion volume of the *Acts of the Apostles*). But hitherto, all these reports have been compiled at second hand. Now for the first time comes the testimony of a close friend of Jesus, and, as we should expect, it offers a wealth of fresh material.

With great good judgment, Mr. Bar-Zebedee has refrained from going over old ground, except for the purpose of tidying up the chronology which, in previous accounts, was conspicuously lacking. Thus, he makes it plain that Jesus paid at least two visits to Jerusalem during the three years of His ministry—a circumstance which clears up a number of confusing points in the narrative of His arrest; and the two examinations in the ecclesiastical courts are at last clearly distinguished. Many new episodes are related; in particular, it has now become possible to reveal the facts about the mysterious affair at Bethany, hitherto discreetly veiled out of consideration for the surviving members of the Lazarus family, whom rumor had subjected to much vulgar curiosity and political embarrassment. But the most interesting and important portions of the book are those devoted to Christ's lectures in the Temple and the theological and philosophical instructions given privately to His followers. These, naturally, differ considerably in matter and manner from the open-air "talks" delivered before a mixed audience, and shed a flood of new light, both on the massive intellectual equipment of the preacher and on the truly astonishing nature of His claim to authority. Mr. Bar-Zebedee interprets and comments upon these remarkable discourses with considerable learning, and with the intimate understanding of one familiar with his Master's habits of thought.

Finally, the author of these memoirs reveals himself as that delightful *rara avis,* a "born writer." He commands a fine economy and precision in the use of dialogue; his character-sketches (as in the delicate comedy of the blind beggar at the Pool of Siloam) are little masterpieces of quiet humor, while his descriptions of the Meal in the Upper Room, the visit of Simon Bar-Jonah and himself to the Sepulchre, and the last uncanny encounter by the Lake of Tiberias are distinguished by an atmospheric quality which places this account of the Nazarene in a category apart.

How reasonable it all sounds, in the journalese jargon to which we have grown accustomed! And how much more readily we may accept discrepancies and additions when once we have rid ourselves of that notion "the earlier, the purer," which, however plausible in the case of folklore, is entirely irrelevant when it comes to "real" biography. Indeed, the first "Life" of any celebrity is nowadays accepted as an interim document. For considered appreciation we must wait until many contemporaries have gone to where rumor cannot distress them, until grief and passion have died down, until emotion can be remembered in tranquility.

It is rather unfortunate that the "Higher Criticism" was first undertaken at a time when all textual criticism tended to be destructive—when the body of Homer was being torn into fragments, the Arthurian romance reduced to its Celtic elements, and the "authority" of manuscripts established by a mechanical system of verbal agreements. The great secular scholars have already recanted and adopted the slogan of the great archaeologist Didron: "Preserve all you can; restore seldom; never reconstruct." When it came to the Bible, the spirit of destruction was the more gleefully iconoclastic because of the conservative extravagances of the "verbal inspiration" theory. But the root of the trouble is to be found, I suspect (as usual), in the collapse of dogma. Christ, even for Christians, is not quite "really" real—not altogether human—and the taint of unreality has spread to His disciples and friends and to His biographers: they are not "real" writers, but just "Bible" writers. John and Matthew and Luke and Mark, some or all of them, disagree about the occasion on which a parable was told or an epigram uttered. One or all must be a liar or untrustworthy, because Christ (not being quite real) must have made every remark once and once only. He could not, of course, like a real teacher, have used the same illustration twice, or found it necessary to hammer the same point home twenty times over, as one does when addressing audiences of real people and not of "Bible characters."

Nor (one is led to imagine) did Christ ever use any ordinary behavior that is not expressly recorded of Him. "We are twice told that He wept, but never that He smiled"—the inference being that He never did smile. Similarly, no doubt, we may infer that He never said "Please" or "Thank you." But perhaps these common courtesies were left unrecorded precisely because they were common, whereas the tears were (so to speak) "news." True, we have lately got into the habit of headlining common courtesies: the newspaper that published the review of St. John's memoirs would probably have announced on a previous occasion:

PROPHET'S SMILE

The prophet of Nazareth smiled graciously yesterday morning on inviting Himself to lunch with little Mr. Zacchaeus, a tax-collector, who had climbed into a sycamore to watch Him pass.

St. Luke, who has a better sense of style, merely records that: He looked up and saw him, and said unto him, Zacchaeus, make haste and come down; for today I must abide in thy house. And he made haste and came down and received Him joyfully.

Politeness would suggest that one does not commandeer other people's hospitality with a morose scowl, and that if one is "received joyfully" it is usually because one has behaved pleasantly. But these considerations would, of course, apply only to "real" people.

"Altogether man, with a rational mind and human body—." It is just as well that from time to time Cyrus should march out of Herodotus into the Bible, for the synthesis of history and the confutation of heresy.

The Persona Dei: The Image of Truth

I the image of the Unimaginable
In the place where the Image and the Unimaged are one,
The Act of the Will, the Word of the Thought, the Son
In whom the Father's selfhood is known to Himself,
I being God and with God from the beginning
Speak to Man in the place of the Images.
You that We made for Ourself in Our own image,
Free like Us to experience good by choice,
Not of necessity, laying your will in Ours
For love's sake creaturely, to enjoy your peace,
What did you do? What did you do for Us
By what you did for yourselves in the moment of choice?
O Eve My daughter, and O My dear son Adam,
Try to understand that when you chose your will
Rather than Mine, and when you chose to know evil
In your way and not in Mine, you chose for Me.
It is My will you should know Me as I am—
But how? for you chose to know your good as evil,
Therefore the face of God is evil to you,
And you know My love as terror, My mercy as judgment,
My innocence as a sword; My naked life
Would slay you. How can you ever know Me then?
Yet know you must, since you were made for that;
Thus either way you perish. Nay, but the hands
That made you, hold you still; and since you would not
Submit to God, God shall submit to you,
Not of necessity, but free to choose
For your love's sake what you refused to Mine.
God shall be man; that which man chose for man
God shall endure, and what man chose to know
God shall know too—the experience of evil
In the flesh of man; and certainly He shall feel
Terror and judgment and the point of the sword;
And God shall see God's face set like a flint
Against Him; and man shall see the Image of God
In the image of man; and man shall show no mercy.

Truly I will bear your sin and carry your sorrow,
And, if you will, bring you to the tree of life,
Where you may eat, and know your evil as good,
Redeeming that first knowledge. But all this
Still at your choice, and only as you choose,
Save as you choose to let Me choose in you.

Who then will choose to be the chosen of God,
And will to bear Me that I may bear you?

Loving God with All Your Mind

JOHN STOTT

John Robert Walmsley Stott (1921–) is a prominent British Anglican clergyman who is an accomplished writer and noteworthy communicator. Having authored more than fifty books, he has done much to make the Bible accessible to contemporary minds. From 1951 to 1991 he served as the chaplain for Queen Elizabeth II, and he was appointed a Commander of the Order of the British Empire (CBE) in 2006. Although now retired from the pulpit, he remains Rector Emeritus of All Souls Church, London.

Asserting the importance of the exercise of the mind in relation to faith is one of Stott's favorite themes. From the beginning of "Your Mind Matters," he affirms an essential truth: God created every human being with the ability to think. He argues that consideration of faith requires intelligence and critical thinking. Similarly, he takes great care to point out the differences between faith based on emotionalism and one based on rationality.

Why Use Our Minds?

WHY SHOULD CHRISTIANS use their minds?

The first reason will appeal to every believer who longs to see the gospel spread and Jesus Christ acknowledged throughout the world. It concerns the power of men's thoughts to shape their actions. History is full of examples of the influence of great ideas. Every powerful movement has had its philosophy which has gripped the mind, fired the imagination, and captured the devotion of its adherents. One has only to think of the Fascist and Communist manifestos of this century, of Hitler's *Mein Kampf* on the one hand and of Marx's *Das Kapital* and the *Thoughts* of Chairman Mao on the other. A. N. Whitehead sums it up:

> The great conquerors, from Alexander to Caesar, and from Caesar to Napoleon, influenced profoundly the lives of subsequent generations. But the total effect of this influence shrinks to insignificance, if compared to the entire transformation of human habits and human mentality produced by the long line of men of thought from Thales to the present day, men individually powerless, but ultimately the rulers of the world.[1]

Much of today's world is dominated by ideologies which, if not totally false, are alien to the gospel of Christ. We may talk of "conquering" the world for Christ. But what sort of "conquest" do we mean? Not a victory by force of arms. Our Christian crusade is far different from the shameful crusades of the Middle Ages. Listen to Paul's description of the battle: "Our war is not fought with weapons of flesh, yet they are strong enough, in God's cause, to demolish fortresses. We demolish sophistries, and the arrogance that tries to resist the knowledge of God; every thought is our prisoner, captured to be brought into obedience to Christ."[2] This is a battle of ideas, God's truth overthrowing the lies of men. Do we believe in the power of the truth?

Not long after Soviet Russia's brutal suppression of the Hungarian uprising in 1956, Mr. Krushchev referred to the example set by Tsar Nicholas I, whose Russian forces had repressed the Hungarian revolt of 1848. In a debate on Hungary in the General Assembly of the United Nations, Sir Leslie Munro quoted Mr. Krushchev's remarks and concluded his speech by recalling a statement made by Lord Palmerston in the House of Commons on July 21, 1849, on the same subject. This is what Palmerston had said:

> Opinions are stronger than armies. Opinions, if they are founded in truth and justice, will in the end prevail against the bayonets of infantry, the fire of artillery and the charges of cavalry. . . .[3]

I turn now from secular examples of the power of thought to some more specifically Christian reasons for using our minds. My argument now is that the great doctrines of creation, revelation, redemption, and judgment all imply that man has an inescapable duty both to think and to act upon what he thinks and knows.

Created to Think

I begin with creation. God made man in his own image, and one of the noblest features of the divine likeness in man is his capacity to think. It is true that all subhuman creatures have brains, some rudimentary, some more developed. Mr. W. S. Anthony of the Oxford Institute of Experimental Psychology read a paper to the British Association in September 1957 in which he described certain experiments with rats. He put obstacles before their food and water "goal-boxes," which had frustrated them in their attempts to find their way through the maze. He discovered that, faced with the more complicated mazes, his rats showed signs of what he called "primitive intellectual doubt"! That may well be. But if some creatures have doubts, only man has what the Bible calls "understanding."[4]

Scripture assumes and portrays this from the beginning of man's creation. In Genesis 2 and 3 we see God communicating with man in a way that he does not communicate with animals. He expects man to cooperate with him, consciously and intelligently, in tilling and keeping the garden in which he has placed him, and to discriminate—rationally as well as morally—between what he is permitted to do and the one thing he is prohibited from doing. Moreover, God invites man to name the animals, symbolizing the lordship over them which he has been given; and he creates woman in such a way that man immediately recognizes her suitability as his life partner and, as a result, breaks spontaneously into the first love poem ever composed!

This basic rationality of man by creation is everywhere taken for granted. Indeed, Scripture bases upon it the regular argument that since man is different from the animals he should *behave* differently: "Be not like a horse or a mule, without understanding."[5] Consequently, man is mocked and rebuked both when his behavior is more bestial than human ("I was stupid and ignorant, I was like a beast toward thee"[6]) and when the behavior of animals is more human than that of some human beings. For sometimes animals actually outshine humans. Ants are more industrious and more prudent than the human sluggard. Oxen and donkeys tend to give their masters a more obedient recognition than God's people. And migratory birds are better at repentance, for when they go away on migration they always return, whereas some backsliders go and fail to come back.[7]

The theme is clear and compelling. There are many similarities between man and the animals. But animals were created to behave by instinct, human beings (*pace* the behaviorists) by intelligent choice. So when humans fail to do by their own mind and consent what animals do by instinct, they are contradicting themselves, contradicting their creation and their distinctive humanity, and they ought to be ashamed of themselves.

It is quite true that man's mind has shared in the devastating results of the Fall. The "total depravity" of man means that every constituent part of his humanness has been to some degree corrupted, including his mind, which Scripture describes as "darkened." Indeed, the more men suppress the truth of God which they know, the more "futile," even "senseless," they become in their thinking. They may claim to be wise, but they are fools. Their mind is "the mind of the flesh," the mentality of a fallen creature, and it is basically hostile to God and his law.[8]

All this is true. But the fact that man's mind is fallen is no excuse for a retreat from thought into emotion, for the emotional side of man's nature is equally fallen. Indeed, sin has more dangerous effects on our faculty of feeling than on our faculty of thinking, because our opinions are more easily checked and regulated by revealed truth than our experiences.

So then, in spite of the fallenness of man's mind, commands to *think*, to use his mind, are still addressed to him as a human being. God invites rebellious Israel: "Come now, let us reason together, says the Lord."[9] And Jesus accused the unbelieving multitudes, including the Pharisees and Sadducees, of being able to interpret the sky and forecast the weather but quite unable to interpret "the signs of the times" and forecast the judgment of God. "Why do you not judge for yourselves what is right?" he asked them. In other words, why don't you use your brains? Why don't you apply to the spiritual and moral realm the common sense which you use in the physical?[10]

What Scripture teaches concerning man's basic rationality, constituted by his creation and not altogether destroyed by his fall, secular society everywhere assumes. Advertisers may address their appeal to our baser appetites, but they take for granted our ability to distinguish between products; indeed, they often try to flatter the "discriminating" customer. When a crime is first reported by the news media, it is often added that "no motive has yet been discovered." It is assumed, you see, that even criminal behavior has a motivation of some kind. And when our behavior is more emotional than rational, we still insist on "rationalizing" it. The very process called "rationalization" is significant. It indicates that man has been constituted such a rational being that if he has no reasons for his behavior he has to invent some in order to live with himself.

Thinking God's Thoughts

I turn now from creation to revelation. The simple and glorious facts that God is a self-revealing God and that he has revealed himself to man indicate the importance of our minds. For all God's revelation is rational revelation, both his general revelation in nature and his special revelation in Scripture and in Christ.

Take nature. "The heavens are telling the glory of God; and the firmament proclaims his handiwork. Day to day pours forth speech, and night to night declares knowledge. There is no speech, nor are there words; their voice is not heard; yet their voice goes out through all the earth, and their words to the end of the world."[11] That is to say, God speaks to man through the created universe and proclaims his divine glory, although it is a message without words. The message is quite clear, however, and men who stifle its truth are guilty before God. "For what can be known about God is plain to them, because God has shown it to them. Ever since the creation of the world his invisible nature, namely his eternal power and deity, has been clearly perceived in the things that have been made. So they are without excuse, for although they knew God they did not honor him as God. . . ."[12]

Both these passages refer to God's self-revelation through the created order. Although it is a proclamation without speech, a voice without words, yet as a result of it all men to some degree "know God." This assumed ability of man to read what God has written in the universe is extremely important. All scientific research depends upon it, upon a correspondence between the character of what is being investigated and the mind of the investigator. This correspondence is *rationality*. Man is able to comprehend the processes of nature. They are not mysterious. They are logically explicable in terms of cause and effect. Christians believe that this common rationality between man's mind and observable phenomena is due to the Creator who has expressed his mind in both. As a result, in the astronomer Kepler's famous words, men can "think God's thoughts after him."

The same essential correspondence is even more direct between the Bible and the Bible reader. For in and through Scripture God has *spoken*, that is, communicated in words. One may perhaps say that if in nature God's revelation is visualized, in Scripture it is verbalized, and in Christ it is both, for he is "the Word made flesh." Now communication in words presupposes a mind which can understand and interpret them. For words are meaningless symbols until they are deciphered by an intelligent being.

So the second Christian reason why the human mind is important is that Christianity is a revealed religion. I doubt if this point has been better expressed than by James Orr in his book *The Christian View of God and the World*:

> If there is a religion in the world which exalts the office of teaching, it is safe to say that it is the religion of Jesus Christ. It has been frequently remarked that in pagan religions the doctrinal element is at a minimum—the chief thing there is the performance of a ritual. But this is precisely where Christianity distinguishes itself from other religions—it does contain doctrine. It comes to men with definite, positive teaching; it claims to be the truth; it bases religion on knowledge, though a knowledge which is only attainable under moral conditions . . . A religion divorced from earnest and lofty thought has always, down the whole history of the Church, tended to become weak, jejune and unwholesome; while the intellect, deprived of its rights within religion, has sought its satisfaction without, and developed into godless rationalism.[13]

Some people, to be sure, have reached the opposite conclusion. Since man is finite and fallen, they argue, since he cannot discover God by his intellect and God must reveal himself, therefore the mind is unimportant. But no. The Christian doctrine of revelation, far from making the human mind unnecessary, actually makes it indispensable and assigns to it its proper place. God has revealed himself in *words* to *minds*. His revelation is a rational revelation to rational creatures. Our duty is to receive his message, to submit to it, to seek to understand it and to relate it to the world in which we live.

That God needs to take the initiative to reveal himself shows that our minds are finite and fallen; that he chooses to reveal himself to babies[14] shows that we must humble ourselves to receive his Word; that he does so at all, and in words, shows that our minds are capable of understanding it. One of the highest and noblest functions of man's mind is to listen to God's Word, and so to read his mind and think his thoughts after him, both in nature and in Scripture.

I venture to say that when we fail to use our minds and descend to the level of animals, God addresses us as he addressed Job when he found him wallowing in self-pity, folly and bitter complaining: "Gird up your loins like a man, I will question you, and you shall declare to me."[15]

DAVID ELTON TRUEBLOOD

A former chaplain at Harvard and Stanford Universities, David Elton Trueblood (1900–1994) was a distinguished twentieth-century Quaker author and theologian. Besides theological works, he also authored biographies, including one of Abraham Lincoln. In addition to his academic pursuits, Trueblood was an advisor to Presidents Dwight D. Eisenhower and Richard Nixon and a lifelong friend to Herbert Hoover, a fellow Quaker.

A fascinating thinker and engaging writer, Trueblood never tired of exhorting people to pursue the knowledge of God with their mind, engaging both their faith and intellect. In The Knowledge of God *he joined the ongoing debate (which continues today!) about the veracity of religious experience. Noting our modern need to verify every religious experience, he concludes that the scientific community has had a great impact on our thinking. In this selection, he proposes a method of verification to evaluate the religious experience of a group. First, there will be considerable concurrence in their testimony. And second, they each will begin to exhibit new character qualities, like love, joy, and peace.*

The Means of Verification

IN ONE OF his later utterances, at the conclusion of his Terry Lectures at Yale University, Dr. Jung expressed what is probably a common opinion when he asserted that there is no appeal beyond the simple fact of religious experience. "Religious experience," he said, "is absolute. It is indisputable. You can only say that you have never had such an experience, and your opponent will say: 'Sorry, I have.' And there your discussion will come to an end."[1] But will it? We have already given evidence that this is far from the case. There is *much* more to be said, and to be said with relevance, for we must inquire into the general credibility of the speaker as well as his agreement or lack of agreement with other credible reporters. But is this as far as we can go? Perhaps it is, but it would be highly desirable to go farther. What we deeply desire is some added check, roughly comparable to what is called verification in scientific method. We want more than the mere word of a man who says, "Sorry, I have." We want, if possible, some external proof. It is obvious that we cannot have this in the sense that we go beyond experience, but perhaps there is, within experience, that which is publicly observable.

When most people ask whether religious experience can be verified they apparently mean that they want something as convincing as is a photograph in astronomical study. The significance of the photograph lies in the fact that the existence of the object reported has made a difference, in this case the difference being the change of a camera plate or film. We correctly ask, "Was some permanent mark left, a mark which others may see?" When no such effects can be shown, the fact may be as it is asserted, but it is not verified, and we are justifiably skeptical.

This demand for verification is a measure of the degree to which the scientific mentality has permeated our time. Many who consider the knowledge claim so long implicit and explicit in living religion, and are inclined to accept the claim as essentially valid when they have examined the evidence, go on to say that they would be much clearer in their minds if the claim in question could be verified.

The process of verification, itself, may easily be misunderstood. The modern use of the term derives largely from the writings of John Stuart Mill and stood, in his thought, for the process by which certain facts are first deduced from an hypothesis and later these facts are actually discovered. The form of reasoning is as follows:

1. If the hypothesis is true certain facts follow
2. These facts are found
3. Therefore the hypothesis is true.

There can be no doubt that the method of verification, thus stated, is *logically unsound*. To show that facts agree with an hypothesis is not to prove it true, unless we can show how there is no alternative hypothesis which could also account for the facts discovered, and this last is a most difficult task. The logical form is:

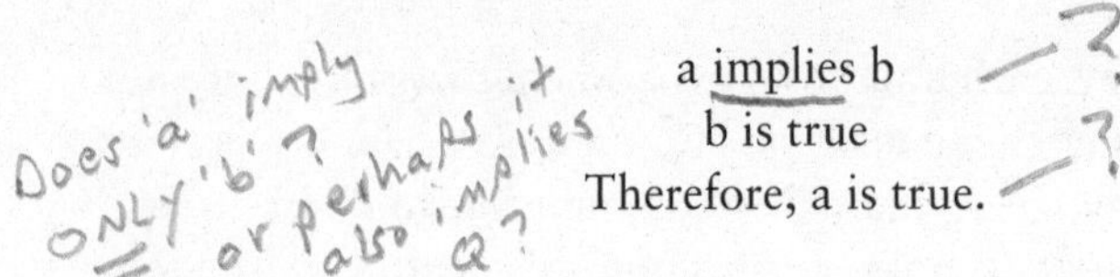

a implies b
b is true
Therefore, a is true.

When we see the method of verification reduced to this form we realize quickly that it is a perfect illustration of the formal fallacy known as the "affirmation of the consequent." This very common fallacy consists in supposing that a condition and its consequent are convertible, or that we can argue backward from effects to causes. If a government is good and just, the citizens will not revolt: hence we might argue that the government of certain countries is good and just. But there might be other reasons for the failure to revolt, such as a military dictatorship so strict that revolt can never get under way.

But, if verification rests on a fundamentally fallacious process, why has it come to play such an important part in modern thought, and especially in scientific method? The reason is that this process, unsatisfactory as it may be, is often the best or the only method that is available. There are many situations in which it is not possible to make a direct observation of the matter under discussion, but in which we can observe *something about it,* if we observe consequences. The following example will make this clear. We cannot confirm by direct observation that the sun and the planet Mars attract each other proportionally to their masses, and inversely as the square of their distances. But we can know what some of the consequences of this hypothesis are, one being that the planet's orbit is an ellipse with the sun at the focus. Then, as a matter of fact, we can find that Mars is observed to be at different points of an ellipse on stated occasions.[2]

In such an astronomical example we are still committing the fallacy of affirming the consequent, but we do not doubt the truth of the conclusion, partly because we cannot readily think of an alternative hypothesis. Even Professor Joseph, distinguished exponent of the classical logic, admits that "in practice we often have to be content with verification."[3] In many areas of experience there is no such thing as rigorous proof and we have to content ourselves with what is called the weight of evidence.

It has been difficult for later thinkers to improve upon Sir Isaac Newton's statement of both the weakness of verification and the practical necessity of dependence upon it.

> And although the arguing from experiments and observations by induction be no demonstration of general conclusions yet it is the best way of arguing which the nature of things admits of, and may be looked upon as so much the stronger, by how much the induction is more general.

Recognizing that the process of verification, even though formally unsatisfactory, is the only one available, we make every effort to refine the process and thereby lessen the likelihood of error. Thus we may deduce a number of complicated consequences and note whether all are found, or we may test the effects under a variety of circumstances in a variety of places. *We overcome a fallacy by committing it in sufficient amount in a refined fashion.*

A good example of how, by careful refinement of deductions and observations, we seek to escape the fallacy of the affirmation of the consequent is that of the empirical evidence for the existence of atoms. We have it on good authority that our sole evidence of the existence of atoms is of this character, inasmuch as they cannot be directly observed though the consequences of there being atoms can be observed.[4]

If we could find something in religion as convincing as is the indirect observation possible in regard to atoms we should be satisfied, even though it would not constitute strict proof. Taken in conjunction with the considerations which we have brought forward in earlier chapters of this volume, we should be justified in supposing it logically important.

At first it seems hard to see how there can be a process of verification in regard to the alleged knowledge of God, but the method is not really far to seek. The knowledge of God, since it necessarily takes place in the privacy of the individual's mind, is something which, in the nature of the case, another person cannot observe. But another person *can observe what the subject does.* It is possible to observe something of the quality of his life and the way he responds to situations of various kinds.

We can make a reasonably accurate deduction with which to begin. If men have known the Living God we have a right to expect two consequences. First, it is reasonable to suppose that they would tell about Him and that, after making necessary allowances for individual differences, there would be a substantial agreement in what they report. Second, it is reasonable to suppose that they would show new qualities of character, especially in joy, peace, courage, and human love. This is reasonable because the fact that God is, if true, is the most important fact in the world. We naturally expect that those who have had a glimpse of divine love will exhibit more courageous love in their lives than they have had before. We do not expect perfection, but we expect the experience to make a difference.

It has already been shown that the first of these two consequences is found in fact; there is substantial agreement such as we expect if the reported knowledge refers to a real object. It is not complete agreement and we are glad it is not, for we should be suspicious of collusion in that case. What we find is substantial agreement and a significant convergence in mature religious experience, as against the diversity in savage religion. Maturity, so considered, has little relation to chronology.

Our chief interest, in this final chapter, is in the second consequence, that of a new quality of life, which is publicly observable. In religion we cannot reasonably look for a mark on photographic plates, but we can reasonably look for a mark on human lives. If the experience of God is what men claim it is, we should expect to see a general change in their character; we should expect them to walk with a new step. It is this that we can check abundantly in a way that should be convincing to the open-minded. The evidence of altered lives, including both new strength and new tenderness, is so great that only a small portion of it has ever been committed to print. Not all of those who have reported religious experience have demonstrated "the fruits of the spirit," but, in considering evidence of this kind, we are concerned not so much with what is universal as with what is typical. We can show the typical verification through moral strength, by pointing to characteristic experiences in different settings.

In presenting the fruits of the spirit as evidence of the truth of the basic religious claim, we are by no means adopting a merely pragmatic conception of the meaning of truth. There are in the world untruths that are morally efficacious, at least for a time. We do not hold that all things which "work" are true, though we do hold that all things which are true may reasonably be expected to "work."

When, therefore, we point to the moral efficacy of religious experience we are not presenting a conclusive proof, but are engaging in precisely the same "affirmation of the consequent" on which all scientific verification depends and which approached proof as the body of the evidence increases, especially under a variety of situations. The effects of religious experience do no stand alone, but are part of the cumulative proof, according to which the problem is approached from several angles at once.

The evidence to be gleaned by a consideration of the new quality of life resulting from religious experience seems, at first, to be canceled by the fact that many crimes have been committed in the name of religion. It must be frankly admitted that there have been such crimes. The truth is that religion may be extremely harmful as well as beneficial both to its adherents and to the human race generally. It has sometimes blinded men to the glories of art, and it has often inspired vindictive crusades against unbelievers. The present sickness of civilization is marked, not so much by absence of religion, as by the emergence of new and dangerous movements, religious or quasi-religious in character. This is demonstrated by the kind of devotion they elicit from their members. Living men are held in an esteem which has a dangerously religious quality about it.

After all this has been openly conceded, however, there remains such a body of evidence concerning what Saint Paul called the fruits of the spirit that it is wonderfully convincing. This suggests that hypothesis that the evils just mentioned have come from false or perverted religion, for they do not belong to the mainstream. By the side of the cruelty and lust which religion has encouraged, we must place the overcoming joy with which millions in many generations have met life, including the persecutions of the cruel. The negative evidence provided by the Puritan hangmen in Boston is more than balanced by the amazing spirit of the people who were hanged. It was this kind of joy which so impressed the scientific mind of Romanes that he made it the keystone of the projected work of his mature years. . . .

Thus we have a working basis on which to judge alleged religious insight. If, in the long run, it does not give love and power and joy, it is not based on reality. Here we are at last on firm ground, for, though the affirmation of the consequent is a formal fallacy, the negation of the consequent is not. If x implies y, and y is false, we can be sure that x is false. By this method we can test various alleged experiences which we already have reason to doubt. The alleged experiences, of what is called spiritualism, are suspect on this account. There have now been many years in which these experiences have been claimed, but no one seriously supposes that results like those mentioned above have been produced. The messages seem uniformly trivial and the crop of saints seems slight. This gives some indication of the various ways in which we can apply the pragmatic test of the true and lying or deceived prophets. Much of what goes by the name of religion will not pass this test.

We are now in a position to bring our analysis to a conclusion. We have sought to inquire into the tremendous claim that men actually have knowledge *of* God, and not merely knowledge *about* God. We have shown that the facts cannot reasonably be accounted for except on the supposition of objective reference. This must not be considered as *proved,* for it cannot be established in a coercive manner or beyond a shadow of a doubt. As we have proceeded, however, we have come to see that alleged religious knowledge is in the same position as other knowledge in this regard.

That good and great as well as humble men have long claimed to have a knowledge of God is our initial fact. A philosophical system which neglects or minimizes this fact is itself on trial. The theory that this experience is due to a real relation to the God whom we address in prayer is the only one which offers a satisfactory explanation of all the known facts of religious experience. The chief alternative theory, that of projection, fails to explain many of these facts and is directly contradicted by some. The illogicality of rival theories, plus the objective verification of the theory that does explain, gives as good evidence as is usually available in this world.

It will be noted that much of our thought has been devoted to a removal of logical difficulties. There has been an important reason for this. The positive evidence is already on the side of the realistic interpretation, and it would be believed by everybody, were not certain difficulties presented. If the greatest souls in history have testified to the objective reality of the God known in prayer, *as they have,* and if this has been matched in the experience of countless humble souls, *as it has,* and if, furthermore, this has resulted in a new kind of overcoming joy, *as it has,* then the burden of proof rests not with the exponents of religious knowledge, but with its critics. Apart from specific objections, it is naturally accepted like any other knowledge, with a similar recognition of its possible errors, and a similar need of rational interpretation, but as being essentially reliable. If we remove these specific objections which turn out, upon analysis, to be chiefly logical in nature, we "do more than merely negative work of merely criticizing the critic," we leave the realistic thesis in possession of the field. It is therefore appropriate to end our study with highly significant words from the pen of Baron von Hügel:

> And as our removal of objections to the reality of an external world necessarily establishes its reality for us—because there is the vivid impression, the sense of a trans-human reality all around us, which clamors to be taken as it gives itself, and which was only refused to be thus taken because of those objections; so now our removal of objections to the reality of the Superhuman Reality necessarily establishes the reality for us—since there, again, is the vivid impression, the sense of a still deeper, a different, trans-human Reality which penetrates and sustains ourselves and all things, and clamors to be taken as It gives Itself.

KEITH WARD

The Reverend Professor John Stephen Keith Ward (1938–) is one of England's foremost philosopher-theologians. Among other distinctions, he is a Fellow of the British Academy, until recently Regius professor of Divinity at the University of Oxford, and retired as the Canon of Christ Church, Oxford. In addition to academics, he is also passionately involved in the dialogue between different religious traditions; thus from 1992 to 2001 he served as joint president of the World Congress of Faiths (WCF).

For Ward, loving God with a person's mind begins by embarking on a reasonable and essential intellectual search for the transcendent. The following selection is taken from his book The Case for Religion. *Starting from a point of view that religion is a worthy human pursuit at all times in history, Ward leads the reader in a quest to define words such as "religion," "faith," and "transcendence," and to challenge the notion that religion is merely a social construct.*

Religion and the Transcendent

In Search of a Definition

It is very difficult to know what religion is. That does not stop people being vehemently for it, or against it. But it turns out that they are often for or against very different things. And when it comes to defining religion, almost anything goes.

Many colleges in America and Europe have courses on "Religion." These courses usually start with a lecture entitled "What Is Religion?" After running through a few dozen definitions, the lecturer almost invariably concludes that nobody knows what religion is, or is even sure that there is such a thing. The courses continue to be called courses on religion, however, because that sounds better than having a course entitled, "I Do Not Know What I Am Talking About."

The problem became clear when, in the 2001 government census in Britain, thousands of people put down their religious affiliation as "Jedi Knight." This is not quite as absurd as it might sound. Jedi Knights wear funny clothes, are in close contact with an invisible Force, and often pronounce platitudes with great profundity. Is that enough to make this a religion? If it is a religion, it has great tax advantages. But how can we decide? Could my grandmother get tax exemption if she started a new religion in her living room? What about Scientologists, pagans, Druids, and *X-Files* devotees?

In recent years many scholars, both in anthropology and in social and cultural studies, have queried whether "religion" is an appropriate or even an identifiable subject of study. Wilfred Cantwell Smith, in *The Meaning and End of Religion*, argued that the concept of religion is "recent, Western-and-Islamic, and unstable," and that the term should be dropped.[1] It is recent, because in Europe the word "religion" at first meant the observance of ritual regulations. Later it most often meant "piety" or "worship." So to be religious was to be pious, and "true religion" was, in Augustine for instance, true piety or devotion. However, in the seventeenth century, Cantwell Smith argues, the word "religion" came to have a new meaning, of a system of doctrines, and "true religion" came to mean the true set of doctrines. This, he suggests, makes religion into a matter of having correct beliefs, whereas it should be, and usually was before the seventeenth century, a matter of personal faith and experience.

The term "religion" is Western, he goes on to say, because a great many cultures, such as the Chinese or Indian, do not have a word for "religion," and so the word does not quite capture what they do when they are being religious. Finally, the term "religion" is unstable, because it can mean so many different things, and it deceives people into asking useless questions such as "What is the essence of religion?" When they ask that question, they either come up with something suspiciously like what they themselves believe or, if they are atheists, something that is obviously ridiculous. Either way, the question is simply not profitable, and we should stop asking it.

What Cantwell Smith objects to is labeling a whole lot of different things in very different cultures "religions." Then each religion is seen as a total isolated system, which competes with others, and is a fixed entity whose essence is clear, precise and exclusive. This, he says, turns a matter of living faith into a set of abstract, "frozen" doctrines, as though there were a number of "religions," each with a fixed essence. He recommends that we should speak instead of many cumulative traditions, which are always in flux, always changing, and closely intermingled with their own histories and cultures. We can separate this from the lived experience of faith, of personal relation to the Transcendent. He hoped, when he wrote the book in 1962, that we might have stopped using the word "religion" by the year 1987. Like most prophecies, this one has turned out to be completely false—and he himself helped to make it false by calling his book *The Meaning and End of Religion,* and writing it so well that it was still on sale well after 1987. There is something slightly paradoxical about a book about religion, the argument of which is that no one should write books about religion any more.

It is an excellent book, and its main argument, with which I wholly agree, and which this book also tries to advocate, is that we should not view religions as discrete and fixed sets of competing doctrines. We should pay close attention to many faiths, seeing each one as a dynamic, fluid and culturally influenced complex, the heart of which is a living personal quality of faith in a transcendent reality. The irony is that, in saying this, Cantwell Smith is precisely advocating a view of what the "essence of religion" is, as distinct from its many cultural forms. He is not at all saying that there is no such thing as religion.

Other writers, usually anthropologists, have argued that it is artificial to separate religion from the general cultural life of a society. We may speak of the beliefs and practices of various cultures, and the way they change in response to new environmental and economic pressures and opportunities. But cultures are very diverse, and it is not helpful to invent general categories into which we try to force this diversity.

It could be argued that it was only when Christendom began to break up that writers such as Herbert of Cherbury (1582–1648) started to speak of "natural religion," an essence that underlies all particular revelations. Religion, for Edward Herbert, consists of five innate ideas: the existence of God, the duties of worship, of moral conduct, and of repentance for sin, and the existence of rewards and punishments after death.[2]

Thus the word "religion" comes, at a particular point in European history, to stand for an essential nature which is supposed to express the common truth of the many diverse religions, whose particular revelations are all in fact false (except for Christianity, whose essence happens to represent the truth most adequately, according to the European thought at that time). This essence, however, may seem to be only the skeleton of decayed Christian faith. The emphasis on God, on the moral nature of religion, and on final judgment, is what remains of Christianity when its most distinctive dogmas of Trinity, incarnation and atonement have been left behind.

So "religion" became established in Europe as a post-Christian, minimal notion, allegedly founded on pure reason, which could be used as a criterion in the light of which all particular religions could be found wanting, especially those of foreign, heathen lands. This idea of religion supported the ideology of growing European colonialism, in its mission to bring primitive and savage races under the benevolent shade of civilization (and to subjugate them economically in the process).

Thus seen, the use of the term "religion" becomes part of a colonizing process, by which all people are persuaded or forced to use a term that subsumes their own culture and belief-system under a European pattern. That in turn subtly undermines their belief-system, by transmuting it into one among many competing "religions," whose true inner essence turns out to be just that recommended by the colonial powers of liberal democracy. The European colonization of the savage mind triumphs when religions become options to be freely chosen, and options which in the end must be judged by criteria of reason which in fact embody the bourgeois, liberal, aristocratic morality of capitalist Europe.[3]

There is just enough truth in all this to make any European, and any American too, rather uncomfortable. It is, however, difficult to see what positive alternative is being recommended. It could be that each culture must be studied strictly as a whole on its own terms, without trying to subsume it under general global categories of explanation. But that would be to make any cross-cultural understanding impossible or at least undesirable. The study of religion would be subsumed under Cultural Studies, or it would perhaps disappear as a politically incorrect subject, which had always disguised a liberal secularizing agenda for sanctioning the superiority of the West.

Ironically, it could be argued that Cantwell Smith himself, the advocate of the end of the concept of "religion," falls prey to the charge of cultural imperialism. He states that the many cumulative traditions are grounds for individual faith in Transcendence. But in using the concept of "Transcendence," he is focusing attention on a supernatural reality and on the possibility of personal experience of it. A critic could say that he is using what is precisely a liberal, post-Christian term to characterize what he sees as a universal object of human belief. Whereas Lord Herbert had spoken of an innate idea of God, Cantwell Smith goes further in denuding the religious object of content, and is left with the bare idea of "the Transcendent." He has thereby left all particular religious traditions behind—none of them worship just the Transcendent. Yet he retains a minimal content, for "the Transcendent" is that which is beyond and greater than the immanent or the everyday. Thereby he is picking out precisely what he thinks is central to religion. He is himself, an unfriendly critic could say, continuing the secularizing liberal program of viewing religion as a discrete cultural option, suggesting that its real essence is so vague as to be without significant social impact, and thus downgrading all specific revelations in favor of a cultivated, reasonable, tolerant and voluntaristic view of religion as one cultural activity among others, for those who like that sort of thing. The ideology of the West has triumphed, even in the work of one of its chief critics!

The Sigh of the Oppressed

Explanations of Religion as a Social Construct

Religious believers think that there is a transcendent or supernatural reality, that some knowledge of it is possible, and that such knowledge will help to achieve human good. There is an important claim to truth in religion. Believers think that their images speak, however inadequately, of that which is most truly real, and of ultimate significance for their lives and for the human future.

The strange thing is that many of the best-known writers who have studied religion as a global phenomenon in the last one hundred and fifty years have denied this fact. Or at least they thought that religious believers were deceived about the real nature of what they were doing. Believers may think they are speaking of an objective spiritual reality. They may indeed be referring to something. But that thing is not what they think. It is incumbent upon unbelievers to give some account of how religious beliefs arise and become so very important to vast numbers of people, many of them intelligent and morally sensitive people. The believers' account is, of course, that since there is such a reality, it will become known, or will even make itself known, to those who seek it. The "making known" may not be immediate, definite, and unmistakably clear. It may be, as most human knowledge is, a gradually developing matter, involving many imaginative hypotheses, much culturally influenced experience, and a cumulative tradition of wisdom. But basically, the hope is that humans will gradually grow in knowledge of what spiritual reality is like.

For the unbeliever, this whole religious quest must be based on an illusion. The trouble is that the illusion does not seem to be fading away. It seems firmly rooted in human nature. That does require some explanation. Atheists who have studied religion have obligingly come up with explanations, though it is questionable whether they are very convincing. The fact that there are so many different explanations, each claiming to be the truly explanatory one, is not a very good start.

Such explanations fall into three main groups. There are explanations such as those of Tylor and Frazer, which see religion as a primitive form of science, long outdated. There are explanations in psychological terms, showing how religious beliefs originate in various states of mind, usually subconscious, which rise to consciousness in dreams or visions. There are explanations in social terms, seeing how religious beliefs help to consolidate certain forms of social order, or perhaps compensate for the inability to gain social satisfaction. A modern variant, evolutionary psychology, tries to show how some beliefs have been conducive to survival in human prehistory, and have continued to be selected because of their efficacy in sustaining specific sorts of society.

The import of all these forms of explanation is to show how such a false system of beliefs could become so important and enduring in human life. If the beliefs were not false, the best form of explanation, and the only adequate one, would show how humans could become acquainted with the spiritual reality that such beliefs postulate. Other forms of explanation could be significant parts of a total explanation. Intellectual forms of explanation might be, not in terms of primitive science, but in terms of a metaphysical vision of reality as fundamentally based on mind or Spirit. Psychological forms of explanation might not show the growth of neuroses in religion, but ways in which religious belief can contribute to mental health and stability, or to personal integration. Social forms of explanation do not have to be in terms of reinforcement of the status quo or compensation for social disadvantage. They could be in terms of the reinforcement of social ideals and personal empowerment for moral action. These forms of explanation can, in other words, give a much more positive interpretation of religion. But the success of a positive account would probably depend on the claims of religion being accepted as true by the believer. It would be difficult to accept a religious view solely on the grounds that it would provide a coherent metaphysical vision of reality, that it contributes to mental health, or that it reinforces social ideals. We might be very happy that it does these things, but we would also need to think that it was true, if all these positive effects were not to be undermined by our knowledge that they were based on illusion. I might be very cheerful if I could make myself believe that I had won the lottery. But if I also really knew that there was no lottery, and that I had not won it, it would be hard to maintain my cheerfulness for very long.

Faith and the Problem of Evil and Suffering

ART LINDSLEY

Since the late 80s, Arthur "Art" Lindsley (1951–) has been a scholar-in-residence at the C. S. Lewis Institute in Annandale, Virginia. Analyzing the works and philosophy of Lewis in light of the reasons they matter today is a passion for Lindsley. Likewise, he considers the next generation as pivotal in fashioning belief and the understanding of ideas. Along with his wife, Connie, he teaches young professionals through an organization they founded called Oasis.

Lindsley defends strongly the merits of truth, specifically in light of the popularity of postmodernism. In the excerpt chosen here, taken from his book True Truth: Defending Absolute Truth in a Relativistic World, *Lindsley sets out to answer some important questions such as: Is it possible honestly to say there is no such thing as evil? And is it possible to live in a world where everything (every behavior, every thought, every action) is right and nothing is deemed otherwise? He challenges conventional thinking while defining and explaining key concepts such as good, evil, morality, and justice.*

No Room for Evil

IF THERE ARE no absolutes, then we cannot say anything really is evil or, for that matter, good. The problem is, we know better.

G. K. Chesterton once said, "People have given up on the idea of original sin when it's the only doctrine of Christianity that can be empirically proven." Look at the murderous reigns of Hitler and Stalin, the killing fields of Cambodia, "ethnic cleansing" in Bosnia, the stealing of food from starving people in Somalia, terrorist attacks such as those on September 11, 2001, and the crime that ravages our streets every day. Looking at these events, can we really say, "There is no evil"?

The difficult question often asked is, Why does an all-good, all-powerful God allow evil? Christian theologians have wrestled with this question with no little success. I wish to point out, however, that the reliability of evil serves to provide a strong argument for God's existence.

Before C. S. Lewis became a believer, it was his intellectual struggle with the problem of evil that prevented him from listening to the claims of Christ. "If a good God made the world," he asserted, "why has it gone wrong?" He refused to listen to Christian replies, supporting that such arguments were merely an attempt to avoid the obvious. Was not the universe cruel and unjust? In Lewis's opinion Lucretius had stated the problem well. "Had God designed the world it would not be a world so frail and faulty as we see."[1] Lewis called this the "argument from undesign."

It gradually dawned on Lewis, however, that he had no basis in his atheism for the idea of justice or injustice. He said,

> But how had I got this idea of just and unjust? A man does not call a line crooked unless he has some idea of a straight line. What was I comparing this universe with when I called it unjust? If the whole show was bad and senseless from A to Z, so to speak, why did I, who was supposed to be a part of the show, find myself in such violent reaction against it? A man feels wet when he falls into water because man is not a water animal: a fish would not feel wet. Of course I could have given up my idea of justice by saying it was nothing but a private idea of my own. But if I did that, then my argument against God collapsed too—for the argument depended on saying that the world was really unjust, not simply that it did not happen to please my private fancies. Thus in trying to prove that God did not exist—in other words, that the whole of reality was senseless—I was forced to assume that one part of reality—namely my idea of justice was full of sense. Consequently atheism turns out to be too simple.[2]

If there is evil, Lewis concluded, there must be a fixed, absolute, "outside this world" standard by which we can know it to be really evil. If there is a real evil, then we must have a fixed standard of good by which we judge it to be evil. This absolute standard of goodness suggests a God who is himself this absolute, infinite standard.

Throughout history, in fact, there has never been anything like a totally different morality where, in every case, "good" is "evil" and "evil" is "good." Lewis documented this in the appendix of *The Abolition of Man,* using illustrations from the ancient Egyptians, Babylonians, Hindus, Chinese, Greeks, Romans, and others. What would a totally different morality look like? Lewis wrote:

> Think of a country where people were admired for running away in battle, or where a man felt proud of double crossing all the people who had been kindest to him. You might just as well try to imagine a country where two and two made five. Men have differed as regards what people you ought to be unselfish to—whether it was only your own family, or your fellow countrymen, or everyone. But they have always agreed that you ought not to put yourself first. Selfishness has never been admired. Men have differed as to whether you should have one wife or four. But they have always agreed that you must not simply have any woman you liked.[3]

In Romans 1.29–32 the apostle Paul gave a long list of evils he assumed everyone knows:

> being filled with all unrighteousness, wickedness, greed, evil; full of envy, murder, strife, deceit, malice; they are gossips, slanderers, haters of God, insolent, arrogant, boastful, inventors of evil, disobedient to parents, without understanding, untrustworthy, unloving, unmerciful; and although they *know the ordinance of God,* that those who practice *such things* are worthy of death, they not only do the same, but also give hearty approval to those who practice them. [*emphasis added*]

Paul contended that each of the evils in the list is, in fact, known by all people. He described this law as "written in their hearts," or on their consciences (Rom 2.15). This conscious awareness of the law can be dulled or perhaps (in the case of a sociopath) lost, but it is usually retained to some degree even in the most calloused people. Even totalitarian dictators or terrorists show care for their own families and have friendships with some people around them. The so-called Mob has its own code of behavior toward those of its own inner circle, even though this code may not apply to those outside.

There seems to be a universal agreement on first principles with some disagreement on secondary issues. If there is real evil then there must be an absolute standard by which it can be judged to be so. If there is injustice, there must be a standard of justice. The alternatives are these: (1) to make all moral statements meaningless and absurd, or (2) to reduce them to arbitrary personal preference, thus making statements about evil mere matters of sentiment.

The Cultural Move

Some try to avoid this impasse by attempting to construct an ethic based on that which is good for society. They reason that it is possible to get a sufficient number of people to agree to a "categorical imperative" (said Immanuel Kant, 1724–1804) to do only that which we would will to become a universal standard. Others suggest that we could make it our goal to be impartial, standing behind a "veil of ignorance" (said John Rawls), so that our bias does not distract. *Then* we can construct a basis for social ethics.

Murder, for example. We might begin by arguing that outlawing murder would be in the interest of preserving society. This is undoubtedly true. If people regularly killed other people, society would be chaotic and unsafe. If murder were practiced on a large scale, it would soon deplete the numbers of people in that society. Outlawing murder *will* preserve society.

However, some could question whether our society *ought* to be preserved. Terrorists, for example, want to destroy the United States no matter how many people are killed. On what basis, then, ought the U.S. to be protected? And what do you say to those who rejected the "categorical imperative" or the "veil of ignorance"? Is murder intrinsically wrong? If so, it is evil and must have an absolute standard by which it is judged to be so. Is the prohibition of murder only in the pragmatic interests of the culture, and it is wrong merely because it is supported by the majority of that society? If so, then we can say, "We are the majority. We say murder is wrong. If you murder, we will arrest you and put you in jail. Might makes right." In this case murder is only wrong because the majority says so. You have gathered a sufficient group around this law (or any other law) to gain its approval.

The reason that such attempts can never work is principal. You cannot get "ought" out of "is." On this point Lewis argued,

> Free from propositions about fact alone no practical conclusion can ever be drawn. *This will preserve society* cannot lead to *do this* except by the mediation of *society ought to be preserved. This will cost you your life* cannot lead directly to *do not do this*: it can lead to it only through a felt desire or an acknowledged duty of self-preservation. The Innovator is trying to get a conclusion in the *imperative mood* out of premises in the *indicative mood*; and though he continues trying to all eternity, he cannot succeed for the thing is impossible.[4]

In a discussion over a moral question, charges may be made: "Who are you to try to impose your morality on me?" In other words, the charge is "Says who?" or "Whose morality and whose justice?" The same question could be asked by a minority challenging the majority: "Who are you, majority, to impose your morality on us?"

MAJORITY: "This will preserve society."
MINORITY: "I do not want this society preserved. I will not accept your laws."
MAJORITY: "Then we will arrest you."
MINORITY: "Again, who are you to impose your morality on me?"
MAJORITY: "Says us."

Atheist and Yale law professor Arthur Leff published a legal essay in the *Duke Law Journal* (1979) entitled "Unspeakable Ethics, Unnatural Law." It came to be considered a classic. In it he argued that there is no normative system of ethics based in anything other than the bare assertion of human will. The common cultural move will not work because of what he called "the grand sez who." Interestingly, though an atheist, he did admit that "sez God" would provide a solid basis for ethics and law.

He started his essay by saying,

> I want to believe—and so do you—in a complete transcendent and immanent set of propositions about right and wrong; findable rules that authoritatively, and unambiguously direct us how to live righteously. I also want to believe—and so do you—in no such thing, but rather that we are wholly free, not only to choose for ourselves what we ought to do, but decide for ourselves, individually and as a species, what we ought to be. What we want, heaven help us, is simultaneously to be perfectly ruled and perfectly free, that is, at the same time to discover the right and the good and to create it. . . . My plan for this article then, is as follows. I shall try to prove to your satisfaction that there cannot be any normative system ultimately based on anything except human will.[5]

Leff argued that much of the current debate on the foundation of law is rooted in this tension between "found law" and "made law." There is a corresponding tension between these two particularly because we may fear that in the end "we are able to locate nothing more attractive, or more final, than ourselves."[6] In order to find "normative propositions," we must find one that is immune from criticism—unchallengeable. Why would it be wrong to violate the command "Thou shalt not commit adultery"? To put it in other words, when would it be impermissible to put forward the schoolyard or barroom trump card—"the grand sez who"? In order to do this, we would have to find an evaluator above being evaluated. The evaluator must be "the unjudged judge, the unruled legislator, the premise maker who rests on no premises, the uncreated creator of values. Now, what would you call such a thing if it existed? You would call it Him."[7]

The reason, Leff said, I ought not commit adultery would be if and only if the speaker is God. A God-grounded system has no "analogues." If God does not exist, no one can take his place. "Anything that took his place would also be Him."[8] A statement like "You ought to do X" would be binding only if the speaker had the power to make X good. Under what circumstances can someone propose an ethical statement that withstands the cosmic "Says who?"

"There are no such circumstances . . . there is no one like the Lord," Leff continued.

> If he does not exist, there is no metaphoric equivalent. No person, no combination of people, no document however hallowed by time, no process, no premise, nothing is equivalent to an actual God in this central function as the unexaminable examiner of good and evil. The so-called death of God turns out to have been just His funeral; it also seems to have effected the total elimination of any coherent, or even more than momentarily convincing, ethical or legal system.[9]

If law cannot be in God, Leff argued, then the only possible alternative is to say that the law is in us—one of us, some of us, all of us. We can either sing, "We're free of God," or "Oh, God, we're free." We need then to ask, who among us *ought* to be able to declare a law that ought to be obeyed? We could make each individual create his or her own law, so that each person becomes, in effect, a godlet. But then who decides the rules among these multiplicities of "gods"? If there is conflict, who ought to give way? You could set up rules that govern "inter-divinity transactions" that suggest that godlets should not use force or fraud to accomplish their ends. "What you could not do is defend it on the basis of Godlet preference."[10] The "whatever is true for me is true for me and whatever is true for you is true for you" philosophy makes evaluating any respective claims impossible.

We could try to get out of this dilemma by counting noses or by discriminating among the qualities of the "ethical boxes." Counting noses does not, however, make the result "right" and other preferences "wrong." And could we judge the quality? It seems not, because there can be no fixed or absolute standards by which we can judge good/bad or better/best when each person is his or her own godlet.

Many people have nevertheless taken this second route. They have a "considered" view or a "serious and reflective view" or have reached a "reflective equilibrium" or have an imagined "veil of ignorance." Who is to decide which position is more "considered" and who says that the more "considered" position is more ethical or right? You could start with a declaration that some basic belief is good and build from there, but then that basic belief would have to be "good" to someone. Perhaps you could gain a considerable following that agrees that this starting proposition is good, but how do we evaluate this claim? Leff went on to say, "*There is no such thing as an unchallengeable evaluative system.* There is no way to prove one ethical system superior to any other, *unless* at some point an evaluator is asserted to have the final, uncontradictable, unexaminable word. That choice of unjudged judge, whoever is given the role, is itself, strictly speaking arbitrarily."[11]

In Robert Nozick's book *Anarchy, State, and Utopia,* he asserted, "Individuals have rights, and there are things no person or group may do to them [without violating their rights]."[12] This seems reasonable enough, but if individuals have rights—*says who?* Also, who decides the rules when people who have equal rights differ about what is to be done? Richard Posner put forward an ethical system in which no person may dominate any other.[13] This is great when two individuals or more decide to make this "deal" with each other. However, what if someone refuses this deal? All you can say is, "No deal." You could get a lot of people to agree on the above assumptions, but if questioned with the "grand sez who," the only final answer is "sez us."

Leff concluded the article with this statement:

> All I can say is this: it looks as if we are all we have. Given what we know about each other and ourselves, this is an extraordinarily unappetizing prospect. . . . Neither reason nor love nor terror, seems to have worked to make us "good," worse than that, there is no reason why anything should. Only if ethics were unspeakable by us could law be unnatural and unchallengeable. As things stand now, everything is up for grabs. Nevertheless:
>
> *Napalming babies is bad.*
> *Starving the poor is wicked.*
> *Buying and selling each other is depraved.*
> *Those who stood up and died resisting Hitler, Stalin,*
> *Amin, Pol Pot, and*

General Custer, too, have earned salvation.
Those who acquiesced deserve to be damned.
There is in the world such a thing as evil.
All together now—sez who?
God help us![14]

Postmodernists like Richard Rorty, Stanley Fish, and Alistair McIntire all understand this critique. They give up a rational basis for ethics but wrongly assume that "sez God" can equally be rejected. . . . It is important to consider the ancient dilemma: Is something right because God says it is or does God say it because it is right? In the former case, God's will seems arbitrary (he just says it). In the latter case, it seems there is a standard higher than God (the right or good). The classic answer to this dilemma is that there is a third option: the good is rooted in the character of God himself. In fact, God's revelation of his will in Scripture is a reflection of his character and it also fits how he has made us. What God "sez" is like the owner's manual of a car. If you violate what it says, the car will not run at all or will at least not run well. God's will is our self-interest now and eternally, and is not unnecessarily restrictive.

We Need to Point Out Inconsistencies

Even though he remained an atheist, Arthur Leff provided us a brilliant critique of attempts to ground an ethical system without God. Sadly, Leff died of cancer in 1984 at age forty-eight. I wish someone had had the opportunity to move him toward an adequate basis for his highest aspirations. If there is evil, and he knew that there was, he could have been asked, "Why do you not believe in the unjudged judge, the unruled legislator, the uncreated creator of values, the unnatural law and that which is unchallengeable by the 'grand sez who'? Are there objections we could clear up? Are there some things that need to be explained? If there is evil, there must be an absolute good in order for us to judge it to be really evil. If there is absolute good or evil, it is hard to resist the conclusion that there must be a God who is good, allowing us to say, 'Sez God.'"

If someone is not yet willing to admit that evil exists, perhaps that person could be gently moved toward the logical conclusion of his or her false assumptions. For instance, journalist Arthur Koestler interviewed a Japanese expert in Buddhism, who denied the existence of good and evil.

KOESTLER: You favor tolerance towards all religions and political systems. What about Hitler's gas chambers?
BUDDHIST: That was very silly of him.
KOESTLER: Just silly, not evil?
BUDDHIST: Evil is a Christian concept. Good and evil exist only on a relative scale.[15]

Many may not be willing to go so far. For instance, a believing friend of mine took graduate classes under Richard Rorty, a leading postmodern philosopher. In one such class he met a woman who was Jewish by heritage but was actually an atheist and a feminist. Being influenced by Rorty's teaching, she claimed there were no absolutes. My friend, knowing what she cared about, said, "I can prove to you that you believe in absolutes."

"No, you can't!"

"Yes, I can. I'll give you two: rape and the Holocaust are morally wrong."

She thought for a while and said, "You're right." Yet she had no basis on which to hold these values.

One time, in a graduate class, Rorty was talking about how the abolition of slavery was achieved. He pointed out that the cultural paradigm changed, which allowed the abolition to be possible. In other words, when a community has moral beliefs and principles that contradict a certain action, only then can that action be said to be unjust for them. My friend, who is African American, raised a question.

FRIEND: If that paradigm had not changed, would the horrible abuses of slavery (kidnapping, harsh treatment, many deaths on slave ships, and so on) be wrong?
RORTY: But it did change.
FRIEND: But if it did not, would it be wrong?
RORTY: But it did change.
FRIEND: But what if it did not?

RORTY: If the community held no belief inconsistent with it, I don't think we could call it unjust for them.

FRIEND (with passion): That is unacceptable!

Rorty said that was the best he could offer. The classroom fell into silence. A number of students came up after class and thanked my friend for asking the question. In this case Rorty finally answered the question. In other situations his stated policy is to ignore or evade. He advocates that you should not "play the game" by others' rules. Once a student of mine asked Rorty in a public setting about how his postmodern pragmatism dealt with the Holocaust. He abruptly responded, "I don't answer that kind of question anymore."

In his published writings he does, however, answer the question of the Holocaust more directly. In a classic autobiographical essay, "Trotsky and Wild Orchids," Rorty complained that his view "is often referred to dismissively as 'cultural relativism.'"

> But it is not relativistic if that means saying that every moral view is as good as every other. Our moral view is *I firmly believe, much better* than any compelling view, even though there are many people to whom you will never be able to convert to it. It is one thing to say, falsely, that there is nothing to choose between the Nazis and us. It is another thing to say, correctly, that there is no neutral, common ground to which a philosophical Nazi and I can repair to argue out our differences.[16]

If there is "no neutral, common ground" to settle the debate with the Nazis, then why is Rorty's view "much better"? It would seem that it is better because he "firmly believes" that it is—"sez Rorty" or "sez Rorty's community." In an essay in the *Human Rights Reader,* Rorty suggested that the basis for human rights is not rationality or moral law but "what Baier calls 'a progress of sentiments.' . . . It is the result of what I have been calling 'sentimental education.'"[17]

So the basis for morality, in Rorty's view, is "sentiment." We are back to preferences and tastes. But whose sentiments? Rorty's? A Nazi's? Or someone else's? Since morality is not based on a neutral ground, it is merely a matter of arbitrary personal preference. Many might (rightly) agree with Rorty's sentiments contra Nazism, but what if someone holds opposite sentiments? How do we decide between them? I quite agree that we need an education of sentiments, but in the absence of a standard of justice or good, we would not know which sentiments to choose. I would suggest that Rorty's conscience is better than his philosophy at this point.

James Miller, an author sympathetic to postmodernism, wrote *The Passion of Michel Foucault,* in which he argued that many of Foucault's American followers (Rorty included) put a rather attractive face on Foucault's radical version of postmodern philosophy:

> Most of these latter-day American Foucaultians are high-minded democrats; they are committed to forging a more diverse society in which whites and people of color, straights and gays, men and women, their various ethnic and gender differences intact, can nevertheless all live together in compassionate harmony—an appealing if difficult goal, with deep roots in the Judeo-Christian tradition.[18]

Notice that this postmodern vision (a la Rorty's respect for kindness) had deep, though unacknowledged, roots in the Judeo-Christian tradition. You can almost hear Christ's "love your neighbor" or Paul's there is "no Jew nor Greek, slave nor free, male nor female." Miller admitted, though, that Foucault's work is "far more unconventional" and disturbing. Foucault, more consistently, wanted to destroy everything that is claimed to be "right" by Western culture. Miller noted as well that Foucault's destruction targets extended to "nearly everything that passes for 'right' among a great many of America's left-wing academics."[19]

Foucault wanted to maintain that there are no limits, no divisions, no boundaries between good and evil, reason and unreason, subject and object. Much more radical than other postmodernists, Foucault focused often on the motto "Be cruel" and on images of torture and death.

Foucault expressed this boundary smashing especially in his views of sexuality. Foucault pursued his philosophy in practice, engaging in sadomasochism and in anonymous gay sex in San

Francisco bathhouses. He contracted AIDS and died in 1985 as a result. Miller titled one chapter in his biography "Be Cruel." Miller's interest in writing this biography was provoked by rumors that Foucault had deliberately infected others with AIDS. He found this suggestion troubling and searched for answer to this charge throughout his book. Fortunately, he found no evidence to verify these rumors. What I find interesting is that Miller and others would be so troubled by this, if it were the case, given Foucault's stated philosophy.

Foucault definitely shows us a darker, more Nietzschean side of relativism that pushes beyond limits that even most relativists find abhorrent. We might ask relativists what stops them from advocating the worst atrocities.

New Age

Earlier, we noted that New Age beliefs hold reality to be contradictory, or "nondual," in accordance with the principle of nondistinction. If all is one, then there are no real distinctions in the world and all apparent distinctions are illusory, a state or condition called *Maya*. This leads to the conclusion that matter, time, and space, and the distinctions between true and false, good and evil, are illusory as well.

Most people do not realize how pervasive this denial of the reality of "good" and "evil" is in Eastern religion. The following are some examples.

Mythologist Joseph Campbell (1904–1987), in a PBS interview with Bill Moyers, called good and evil mere "apparitions of temporality." Struggling with the implications of this idea, Campbell went to a Hindu guru and asked him whether we must say yes or no to things normally considered evil, things like brutality and vulgarity. The guru thought about it and responded, "For you and me, we must say 'yes.'"

Rajneesh, who had a considerable following nationally and internationally, said, "We have divided the world into the good and the evil. The world is not so divided. The good and evil are our valuations. . . . Valuation is human. It is our imposition, it is our projection. . . . There is no good; there is no bad. . . . So, do not impose on the creative process (God) your own feelings, your own valuations;

rather, if you want to know the Creator, Creative Process, go beyond these dualisms."[20]

Zen master Yun-Men once said, "I want you to get the plain truth; be not concerned with right and wrong; the conflict between right and wrong is sickness of the mind."[21]

Herman Hesse, in his rendering of the life of Buddha, *Siddhartha*, said, "The world . . . is not imperfect or slowly evolving along a path to perfection. No, it is perfect at every moment. . . . Therefore, it seems to me that everything that exists is good—death as well as life, sin as well as holiness, wisdom as well as folly."[22]

I have personally met many New Age leaders who would agree with this view theoretically but who, I am convinced, would not dream of applying it in sinister, malicious, or cruel acts. Nor do I think the authors mentioned here would torture people. However, it is important to underline that there would be no reason, based on their views, to prohibit such cruelty from being practiced. The principle of nondistinction that makes it difficult for those in the New Age to talk about that which is true or false also makes it difficult, if not impossible, to speak of good and evil.

Neopaganism

At a meeting of neopagans, the participants put together "13 Principles." One was "We do not accept the concept of 'absolute evil' nor do we worship any entity known as 'Satan' or the 'Devil.'"[23] In their view Satanism is a Christian heresy because it involves inverting and rebelling against the biblical God and therefore assumes the biblical worldview—a worldview they reject. Not only do they reject the "absolute evil" of Satan, but they also reject any distinction between good and evil. Erica Jong said, "Satanists . . . accept the duality between good and evil; pagans do not. . . . Pagans see good and evil as allied, in fact, indivisible."[24]

Another neopagan advocate, Starhawk, said of the goddess: "The nature of the Goddess is never single. . . . She is light and darkness, the patroness of love and death, who makes all possibilities. She brings forth comfort and pain. . . . As Crone, she is the dark face of life that demands death and sacrifice. . . . In Witchcraft, the dark waning aspect of the God is not evil—it is a vital part of the natural structure."[25]

One of the predecessors of neopaganism, Alistair Crowley, said in 1903 that the only rule of witchcraft was "Do what thou wilt shall be the whole of the Law."[26] This has continued to be the Wiccan "Rede," or rule for living, with only one addition: "Harm none and do as you will." While I am glad that "harm none" was added, it begs the question "Is harming really evil and not harming really good?" "Harm none" sounds curiously like a negative way of saying, "Love your neighbor"—the Golden Rule.

Which Is True or Good?

If atheism, postmodernism, pantheism, and neopaganism agree on anything, it is that there are no absolutes, no fixed points, no ultimate basis from which to talk about real good and real evil. The existence of real evil would, in fact, make each of these worldviews false, because none has a means to account for evil. If there is no such thing as good or evil, then Judaism, Islam, and Christianity are all false. And though relativists would be loath to make such a statement, it must be said: one view must be wrong and one must be right. You cannot have it both ways.

DESMOND TUTU

The word that most aptly describes the life and legacy of The Most Reverend Desmond Tutu (1931–) is reconciliation. He is best known for his role in the peaceful restoration of justice for all in South Africa, triumphing over the long and prejudicial history of apartheid. Tutu is a dedicated defender of human rights, and continues to advocate on behalf of the oppressed around the world. In 1984 he became only the second South African to receive the prestigious Nobel Peace Prize. He has also received the Albert Schweitzer Prize for Humanitarianism and the Gandhi Peace Prize, in 2005.

As the first black South African Anglican Archbishop (now retired), he remains a highly visible clergyperson in today's world. Both as a speaker and a writer, Tutu communicates on a variety of topics concerning faith in a gentle and accessible way. From his book God Has a Dream: A Vision of Hope for Our Time, *Tutu leads the reader to consider the character of God, paying particular attention to the problem of suffering and God's moral law in the universe. He does this not as one who is pointing a finger, but as a fellow journeyman, one who has witnessed large-scale injustice and still finds ample reason to have faith and hope in the face of suffering.*

God Believes in Us

DEAR CHILD OF God, I write these words because we all experience sadness, we all come at times to despair, and we all lose hope that the suffering in our lives and in our world will ever end. I want to share with you my faith and my understanding that this suffering can be transformed and redeemed. There is no such thing as a totally hopeless case. Our God is an expert at dealing with chaos, with brokenness, with all the worst that we can imagine. God created order out of disorder, cosmos out of chaos, and God can do so always, can do so now—in our personal lives and in our lives as nations, globally. The most unlikely person, the most improbable situation—these are all "transfigurable"—they can be turned into their glorious opposites. Indeed, God is transforming the world now—through us—because God loves us.

This is not wishful thinking or groundless belief. It is my deep conviction, based on my reading of the Bible and of history. It is borne out not only by my experience in South Africa but also by many other visits to countries suffering oppression or in conflict. Our world is in the grips of a transformation that continues forward and backward in ways that lead to despair at times but ultimately redemption. While I write as a Christian, this transformation can be recognized and experienced by anyone, regardless of your faith and religion, and even if you practice no religion at all.

Dear Child of God, it is often difficult for us to recognize the presence of God in our lives and in our world. In the clamor of the tragedy that fills the headlines we forget about the majesty that is present all around us. We feel vulnerable and often helpless. It is true that all of us are vulnerable, for vulnerability is the essence of creaturehood. But we are not helpless and with God's love we are ultimately invincible. Our God does not forget those who are suffering and oppressed.

During the darkest days of apartheid I used to say to P. W. Botha, the president of South Africa, that we had already won, and I invited him and other white South Africans to join the winning side. All the "objective" facts were against us—the pass laws, the imprisonments, the teargassing, the massacres, the murder of political activists—but my confidence was not in the present circumstances but in the laws of God's universe. This is a *moral* universe, which means that, despite all the evidence that seems to be to the contrary, there is no way that evil and injustice and oppression and lies can have the last word. God is a God who cares about right and wrong. God cares about justice and injustice. God is in charge. That is what had upheld the morale of our people, to know that in the end good will prevail. It was these higher laws that convinced me that our peaceful struggle would topple the immoral laws of apartheid.

Of course, there were times when you had to whistle in the dark to keep your morale up, and you wanted to whisper in God's ear: "God, we know You are in charge, but can't You make it a little more obvious?" God did make it more obvious to me once, during what we call the Feast of the Transfiguration. Apartheid was in full swing as I and other church leaders were preparing for a meeting with the prime minister to discuss one of the many controversies that erupted in those days. We met at a theological college that had closed down because of the government's racist policies. During our discussions I went into the priory garden for some quiet. There was a huge Calvary—a large wooden cross without corpus, but with protruding nails and a crown of thorns. It was a stark symbol of the Christian faith. It was winter, the grass was pale and dry, and nobody would have believed that in a few weeks' time it would be lush and green and beautiful again. It would be transfigured.

As I sat quietly in the garden I realized the power of transfiguration—of God's transformation—in our world. The principle of transfiguration is at work when something so unlikely as the brown grass that covers our veld in winter becomes bright green again. Or when the tree with gnarled leafless branches bursts forth with the sap flowing so that the birds sit chirping in the leafy branches. Or when the once dry streams gurgle with swift-flowing water. When winter gives way to the spring and nature seems to experience its own resurrection.

The principle of transfiguration says nothing, no one and no situation, is "untransfigurable," that the whole of creation, nature, waits expectantly for its transfiguration, when it will be released from its bondage and share in the glorious liberty of the children of God, when it will not be just dry inert matter but will be translucent with divine glory.

Many of us can acknowledge that God cares about the world but can't imagine that God would care about you or me individually. But our God marvelously, miraculously, cares about each and every one of us. The Bible has this incredible image of you, of me, of all of us, each one, held as something precious, fragile in the palms of God's hands. And that you and I exist only because God is forever blowing God's breath into our being. And so God says to you, "I love you. You are precious in your fragility and your vulnerability. Your being is a gift. I breathe into you and hold you as something precious."

But why, we ask in our disbelief and despair, would God care about *me*? The simple reason is that God loves you. God loves you as if you were the only person on earth. God, looking on us here, does not see us as a mass. God knows us each by name. God says, "Your name is engraved on the palms of My hands." You are so precious to God that the very hairs of your head are numbered. "Can a mother," God asks, "forget the child she bore?" That is a most unlikely thing, quite unnatural, but it could happen. God says, even if that most unlikely thing were to happen, God's love wouldn't allow Him to forget you or me. We are those precious things that God carries gently. God carries each one of us as if we were fragile because God knows that we are. You are precious to God. God cares for you.

Many people believe that they are beyond God's love—that God may love others but that what they have done has caused God to stop loving them. But Jesus by his example showed us that God loves sinners as much as saints. Jesus associated with the scum of society. And Jesus taught that he had come to seek and to find not the righteous but the lost and the sinners. He scandalized the prim and proper people of his day who believed that he was lowering standards horribly badly. Now anyone could enter heaven. He companied not with the respectable, not with the elite of society, but with those occupying the fringes of society—the prostitutes, the sinners, the ostracized ones. You see, Jesus would most probably have been seen in the red-light district of a city. Can you imagine if they saw me there walking into a brothel to visit with what are often called the women of easy virtue? Who would say, "We're quite sure the archbishop is there for a pastoral reason"? But that's exactly what Jesus did. Someone might look like a criminal or a drug addict, but these societal outcasts remain God's children despite their desperate deeds.

I saw the power of this gospel when I was serving as chairperson of the Truth and Reconciliation Commission in South Africa. This was the commission that the postapartheid government, headed by our president Nelson Mandela, had established to move us beyond the cycles of retribution and violence that had plagued so many other countries during their transitions from oppression to democracy. The commission gave perpetrators of political crimes the opportunity to appeal for amnesty by telling the truth of their actions and an opportunity to ask for forgiveness, an opportunity that some took and others did not. The commission also gave victims of political crimes an opportunity to unburden themselves from the pain and suffering they had experienced.

As we listened to accounts of truly monstrous deeds of torture and cruelty, it would have been easy to dismiss the perpetrators as monsters because their deeds were truly monstrous. But we are reminded that God's love is not cut off from anyone. However diabolical the act, it does not turn the perpetrator into a demon. When we proclaim that someone is subhuman, we not only remove for them the possibility of change and repentance, we also remove from them moral responsibility.

We cannot condemn anyone to be irredeemable, as Jesus reminded us on the Cross, crucified as he was between two thieves. When one repented, Jesus promised him that he would be in paradise with him on that same day. Even the most notorious sinner and evildoer at the eleventh hour may repent and be forgiven, because our God is preeminently a God of grace. Everything that we are, that we have, is a gift from God. He does not give up on you or on anyone for God loves you now and will always love you. Whether we are good or bad, God's love is unchanging and unchangeable. Like a tireless and long-suffering parent, our God is there for us when we are ready to hear His still, small voice in our lives. (I refer to God as He in this book, but this language is offensive to many, including me, because it implies that God is more of a He than a She, and this is clearly not the case. Fortunately, in our Bantu languages in South Africa we do not have gendered pronouns and so we do not face this problem. To avoid cumbersome usage in English, I have chosen to follow convention here, but I apologize to the reader for this grammatical necessity but spiritual inaccuracy.)

So why, you may ask, if God is actively working with us to transfigure and transform the world does He allow us to do evil to one another? The problem of evil is an important one and this question is not to be answered lightly. I have heard and seen many examples of the cruelty that we are able to visit on one another during my time on the commission and during my travels.

I was devastated as I listened to one former member of the security forces describe how he and others shot and killed a fellow human being, burned his body on a pyre, and while this cremation was going on actually enjoyed a barbecue on the side. And then he no doubt went home and kissed his wife and children. When I was serving as the president of the All Africa Conference of Churches, I went to Rwanda one year after the genocide there that claimed the lives of more than half a million people. I saw skulls that still had machetes and daggers embedded in them. I couldn't pray. I could only weep.

If we are capable of such acts, how can there be any hope for us, how can we have faith in goodness? There very well may be times when God has regretted creating us, but I am convinced that there are many more times that God feels vindicated by our kindness, our magnanimity, our nobility of spirit. I have also seen incredible forgiveness and compassion, like the man who after being beaten and spending more than a hundred days in solitary confinement said to me we must not become bitter, or the American couple who established a foundation in South Africa to help the children of a black township where their daughter had been brutally murdered.

Yes, each of us has the capacity for great evil. Not one of us can say with certainty that we would not become perpetrators if we were subject to the same conditioning as those in South Africa, Rwanda, or anywhere that hatred perverts the human spirit. This is not for one minute to excuse what was done or those who did it. It is, however, to be filled more and more with the compassion of God, looking on and weeping that His beloved children, our beloved brothers or sisters, have come to such a sad state. But for every act of evil there are a dozen acts of goodness in our world that go unnoticed. It is only because the evil deeds are less common that they are "news." It is only because we believe that people *should* be good that we despair when they are not. Indeed, if people condoned the evil, we would be justified in losing hope. But most of the world does not. We know that we are meant for better.

The Bible recognizes that we are a mixture of good and bad. We must therefore not be too surprised that most human enterprises are not always wholly good or wholly bad. Our ability to do evil is part and parcel of our ability to do good. One is meaningless without the other. Empathy and compassion have no meaning unless they occur in a situation where one could be callous and indifferent to the suffering of others. To have any possibility of moral growth there has to be the possibility of becoming immoral.

God has given us space to be authentically human persons with autonomy. Love is something that must be given freely. If God is saying, I would like you to obey Me, then that must leave the possibility of disobeying God. Because God takes the risk of real relationships, there is the possibility that those relationships are going to splinter, and they often do.

At times of despair, we must learn to see with new eyes like the prophet Elisha. The Bible tells us that Elisha and his servant were surrounded by a host of enemies. But the prophet remained strangely calm and somewhat unconcerned while his servant grew ever more agitated. The prophet asked God to open the servant's eyes and the servant then saw that those who were on their side were many times more than those against them. This is not just an old story. This is a way to see that you are not alone in your struggle for justice. There are many of you who are working to feed the orphan and the widow. There are many who are working to beat swords into plowshares. There is hope that nightmares will end, hope that seemingly intractable problems will find solutions. God has some tremendous fellow workers, some outstanding partners.

Each of us has a capacity for great evil but also for great good, and that is what convinces God that it was worth the risk of creating us. It is awesome that God the omnipotent One depends on us fragile and vulnerable creatures to accomplish God's will and to bring justice and healing and wholeness. God has no one but us. As the great African saint Augustine of Hippo put it, "God without us will not as we without God cannot."

I have often told the story of the rustic priest in Russia who was accosted by a brash young physicist who had rehearsed all the reasons for atheism and arrogantly concluded, "Therefore I do not believe in God." The little priest, not put off at all, replied quietly, "Oh, it doesn't matter. God believes in you."

God *does* believe in us. God relies on us to help make this world all that God has dreamed of it being.

Seeing with the Eyes of the Heart

Dear Child of God, I am sorry to say that suffering is not optional. It seems to be part and parcel of the human condition, but suffering can either embitter or ennoble. Our suffering can become a spirituality of transformation when we understand that we have a role in God's transfiguration of the world. And if we are to be true partners with God, we must learn to see with the eyes of God—that is, to see with the eyes of the heart and not just the eyes of the head. The eyes of the heart are not concerned with appearances but with essences, and as we cultivate these eyes we are able to learn from our suffering and to see the world with more loving, forgiving, humble, generous eyes.

We tend to look on suffering as something to be avoided at all costs, and yes, we need to work to remove suffering whenever and wherever we can in our lives and in the lives of others. But in the universe we inhabit there will always be suffering. Even if God's dream were to come true, there would still be pain in childbirth, torment in illness, and anguish in death. Sadness, longing, and heartache would not disappear. They would be lessened greatly but never ended. This should not discourage us. It should simply allow us to see suffering—and our role in decreasing it—differently. When we are able to see the larger purpose of our suffering, it is transformed, transmuted. It becomes a redemptive suffering.

In our universe suffering is often how we grow, especially how we grow emotionally, spiritually, and morally. That is, when we let the suffering ennoble us and not embitter us. In God's universe, while we are not free to choose whether we suffer, we are free to choose whether it will ennoble us or instead will embitter us. Nelson Mandela spent twenty-seven years in prison, eighteen of them on Robben Island breaking rocks into little rocks, a totally senseless task. The unrelenting brightness of the light reflected off the white stone damaged his eyes so that now when you have your picture taken with him, you will be asked not to use a flash. Many people say, "What a waste! Wouldn't it have been wonderful if Nelson Mandela had come out earlier? Look at all the things he would have accomplished."

Those ghastly, suffering-filled twenty-seven years actually were not a waste. It may seem so in a sense, but when Nelson Mandela went to jail he was angry. He was a young man who was understandably very upset at the miscarriage of justice in South Africa. He and his colleagues were being sentenced because they were standing up for what seemed so obvious. They were demanding the rights that in other countries were claimed to be inalienable. At the time, he was very forthright and belligerent, as he should have been, leading the armed wing of the African National Congress, but he mellowed in jail. He began to discover depths of resilience and spiritual attributes that he would not have known he had. And in particular I think he learned to appreciate the foibles and weaknesses of others and to be able to be gentle and compassionate toward others even in their awfulness. So the suffering transformed him because he allowed it to ennoble him. He could never have become the political *and* moral leader he became had it not been for the suffering he experienced on Robben Island. So much was anger replaced with forgiveness that he invited his former jailer to be a VIP guest at his inauguration.

In jail he became an instrument of good where previously there had been so much evil. It seems that in this universe redemption of any kind happens only through some form of suffering. However, it is possible to be in jail for twenty-seven years and come out of that experience of suffering angry, bitter, wishing to pay back those who jailed you. Or you can be in jail for twenty-seven years and instead of your experiences becoming a negative influence on your life, they can become a positive influence and, in fact, amazingly even an enriching one. Thank God for South Africa that this was the case for Nelson Mandela.

The texture of the suffering is changed when we see it and begin to experience it as being redemptive, as not being wasteful, as not being senseless. We humans can tolerate suffering but we cannot tolerate meaninglessness. This is what I mean when I say we can transform our suffering into a spirituality of transformation by understanding that we have a role in God's transfiguration of the world. Even our own suffering serves to remove the dross, just like it did for Mandela, to burn away the impurities and allow us to fulfill our role in God's plan.

ELIE WIESEL

Eliezer "Elie" Wiesel (1928–) is one of the twentieth century's most venerated Jewish humanitarians, writers, professors, and political activists. He also is a survivor of the Holocaust. His internationally acclaimed work Night *is an intimate account of his courageous survival in the face of horrific brutality and utter humiliation in several Nazi concentration camps. In his 1986 Nobel Peace Prize address, Wiesel focused on what has become known as the defining themes of his life: peace, atonement, and human dignity.*

Teaching is integral for Wiesel so that humanity does not fall into forgetfulness. He fervently believes that our memories of the past must be joined to the present.

In 1987 French journalist Philippe-Michaël de Saint-Cheron interviewed Wiesel, and the exchange was subsequently published in a book called Evil and Exile. *The following selection is taken from that book and follows a question-and-answer format. Wiesel specifically wrestles with the concepts of evil and suffering, evil and love, and responsibility and meaning.*

Evil

PHILIPPE DE SAINT-CHERON: *How do you reconcile the ideas of providence and silence, or what Buber called the eclipse of God? Do you feel that providence died during the Shoah? What possible meaning can it have today, when it is clearly so sorely lacking?*

ELIE WIESEL: There are some paradoxes that I have to accept. I simply have no choice. That particular one is essential, and it is equally essential to face it, though I have found no way to resolve it. I do not understand it now, and I never will. I first asked this question more than forty years ago, and it is as valid today as ever. My only answer is that I would not like to see any one point of view prevail over the others. On the contrary, this must remain an open question, a conflict.

You would not argue that theodicy died in Auschwitz or that providence no longer exists?

I certainly do not agree with those who say: faith alone exists, faith stands above all else. That would amount to saying: have faith, and that's that. But neither would I agree with the claim that theodicy is dead. The moment an answer is given, I get suspicious; as a question, I accept it.

Isn't it true that every human being's life is dominated by the accident of having been born in one place and not in the other?

On the contrary, in the Jewish tradition we believe that there is divine intervention, almost a divine choice. God foreordains each soul before its birth; each soul is His treasure, and He watches over it personally. There are no guardian angels. It is the Lord Himself who takes charge of His souls. In the midrashic legend, there is a sort of image depicting God giving life to a soul. It is He who wanted you to be born in one place and I in another. That is why I like to think that in this instance chance is not involved at all.

But consider the death of so many thousands of children, in places like Ethiopia and Somalia, Vietnam and Cambodia. Doesn't that attest to the absolute meaninglessness, the fundamental absurdity, of the human condition, after what you call the Event?

How can you reconcile this basic absurdity with the meaning of Jewish faith?

Yes, it is absurd, tragically absurd. It shows that our world has learned nothing. Perhaps there is nothing to learn; perhaps it is so far beyond our understanding that we cannot draw any conclusions. But we have to make the effort, and today even that is lacking. The fact that there is still so much suffering and so much agony, so many deaths and so many victims, shows that we—and all our contemporaries—have failed to bring man's deeds into line with his capacities.

Isn't this a terrible failure of human thought, and perhaps also of religion?

In this case the issue is not religion, but thought. The failure of religion came earlier, during the Whirlwind. It was then that we realized religion was no longer an effective pillar or source of strength or truth. For the most part, the killers had been baptized. They had been reared under Christianity, and some of them even went to church, to mass, and probably to confession. Yet still they killed. That showed that there was no barrier in Christianity preventing the killers from doing their evil. What we are seeing today, on the other hand, is a failure of humanity, perhaps a failure of rationalism, but certainly a failure of politics and commitment, a failure of all systems, of philosophy, and of art.

Can this meaninglessness be reconciled with the meaning of religious faith?

My view is that faith must be tested. If it is unbroken, then it is not whole. "There is nothing so whole as a broken heart," Rabbi Nahman of Bratzlav once said. But in our epoch, I would say, there is nothing so whole as broken faith. Faith must be tested. But it must not remain severed or sundered. We must press on, facing up to what happened in the past and what is happening in the world today. We can no longer simply accept faith as such. We must first pass through a period of anguish, then one of respite, ultimately recovering and rediscovering the faith of our Masters. Because without faith we could not survive. Without faith our world would be empty.

In the terrifying twenty-sixth chapter of Vayikra (Leviticus), the word qeri *occurs seven times in succession. Most translations render it as "defiance," or "with harshness, stubbornness." But Rabbi Ben Ouziel in the Talmud, Maimonides in his epistle to Yemen, and André Neher (among others) have translated this word as* chance*. Neher, for instance, translates: "If you choose the covenant, I will be with you in the covenant. If you choose chance, I will yet be with you in chance." How do you interpret this duality, this coun-*

terposition between Obedience and Chance, between the choice of Covenant and the choice of Chance?

I agree. In my view, this is the only meaning: *qeri* means chance. On another level, it also connotes chaos, which is the enemy of everything the Jewish religion holds dear. Chaos is worse than chance, worse than anything, because if there is chaos, then Good is not good and Evil is boundless. It is the original *tohu va bohu. Qeri* is therefore chance, and with chance anything is possible. Covenant, on the contrary, is a response to chance. We have a choice between Covenant and Chance, and it is incumbent upon us to formulate that choice, to accept it, and to make it. Moreover, it is a choice that must be made daily. Each and every day we have the power, the privilege, of saying to ourselves: today either I partake of Covenant or I am here by chance.

Isn't this the first question we ask ourselves within faith itself?

Except that within faith we must sometimes take our stand against chance, but never against Covenant. In other words, I can protest against God within the Covenant, but not outside it.

Recently you said, "it is my faith, my confidence in God and His promises, that has been shaken." On the other hand, you have also said that although you are sometimes for God and often against Him, you are never without Him.

That is exactly how I would describe my relationship to my faith. I have never forsaken it, and it has never forsaken me. Whatever has been shaken has been shaken within faith, for faith has always been present. The question was: what is happening in the world, why is it happening, according to what design? So yes, there is a shaking of faith, but there is also faith, and there is protest against faith precisely because it has been shaken.

Have you ever found it impossible to say certain prayers?

Not any more, but it used to happen to me often. Today I know that heartbreak exists, and that prayer is tied to heartbreak. In the morning prayer, for instance, there is a phrase that says *Ashrenu ma-tov 'helkenu,* "happy are we with our destiny! How pleasant is our fate! How precious is our heritage!" When I think that I recited that prayer in the camp, along with hundreds of my comrades, that we said it again and again! How could we have said such a prayer? Yet we did. So I tell myself that if we said it in the camp, what right do I have to stop saying it today?

Yet there are dreadful—perhaps even dreadfully unutterable—prayers in the Rosh Hashanah [New Year] ritual, in which we say that on Yom Kippur [the Day of Atonement] the book of God records the fate of those who will live and those who will die in the course of the year, whether by illness or famine, war or fire, flood or epidemic. How can we recite such prayers?

Nevertheless, I accept them.

But shouldn't they be understood metaphorically and allegorically rather than literally?

Of course they should be understood metaphorically. Which simply means: I believe that there is some connection between what we do and what happens to us.

But what is the connection between these prayers and the thousands of starving people in Africa and elsewhere? Could they prevent famine by doing something different, by believing in something else?

It is our duty to see to it that these thousands of people suffer less, and that fewer of them—or none at all—die of famine. Which simply means that in one way or another, we are responsible for their fate.

In the darkest and most terrible moments of doubt and despair, what was your response to the summons in Devarim (Deuteronomy): "Choose life that you may live"? In particular, what meaning do you attach to the second clause of the verse: that *you may live? Why the repetition? Could one choose life that one might not live?*

One could choose life so as not to live and one could live life so as to proclaim the end of life. Nietzscheans and the philosophers of the absurd speak of life against life. What the Torah is saying is that one must choose life in order to live and to sanctify life. In my view, we must first of all say, "choose life." And second: "choose the living." A single living being is more important than all the dead who have gone before.

In this sense, your memory and your work are for the living?

I write for the living, but I would also like to reconcile them to the dead, for in our century a terrible breach has opened between the living and the dead. It may be that the two are also divided by a terrible rage, and that's why I think it is high time to try to reconcile them.

Responsibility and Meaning

PHILIPPE DE SAINT-CHERON: *Can the ethic that runs through our entire Bible be seen as a response to a world in which the most basic human rights can be (and are) trampled underfoot, a response to a civilization whose morality teaches that anything that is possible is permissible, and in which, it would seem, we have no rights but only duties?*

ELIE WIESEL: It is the only response. There is no other. There is so much violence in this world, so much terror and inhumanity, that we must try to return to an ancient wisdom. What are ethics, at bottom? They are laws that govern the relations between human beings. They govern the relationship between me and others, not between me and God. So long as these ethics are not explored, shared, and adopted, we are in danger.

Do you think that man's wisdom has evolved as quickly as science and technology, or is the gap between them wider than ever?

The gap can be measured in light-years. This is one of the reasons why we often feel such despair. In medicine, the sciences, nuclear physics, computer technology, the human race has made more progress in the past fifty years than in the previous three thousand. But in philosophy, literature, poetry, religion, and morality, there has been very little progress at all. True, from time to time we see an advance here and there; but it is slow, maddeningly slow.

How have Jewish tradition and Hasidism interpreted Evil and death? In Isaiah we read: "I form the light and create darkness: I make the peace and create evil: I, the Lord, do all these things."

And in the first book of Samuel, Hannah proclaims: "The Lord puts to death and gives life." Is Adam and Eve's offense the cause of the death and evil that has dwelled within man?

This is primarily a philosophical idea advanced in opposition to the notion of divine duality: a god of good and a god of evil. Isaiah was proclaiming the oneness of God. God is one; He is everywhere. And if He is everywhere, then He is in evil and injustice too, and also in the supreme evil: death. It is man's task to free God of this evil. Every time we extirpate a spark of evil, we hasten the coming of the Messiah.

When we look at the fighting between—and even within—religions, should we not wonder whether historically they have been sources of conflict, disaster, and war, rather than founts of peace and fraternal love?

Up to now, that is indeed the impression they give, what with all the wars, violence, fear, and intolerance. This is not salvation but its opposite. The truth is that it is up to us to change.

Evil and Love

PHILIPPE DE SAINT-CHERON: *It seems to me that raising the question of Evil inevitably raises the question of Good, of love. What are your feelings about the people who were able to demon-*

strate the greatest love, giving of themselves completely, even in the hell of the camps? I have in mind in particular the Polish Franciscan Maximilian Kolbe, whose church declared him the saint and martyr of the camps.

ELIE WIESEL: Personally, I think more about the people I knew, about the Jews—rabbis and laymen alike—who shared tenderness and generosity even in the camps. And indeed, I knew such people. They weren't saints, simply men and women who accepted their fate in very human and very Jewish terms. In fact, for them that meant the same thing, as it does for me as well. There are no saints in Judaism, of course; we do not believe in them. Sainthood is divine. In the Shma Israel we say: *vihitem kedoshim lelohekehm,* may you be sanctified. In place of saints we have the Just; it is they who serve as examples.

For you Evil, or hatred, is still the great question, is it not?

Hatred is Evil and Evil dwells in hatred. The two go hand in hand. They partake of the same phenomenon, the same source. But that is not the problem. The problem is that evil is sometimes done not in its own name but in the name of love. How many massacres have been planned and committed in the name of love! Which brings us back to what we were discussing earlier today: chance and chaos. Think of the *havdala* service that we celebrate at the close of the Sabbath. It marks the border between the holy and the profane—or to put it another way, between good and evil—separating the Sabbath from the rest of the week. The first thing God did in the Creation was to divide the higher from the lower waters. Let good be good and evil be evil; then we know that we must serve one and combat the other. So it is very serious when evil takes on the appearance of good.

In Messengers of God *you wrote: "to watch over a man in pain is more urgent than to contemplate God." But isn't that exactly what contemplating God means to a believer: to live in the path of He who had His prophet say, "He recognized the orphan and the poor and He saw that it was good. That is surely what it is to know me"?*

Of course. But that is not the reason we have to do it. We must do it because a child is thirsty, because a friend is hungry. When I come to that child's aid, I place myself on a certain path, in a certain light. But the reason I must help the orphan is not because I have read that verse of the prophets, but because he is defenseless, and I must aid the child because he is in pain, or because his mother is sick, or because his parents are poor. When I grant such aid and succor, my act draws me closer to the call of the prophets, for God in His Scripture speaks to everyone, myself included. But I repeat, I must try to do good not simply because it is written, but also because it is a human duty, and we cannot shun that which is human. The Bible, in fact, only makes explicit what we must do.

Faith and the Cry for Justice

TIM KELLER

Possessing both a powerful intellect and the real-world experience of a modern, big-city pastor, Tim Keller (1950–) seeks to explore various doubts people have with religion today. In an atmosphere often characterized by hostility, Keller defuses the angst with honest responses to some of the more difficult complaints.

An idea like justice may resonate in our hearts and motivate us to respond to a hurting world. So then how do we answer someone (or our own conscience) who blames religion for perpetuating injustice, both historically and currently? Keller dives into these murky waters by examining some of the misconceptions associated with the behavior of people who are religious. He also tackles the age-old idea that religion breeds violence, dispels some myths about religious people, including the idea of fanaticism, and deals with two equally compelling topics: a look at the word "religion" and a critique of biblical justice. The following reading is taken from The Reason for God.

The Church Is Responsible for So Much Injustice

"I have to doubt any religion that has so many fanatics and hypocrites," insisted Helen, a law student. "There are so many people who are not religious at all who are more kind and even more moral than many of the Christians I know."

"The church has a history of supporting injustice, of destroying culture," responded Jessica, another law student. "If Christianity is the true religion, how could this be?"

MARK LILLA, A professor at the University of Chicago, wrote an account for the *New York Times Magazine* of his "born-again" experience as a teenager. During college he "de-converted" and abandoned his Christian faith. How did it happen? Moving from Detroit to Ann Arbor, Michigan, he entered a Christian community that had a national reputation for spiritual vitality, but it turned out to be a "crushing disappointment." The community was authoritarian and hierarchical, and the members were "dogmatic . . . eager to bring me into the line doctrinally." Disillusioned by the combative and exploitative way he thought they used the Bible to control people's lives, "the thought penetrated my mind—that the Bible might be wrong. . . . It was my first step out of the world of faith . . ."[1]

Many people who take an intellectual stand against Christianity do so against a background of personal disappointment with Christians and churches. We all bring to issues intellectual predispositions based on our experience. If you have known many wise, loving, kind, and insightful Christians over the years, and if you have seen churches that are devout in belief yet civic-minded and generous, you will find the intellectual case for Christianity much more plausible. If, on the other hand, the preponderance of your experience is with nominal Christians (who bear the name but don't practice it) or with self-righteous fanatics, then the arguments for Christianity will have to be extremely strong for you to concede that they have any cogency at all. Mark Lilla's determination that "the Bible might be wrong" was not a pure act of philosophical reflection. He was resisting the way that a particular person, in the name of Christianity, was trying to exercise power over him.

So we have to address the behavior of Christians—individual and corporate—that has undermined the plausibility of Christianity for so many people. Three issues stand out. First, there is the issue of Christians' glaring character flaws. If Christianity is the truth, why are so many non-Christians living better lives than the Christians? Second, there is the issue of war and violence. If Christianity is the truth, why has the institutional church supported war, injustice, and violence over the years? Third, there is the issue of fanaticism. Even if Christian teaching has much to offer, why would we want to be together with so many smug, self-righteous, dangerous fanatics?

Character Flaws

Anyone involved in the life of a church will soon discover the many flaws in the character of the average professing Christian. Church communities seem, if anything, to be characterized by more fighting and party spirit than do other voluntary organizations. Also, the moral failing of Christian leaders are well known. It may be true that the press takes too much pleasure in publicizing them, but it doesn't create them. Church officials seem to be at least (if not more) corrupt than leaders in the world at large.

At the same time there are many formally irreligious people who live morally exemplary lives. If Christianity is all it claims to be, shouldn't Christians on the whole be much better people than everyone else?

This assumption is based on a mistaken belief concerning what Christianity actually teaches about itself. Christian theology has taught what is known as *common grace*. James 1.17 says, "Every good and perfect gift comes down from above . . . from the father of lights." This means that no matter who performs it, every act of goodness, wisdom, justice, and beauty is empowered by God. God gives our good gifts of wisdom, talent, beauty, and skill "graciously"—that is, in a completely unmerited way. He casts them across *all* humanity, regardless of religious conviction, race, gender, or any other attribute to enrich, brighten, and preserve the world.

Christian theology also speaks of the seriously flawed character of real Christians. A central message of the Bible is that we can only have a relationship with God by sheer grace. Our moral efforts are too feeble and falsely motivated to ever merit salvation. Jesus, through his death and resurrection, had provided salvation for us, which we receive as a gift. All churches believe this in one form or another. Growth is character and changes in behavior occur in a gradual process after a person becomes a Christian. The mistaken belief that a person must "clean up" his or her own life in order to merit God's presence is not Christianity. This means, though, that the church will be filled with immature and broken people who still have a long way to go emotionally, morally, and spiritually. As the saying has it: "The church is a hospital for sinners, not a museum for saints."

Good character is largely attributable to a loving, safe, and stable family and social environment—conditions for which we were not responsible. Many have had instead an unstable family background, poor role models, and a history of tragedy and disappointment. As a result, they are burdened with deep insecurities, hypersensitivity, and a lack of self-confidence. They may struggle with uncontrolled anger, shyness, addictions, and other difficulties as a result.

Now imagine that someone with a very broken past becomes a

Christian and her character improves significantly over what it was. Nevertheless, she still may be less secure and self-disciplined than someone who is so well adjusted that she feels no particular need of religious affiliation at all. Suppose you meet both of these women the same week. Unless you know the starting points and life journeys of each woman, you could easily conclude that Christianity isn't worth much, and that Christians are inconsistent with their own high standards. It is often the case that people whose lives have been harder and who are "lower on the character scale" are more likely to recognize their need for God and turn to Christianity. So we should expect that many Christians' lives would not compare well to those of the nonreligious[2] (just as the health of people in the hospital is comparatively worse than people visiting museums).

Religion and Violence

Doesn't orthodox religion lead inevitably to violence? Christopher Hitchens, the author of *God Is Not Great: How Religion Poisons Everything,* argues that it does. In his chapter "Religion Kills," he gives personal accounts of religion-fueled violence in Belfast, Beirut, Bombay, Belgrade, Bethlehem, and Baghdad. His argument is that religion takes racial and cultural differences and aggravates them. "Religion is not unlike racism," he writes. "One version of it inspires and provokes the other. Religion has been an enormous multiplier of tribal suspicion and hatred. . . ."[3]

Hitchens's point is fair. Religion "transcendentalizes" ordinary cultural differences so that parties feel they are in a cosmic battle between good and evil. This is why Hitchens argues that "religion poisons everything." So it would seem Christian nations institutionalized imperialism, violence, and oppression through the Inquisition and the African slave trade. The totalitarian and militaristic Japanese empire of the mid-twentieth century grew out of a culture deeply influenced by Buddhism and Shintoism. Islam is the soil for much of today's terrorism, while Israeli forces have often been ruthless too. Hindu nationalists, in the name of their religion, carry out bloody strikes on both Christian churches and Muslim mosques. All of this evidence seems to indicate that religion aggravates human differences until they boil over into war, violence, and the oppression of minorities.[4]

There are problems with this view, however. The communist Russian, Chinese, and Cambodian regimes of the twentieth century rejected all organized religion and belief in God. A forerunner of all these was the French Revolution, which rejected traditional religion for human reason. These societies were all rational and secular, yet each produced massive violence against its own people without the influence of religion. Why? Alister McGrath points out that when the idea of God is gone, a society will "transcendentalize" something else, some other concept, in order to appear morally and spiritually superior. The Marxists made the State into such an absolute, while the Nazis did it to race and blood. Even the ideals of liberty and equality can be used in this way in order to do violence to opponents. In 1793, when Madame Roland went to the guillotine on trumped-up charges, she bowed to the statue personifying liberty in the Place de la Révolution and said, "*Liberty, what crimes are committed in your name.*"[5]

Violence done in the name of Christianity is a terrible reality and must be both addressed and redressed. There is no excusing it. In the twentieth century, however, violence has been inspired as much by secularism as by moral absolutism. Societies that have rid themselves of all religion have been just as oppressive as those steeped in it. We can only conclude that there is some violent impulse so deeply rooted in the human heart that it expresses itself regardless of what the beliefs of a particular society might be—whether socialist or capitalist, whether religious or irreligious, whether individualistic or hierarchical. Ultimately, then, the fact of violence and warfare in a society is no necessary refutation of the prevailing beliefs of that society.

Fanaticism

Perhaps the biggest deterrent to Christianity for the average person today is not so much violence and warfare but the shadow of fanaticism. Many nonbelievers have friends or relatives who have become "born again" and seem to have gone off the deep end. They soon begin to express loudly their disapproval of various groups and sectors of our society—especially movies and television, the Democratic party, homosexuals, evolutionists, activist judges, members of other religions, and the values taught in public schools. When arguing for the truth of their faith they often appear intolerant and self-righteous. This is what many people would call fanaticism.

Many people try to understand Christians along a spectrum from "nominalism" at one end to "fanaticism" on the other. A nominal Christian is someone who is Christian in name only, who does not practice it and perhaps barely believes it. A fanatic is someone who is thought to over-believe and over-practice Christianity. In this schematic, the best kind of Christian would be someone in the middle, someone who doesn't go all the way with it, who believes it but is not too devoted to it. The problem with this approach is that it assumes that the Christian faith is basically a form of moral improvement. Intense Christians would therefore be intense moralists or, as they were called in Jesus's time, Pharisees. Pharisaic people assume they are right with God because of their moral behavior and right doctrine. This leads naturally to feelings of superiority toward those who do not share their religiosity, and from there to various forms of abuse, exclusion, and oppression. This is the essence of what we think of as fanaticism.

What if, however, the essence of Christianity is salvation by grace, salvation not because of what we do but because of what Christ has done for us? Belief that you are accepted by God by sheer grace is profoundly humbling. The people who are fanatics, then, are not so because they are too committed to the gospel but because they're not committed to it enough.

Think of people you consider fanatical. They're overbearing, self-righteous, opinionated, insensitive, and harsh. Why? It's not because they are too Christian but because they are not Christian enough. They are fanatically zealous and courageous, but they are not fanatically humble, sensitive, loving, empathetic, forgiving, or understanding—as Christ was. Because they think of Christianity as a self-improvement program they emulate the Jesus of the whips in the temple, but not the Jesus who said, "Let him who is without sin cast the first stone" (John 8.7). What strikes us as overly fanatical is actually a failure to be fully committed to Christ and his gospel.

The Biblical Critique of Religion

Extremism and fanaticism, which lead to injustice and oppression, are a constant danger within any body of religious believers. For

Christians, however, the antidote is not to tone down and moderate their faith, but rather to grasp a fuller and truer faith in Christ. The biblical prophets understood this well. In fact, the scholar Merold Westphal documents how Marx's analysis of religion as an instrument of oppression was anticipated by the Hebrew prophets Isaiah, Jeremiah, Amos, and even by the message of the New Testament gospels. Marx, according to Westphal, was unoriginal in his critique of religion—the Bible beat him to it![6]

Jesus conducts a major critique of religion. His famous Sermon on the Mount (Matthew chapters 5, 6, and 7) does not criticize irreligious people, but rather religious ones. In his famous discourse the people he criticizes pray, give to the poor, and seek to live according to the Bible, but they do so in order to get acclaim and power for themselves. They believe they will get leverage over others and even over God because of their spiritual performance ("They think they will be heard for their many words"—Matthew 6.7). This makes them judgmental and condemning, quick to give criticism, and unwilling to take it. They are fanatics.

In his teaching, Jesus continually says to the respectable and upright, "The tax collectors and the prostitutes enter the kingdom before you" (Matthew 21.31). He continuously condemns in white-hot language their legalism, self-righteousness, bigotry, and love of wealth and power ("You clean the outside of the cup and dish, but inside you are full of greed and wickedness. . . . You neglect justice and the love of God . . . You load people down with burdens they can hardly carry, and you yourselves will not lift one finger to help them. . . . [You] devour widows' houses and for a show make long prayers"—Luke 11.39–46; 20.47). We should not be surprised to discover it was the Bible-believing religious establishment who put Jesus to death. As Swiss theologian Karl Barth put it, it was the church, not the world, who crucified Christ.[7]

Jesus followed the lead of the Hebrew prophets such as Isaiah, who said to the people of his day:

> Day after day they seek me out; they seem eager to know my ways, as if they were a nation that does what is right and has not forsaken the commands of its God. They seem eager for God to come near them. "Why have we fasted," they say, "and

> you have not seen it? Why have we humbled ourselves, and you have not noticed?" Yet on the day of your fasting, you do as you please and exploit all your workers. . . . Is not this the kind of fasting I have chosen: to loose the chains of injustice . . . to set the oppressed free and break every yoke? Is it not to share your food with the hungry and to provide the poor wanderer with shelter—when you see the naked, to clothe him . . . ? (Isaiah 58.2–7)

What were the prophets and Jesus criticizing? They were not against prayer and fasting and obedience to biblical directions for life. The tendency of religious people, however, is to use spiritual and ethical observance as a lever to gain power over others and over God, appeasing him through ritual and good works. This leads to both an emphasis on external religious forms as well as greed, materialism, and oppression in social arrangements. Those who believe they have pleased God by the quality of their devotion and moral goodness naturally feel that they and their group deserve deference and power over others. The God of Jesus and the prophets, however, saves completely by grace. He cannot be manipulated by religious and moral performance—he can only be reached through repentance, through the *giving up* of power. If we are saved by sheer grace we can only become grateful, willing servants of God and of everyone around us. Jesus charged his disciples: "Whoever wants to be great among you must be your servant, and whoever wants to be first must be servant of all" (Mark 10.43–45).

In Jesus's and the prophets' critique, self-righteous religion is always marked by insensitivity to issues of social justice, while true faith is marked by profound concern for the poor and marginalized. The Swiss theologian John Calvin, in his commentaries on the Hebrew prophets, says that God so identifies with the poor that their cries express divine pain. The Bible teaches us that our treatment of them equals our treatment of God.[8]

While the church has inexcusably been party to the oppression of people at times, it is important to realize that the Bible gives us tools for analysis and unflinching critique of religiously supported injustice *from within the faith*. Historian C. John Sommerville claims that even strong secular critics of Christianity are really using resources from within it to denounce it.[9] Many criticize the church for being power-hungry and self-regarding, but there are many cultures in which the drive for power and respect is considered a good. Where, then, did we get this list of virtues by which we can discern the church's sins, asks Sommerville? We actually got it from within the Christian faith.

To illustrate this point to his students, Sommerville invites them to do a thought experiment. He points out that the pre-Christian northern European tribes, like the Anglo-Saxons, had societies based on the concept of honor. They were shame-based cultures in which earning and insisting upon respect from others was paramount. The Christian monks who were trying to convert them had a set of values based on charity, on wanting the best for others. To see the difference he asks his students to imagine seeing a little old lady coming down the street at night carrying a big purse. Why not just knock her over and take the purse and its money? The answer of an honor-shame culture is that you do *not* take her purse, because if you pick on the weak you would be a despicable person. No one would respect you and you would not respect yourself. That ethic, of course, is self-regarding. You are focused on how the action will affect your honor and reputation. There is, however, another train of thought to take. You may imagine how much it would hurt to be mugged, and how the loss of money might harm people who depend on her. So you don't take the money because you want the best for her and for her dependants. This is an other-regarding ethic; you are thinking completely about her.

Over the years Sommerville found that the overwhelming majority of his students reasoned according to the second, other-regarding ethic. As a historian, he then showed them how Christian their moral orientation was. Christianity changed those honor-based cultures in which pride was valued rather than humility, dominance rather than service, courage rather than peaceableness, glory rather than modesty, loyalty to one's own tribe rather than equal respect for all.[10]

The typical criticisms by secular people about the oppressiveness and injustices of the Christian church actually come from Christianity's own resources for critique of itself. The shortcomings of the church can be understood historically as the imperfect adoption and practice of the principles of the Christian gospel. Sommerville says that when Anglo-Saxons first heard the Christian gospel message they were incredulous. They couldn't see how any society could survive that did not fear and respect strength. When they did convert, they were far from consistent. They tended to merge the Christian other-regarding ethic with their older ways. They supported the Crusades as a way of protecting God's honor and theirs. They let monks, women, and serfs cultivate charitable virtues, but these virtues weren't considered appropriate for men of honor and action. No wonder there is so much to condemn in church history. But to give up Christian standards would be to leave us with no basis for the criticism.[11]

What is the answer, then, to the very fair and devastating criticisms of the record of the Christian church? The answer is *not* to abandon the Christian faith, because that would leave us with neither the standards nor the resources to make correction. Instead we should move to a fuller and deeper grasp of what Christianity is. The Bible itself has taught us to expect the abuses of religion and it has also told us what to do about them. Because of this, Christian history gives us many remarkable examples of self-correction. Let's look at perhaps the two leading examples of this.

Justice in Jesus's Name

A deep stain on Christian history is the African slave trade. Since Christianity was dominant in the nations that bought and sold slaves during that time, the churches must bear responsibility along with their societies for what happened. Even though slavery in some form was virtually universal in every human culture over the centuries, it was Christians who first came to the conclusion that it was wrong. The social historian Rodney Stark writes:

> Although it has been fashionable to deny it, anti-slavery doctrines began to appear in Christian theology soon after the decline of Rome and were accompanied by the eventual disappearance of slavery in all but the fringes of Christian Europe. When Europeans subsequently instituted slavery in the New World, they did so over strenuous papal opposition, a fact that was conveniently "lost" from history until recently. Finally, the abolition of New World slavery was initiated and achieved by Christian activists.[12]

Christians began to work for abolition not because of some general understanding of human rights, but because they saw it as violating the will of God. Older forms of indentured servanthood and the bond-service of biblical times had often been harsh, but Christian abolitionists concluded that race-based, lifelong chattel slavery, established through kidnapping, could not be squared with biblical teaching either in the Old Testament or the New.[13] Christian activists such as William Wilberforce in Great Britain, John Woolman in America, and many, many others devoted their entire lives, in the name of Christ, to ending slavery. The slave trade was so tremendously lucrative that there was enormous incentive within the church to justify it. Many church leaders defended the institution. The battle of self-correction was titanic.[14]

When the abolitionists finally had British society poised to abolish slavery in their empire, planters in the colonies foretold that emancipation would cost investors enormous sums and the prices of commodities would skyrocket catastrophically. This did not deter the abolitionists in the House of Commons. They agreed to compensate the planters for all freed slaves, an astounding sum up to half of the British government's annual budget. The Act of Emancipation passed in 1833, and the costs were so high to the British people that one historian called the British abolition of slavery "voluntary econocide."

Rodney Stark notes how historians have been desperately trying to figure out why the abolitionists were willing to sacrifice so much to end slavery. He quotes the historian Howard Temperley, who says that the history of abolition is puzzling because most historians believe all political behavior is self-interested. Yet despite the fact that hundreds of scholars over the last fifty years have looked for ways to explain it, Temperley says, "no one has succeeded in showing that those who campaigned for the end of the slave trade . . . stood to gain in any tangible way . . . or that these measures were other than economically costly to the country." Slavery was abolished because it was wrong, and Christians were the leaders in saying so.[15] Christianity's self-correcting apparatus, its critique of religiously supported acts of injustice, had asserted itself.

Another classic case of this is the Civil Rights movement in the United States in the mid-twentieth century. In an important history of the movement, David L. Chappell demonstrates that it was not a political but primarily a religious and spiritual movement. White Northern liberals who were the allies of the African-American civil rights leaders were not proponents of civil disobedience or of a direct attack on segregation. Because of their secular belief in the goodness of human nature, they thought that education and enlightenment would bring out the inevitable social and racial progress. Chappell argues that black leaders were much more rooted in the biblical understanding of the sinfulness of the human heart and in the denunciation of injustice that they read in the Hebrew prophets. Chappell also shows how it was the vibrant faith of rank-and-file African-Americans that empowered them to insist on justice despite the violent opposition to their demands. Thus Chappell says there is no way to understand what happened until you see the Civil Rights movement as a religious revival.[16]

When Martin Luther King Jr. confronted racism in the white church in the South, he did not call on Southern churches to become more secular. Read his sermons and "Letter from Birmingham Jail" and see how he argued. He invoked God's moral law and the Scripture. He calls white Christians to be *more true* to their own beliefs and to realize what the Bible really teaches. He did not say "Truth is relative and everyone is free to determine what is right or wrong for them." If everything is relative, there would have been no incentive for white people in the South to give up their power. Rather, Dr. King invoked the prophet Amos, who said, "Let justice roll down like waters, and righteousness as a mighty stream" (Amos 5.24). The greatest champion of justice in our era knew the antidote to racism was not less Christianity, but a deeper and truer Christianity.

Wilberforce and King were not by any means the only leaders who have turned the tide against injustice in the name of Christ. After apartheid was abolished in South Africa, everyone expected a bloodbath in which former victims would take violent vengeance on their persecutors and former oppressors would defend themselves with force. Instead, Christian leaders like Desmond Tutu set up the remarkable South African Commission for Truth and Reconciliation in the mid-1990s. Its name expressed its principle and mission. It invited victims to come forward to tell their stories publicly. It also invited former perpetrators of oppression and violence to come for-

ward, tell the truth, and ask for amnesty. No side was exempt from appearing before the commission. The commission heard reports of human rights violations and considered amnesty applications from all sides, from the former apartheid state as well as from the African National Congress. Though not without its flaws and critics, the commission helped bring about the transition of majority rule with far less bloodshed than anyone could have expected.

In the late twentieth century the Catholic church in eastern Europe refused to die under Communism. Through "patience, candles, and crosses" it began the chain of events that brought down all those totalitarian regimes. The Polish priest Jerzy Popieluszko, through his preaching and activism, led the movement for a free trade union in Communist Poland in the early 1980s. When he was murdered by the secret police, 250,000 people came to his funeral, including Lech Walesa, whose Solidarity movement would help bring down the Communist government. Many of those who went to his funeral marched past the secret police headquarters with a banner that read "We Forgive."[17] The Christian underpinnings of the resistance movement were unmistakable.

There is a long list of martyrs who stood up for the oppressed in Jesus's name, such as Archbishop Oscar Romero of El Salvador. Romero was made archbishop for his conservative, orthodox, doctrinal views. In his new post he saw irrefutable evidence of chronic and violent human rights abuses by the government. He began to speak out fearlessly against it, and as a result he was shot to death in 1980 while saying Mass.

The famous Lutheran martyr Dietrich Bonhoeffer was pastoring two German-speaking churches in London when Hitler came to power. He refused to stay at a safe distance and returned to his country to head an illegal seminary for the Confessing Church, the Christian congregations that refused to sign an oath of allegiance to the Nazis. Bonhoeffer wrote the classic *The Cost of Discipleship*, in which he critiqued the religion and church of his day. In echoes of Jesus and the prophets, Bonhoeffer revealed that spiritual deadness and self-satisfied complacency made it possible for so many to cooperate with Hitler and turn a blind eye to those being systematically marginalized and destroyed by the Nazis. Bonhoeffer was eventually arrested and hanged.

In his last letters from prison, Bonhoeffer reveals how his Christian faith gave him the resources to give up everything for the sake of others. Marx argued that if you believe in a life after this one you won't be concerned about making this world a better place. You can also argue the opposite. If this world is all there is, and if the goods of this world are the only love, comfort, and wealth I will ever have, why should I sacrifice them for others? Bonhoeffer, however, had a joy and hope in God that made it possible for him to do what he did:

> It is not a religious act that makes the Christian, but participation in the sufferings of God in the secular life. That is metanoia [repentance]: not in the first place thinking about one's own needs, problems, sins, and fear, but allowing oneself to be caught up into the way of Jesus Christ. . . . Pain is a holy angel. . . . Through him men have become greater than through all the joys of the world. . . . The pain of longing, which often can be felt physically, must be there, and we shall not and need not talk it away. But it needs to be overcome every time, and thus there is an even holier angel than the one of pain, that is the one of joy in God.[18]

Why mention all of these examples? They are evidence that Dr. King was right. When people have done injustice in the name of Christ they are not being true to the spirit of the one who himself died as a victim of injustice and who called for the forgiveness of his enemies. When people give their lives to liberate others as Jesus did, they are realizing the true Christianity that Martin Luther King Jr., Dietrich Bonhoeffer, and other Christian voices have called for.

MARTIN LUTHER KING JR.

Honest, reverent, nonviolent, and passionate are some of the characteristics that describe the twentieth century's most influential civil rights activist in the United States—and around the world. Martin Luther King Jr. (1929–1968) led countless marches and sit-ins, crying out for justice for the oppressed minorities in the United States. He invoked the character of God as the necessary agent of change in the hearts and minds of men and women regarding injustice, particularly the evils of racism and segregation.

A brilliant orator, he delivered "A Tough Mind and a Tender Heart" as a sermon decrying the twin dangers of softmindedness (ignorance) and a hardened heart. Like Jesus Christ, whom he followed, King firmly believed we are to love God and others with our minds, using our intellects—but also with our hearts, seeing others as people who must be valued and treated with love and compassion. King was assassinated on April 4, 1968, at a motel in Memphis, Tennessee, at the age of thirty-nine. This excerpt comes from Strength to Love.

A Tough Mind and a Tender Heart

Be ye therefore wise as serpents, and harmless as doves.
(Matthew 10.16)

A FRENCH PHILOSOPHER said, "No man is strong unless he bears within his character antitheses strongly marked." The strong man holds in a living blend strongly marked opposites. Not ordinarily do men achieve this balance of opposites. The idealists are not usually realistic, and the realists are not usually idealistic. The militant are not generally known to be passive, nor the passive to be militant. Seldom are the humble self-assertive, or the self-assertive humble. But life at its best is a creative synthesis of opposites in fruitful harmony. The philosopher Hegel said that truth is found neither in the thesis nor the antithesis, but in an emergent synthesis which reconciles the two.

Jesus recognized the need for blending opposites. He knew that his disciples would face a difficult and hostile world, where they would confront the recalcitrance of political officials and the intransigence of the protectors of the old order. He knew that they would meet cold and arrogant men whose hearts had been hardened by the longer winter of traditionalism. So he said to them, "Behold, I send you forth as sheep in midst of wolves." And then he gave them a formula for action: "Be ye therefore wise as serpents, and harmless as doves."

It is pretty difficult to imagine a single person having, simultaneously, the characteristics of the serpent and the dove, but this is what Jesus expects. We must combine the toughness of the serpent and the softness of the dove, a tough mind and a tender heart.

I

Let us consider, first, the need for a tough mind, characterized by incisive thinking, realistic appraisal, and decisive judgment. The tough mind is sharp and penetrating, breaking through the crust of legends and myths and sifting the true from the false. The tough-minded individual is astute and discerning. He has a strong, austere quality that makes for firmness of purpose and solidness of commitment.

Who doubts that this toughness of mind is one of man's greatest needs? Rarely do we find men who willingly engage in hard, solid thinking. There is an almost universal quest for easy answers and half-baked solutions. Nothing pains some people more than having to think.

This prevalent tendency toward softmindedness is found in man's unbelievable gullibility. Take our attitude toward advertisements. We are so easily led to purchase a product because a television or radio advertisement pronounces it better than any other. Advertisers have long since learned that most people are softminded, and they capitalize on this susceptibility with skillful and effective slogans.

This undue gullibility is also seen in the tendency of many readers to accept the printed word of the press as final truth. Few people realize that even our authentic channels of information—the press, the platform, and in many instances the pulpit—do not give us objective and unbiased truth. Few people have the toughness of mind to judge critically and to discern the true from the false, the fact from the fiction. Our minds are constantly being invaded by legions of half-truths, prejudices, and false facts. One of the great needs of mankind is to be lifted above the morass of false propaganda.

Softminded individuals are prone to embrace all kinds of superstitions. Their minds are constantly invaded by irrational fears, which range from fear of Friday the thirteenth to fear of a black cat crossing one's path. As the elevator made its upward climb in one of the largest hotels in New York City, I noticed for the first time that there was no thirteenth floor—floor fourteen followed floor twelve. On inquiring from the elevator operator the reason for this omission, he said, "This practice is followed by most large hotels because of the fear of numerous people to stay on the thirteenth floor." Then he added, "The real foolishness of the fear is to be found in the fact that the fourteenth floor is actually the thirteenth." Such fears leave the soft mind haggard by day and haunted by night.

The softminded man always fears change. He feels security in the status quo, and he has an almost morbid fear of the new. For him, the greatest pain is the pain of a new idea. An elderly segregationist in the South is reported to have said, "I have come to see now that desegregation is inevitable. But I pray God that it will not take place until after I die." The softminded person always wants to freeze the moment and hold life in the gripping yoke of sameness.

Softmindedness often invades religion. This is why religion has sometimes rejected new truth with a dogmatic passion. Through edicts and bulls, inquisitions and excommunications, the church has attempted to prorogue truth and place an impenetrable stone wall in the path of the truth-seeker. The historical-philological criticism of the Bible is considered by the softminded as blasphemous, and reason is often looked upon as the exercise of a corrupt facility. Softminded persons have revised the Beatitudes to read, "Blessed are the pure in ignorance: for they shall see God."

This has also led to a widespread belief that there is a conflict between science and religion. But this is not true. There may be a conflict between softminded religionists and toughminded scientists, but not between science and religion. Their respective worlds are different and their methods are dissimilar. Science investigates; religion interprets. Science gives man knowledge which is power; religion gives man wisdom which is control. Science deals mainly with facts, religion clearly deals mainly with values. The two are not rivals. They are complementary. Science keeps religion from sinking into the valley of crippling irrationalism and paralyzing obscurantism. Religion prevents science from falling into the marsh of obsolete materialism and moral nihilism.

We do not need to look far to detect the dangers of softmindedness. Dictators, capitalizing on softmindedness, have led men to acts of barbarity and terror that are unthinkable in civilized society. Adolf Hitler realized that softmindedness was so prevalent among his followers that he said, "I use emotion for the many and reserve reason for the few." In *Mein Kampf* he asserted:

> By means of shrewd lies, unremittingly repeated, it is possible to make people believe that heaven is hell—and hell, heaven . . . The greater the lie, the more readily will it be believed.

Softmindedness is one of the basic causes of race prejudice. The toughminded person always examines the facts before he reaches conclusions; in short, he postjudges. The tenderminded person reaches a conclusion before he has examined the first fact; in short, he prejudges and is prejudiced. Race prejudice is based on groundless fears, suspicions, and misunderstandings. There are those who are sufficiently softminded to believe in the superiority of the white race and the inferiority of the Negro race in spite of the toughminded research of anthropologists who reveal the falsity of such a notion. There are softminded persons who argue that racial segregation should be perpetuated because Negroes lag behind in academic, health, and moral standards. They are not toughminded enough to realize that lagging standards are the result of segregation and discrimination. They do not recognize that it is rationally unsound and sociologically untenable to use the tragic effects of segregation as an argument for its continuation. Too many politicians in the South recognize this disease of softmindedness which engulfs their constituency. With insidious zeal, they make inflammatory statements and disseminate distortions and half-truths which arouse abnormal fears and morbid antipathies within the minds of uneducated and underprivileged whites, leaving them so confused that they are led to acts of meanness and violence which no normal person commits.

There is little hope for us until we become toughminded enough to break loose from the shackles of prejudice, half-truths, and downright ignorance. The shape of the world today does not permit us the luxury of softmindedness. A nation or a civilization that continues to produce softminded men purchases its own spiritual death on an installment plan.

II

But we must not stop with the cultivation of a tough mind. The gospel also demands a tender heart. Toughmindedness without tenderheartedness is cold and detached, leaving one's life in a perpetual winter devoid of the warmth of spring and the gentle heat of summer. What is more tragic than to see a person who has risen to the disciplined heights of toughmindedness but has at the same time sunk to the passionless depths of hardheartedness?

The hardhearted person never truly loves. He engages in a crass utilitarianism which values other people mainly according to their usefulness to him. He never experiences the beauty of friendship, because he is too cold to feel affection for another and too self-centered to share another's joy and sorrow. He is an isolated island. No outpouring of love links him with the mainland of humanity.

The hardhearted person lacks the capacity for genuine compassion. He is unmoved by the pains and afflictions of his brothers. He passes unfortunate men every day, but he never really sees them. He gives dollars to a worthwhile charity, but he gives not of his spirit.

The hardhearted individual never sees people as people, but rather as mere objects or as impersonal cogs in an ever-turning wheel. In the vast wheel of industry, he sees men as hands. In the massive wheel of big city life, he sees men as digits in a multitude. In the deadly wheel of army life, he sees men as numbers in a regiment. He depersonalizes life.

Jesus frequently illustrated the characteristics of the hardhearted. The rich fool was condemned, not because he was toughminded, but rather because he was not tenderhearted. Life for him was a mirror in which he saw only himself, and not a window through which he saw other selves. Dives went to hell, not because he was wealthy, but because he was not tenderhearted enough to see Lazarus and because he made no attempt to bridge the gulf between himself and his brother.

Jesus reminds us that the good life combines the toughness of the serpent and the tenderness of the dove. To have serpentlike qualities devoid of dovelike qualities is to be passionless, mean, and selfish. To have dovelike without serpentlike qualities is to be sentimental, anemic, and aimless. We must combine strongly marked antitheses.

We as Negroes must bring together toughmindedness and tenderheartedness, if we are to move creatively toward the goal of freedom and justice. Softminded individuals among us feel that the only way to deal with oppression is by adjusting to it. They acquiesce and resign themselves to segregation. They prefer to remain oppressed. When Moses led the children of Israel from the slavery of Egypt to the freedom of the Promised Land, he discovered that slaves do not always welcome their deliverers. They would rather bear those ills they have, as Shakespeare pointed out, than flee to others that they know not of. They prefer the "fleshpots of Egypt" to the ordeals of emancipation. But this is not the way out. Softminded acquiescence is cowardly. My friends, we cannot win the respect of the white people of the South or elsewhere if we are not willing to trade the future of our children for our personal safety and comfort. Moreover, we must learn that passively to accept an unjust system is to co-operate with that system, and thereby to become a participant in its evil.

And then there are hardhearted and bitter individuals among us who would combat the opponent with physical violence and corroding hatred. Violence brings only temporary victories; violence, by creating many more social problems than it solves, never brings permanent peace. I am convinced that if we succumb to the temptation to use violence in our struggle for freedom, unborn generations will be the recipients of a long and desolate night of bitterness, and our chief legacy to them will be a never-ending reign of chaos. A Voice, echoing through the corridors of time, says to every intemperate Peter, "Put up thy sword." History is cluttered with the wreckage of nations that failed to follow Christ's command.

III

A third way is open in our quest for freedom, namely, nonviolent resistance, that combines toughmindedness and tenderheartedness and avoids the complacency and do-nothingness of the softminded and the violence and bitterness of the hardhearted. My belief is that this method must guide our action in the present crisis in race relations. Through nonviolent resistance we shall be able to oppose the unjust system and at the same time love the perpetrators of the system. We must work passionately and unrelentingly for full stature as citizens, but may it never be said, my friends, that to gain it we used the inferior methods of falsehood, malice, hate, and violence.

I would not conclude without applying the meaning of the text to the nature of God. The greatness of our God lies in the fact that he is both toughminded and tenderhearted. He has qualities both of austerity and of gentleness. The Bible, always clear in stressing both attributes of God, expresses his toughmindedness in his justice and wrath and his tenderheartedness in his love and grace. God has two outstretched arms. One is strong enough to surround us with justice, and one is gentle enough to embrace us with grace. On the one hand, God is a God of justice who punished Israel for her wayward deeds, and on the other hand, he is a forgiving father whose heart was filled with an unutterable joy when the prodigal returned home.

I am thankful that we worship a God who is both toughminded and tenderhearted. If God were only toughminded, he would be a cold, passionless despot sitting in some far-off heaven "contemplating it all," as Tennyson puts it in "The Palace of Art." He would be Aristotle's "unmoved mover," the self-knowing, but not other-loving. But if God were only tenderhearted, he would be too soft and sentimental to function when things go wrong and incapable of controlling what he has made. He would be like H. G. Wells's lovable God in *God, the Invisible King,* who is strongly desirous of making a good world, but finds himself helpless before the surging powers of evil. God is neither hardhearted nor softminded. He is toughminded enough to transcend the world; he is tenderhearted enough to live in it. He does not leave us alone in our agonies and struggles. He seeks us in dark places and suffers with us and for us in our tragic prodigality.

At times we need to know that the Lord is a God of justice. When slumbering giants of injustice emerge in the earth, we need to know that there is a God of power who can cut them down like the grass and leave them withering like the green herb. When our most tireless efforts fail to stop the surging sweep of oppression, we need to know that in this universe is a God whose matchless strength is a fit contrast to the sordid weakness of man. But there are also times when we need to know that God possesses love and mercy. When we are staggered by the chilly winds of adversity and battered by the raging storms of disappointment and when through our folly and sin we stray into some destructive far country and are frustrated because of a strange feeling of homesickness, we need to know that there is Someone who loves us, cares for us, understands us, and will give us another chance. When days grow dark and nights grow dreary, we can be thankful that our God combines in his nature a creative synthesis of love and justice which will lead us through life's dark valleys and into sunlit pathways of hope and fulfillment.

The Harmony of Science and Faith

PAUL BRAND

As a well-renowned surgeon, Paul Brand (1914–2003) spent the majority of his life marveling at the intricacies and complexities of the human body. Born to British missionary parents in southern India, he grew up in a world where exposure to rare diseases and death were a common occurrence. The debilitating nature and shame associated with leprosy drew him to care for and pioneer new research methods for those plagued by it.

In his very first published book, Brand collaborated with popular writer Philip Yancey to introduce his readers to the eternal God who intentionally, with specificity, creates every detail of the human body. He leads us into a world where the fabric of the human body derives its value from its creator. In this piece from Fearfully and Wonderfully Made, *Brand relates a dramatic personal story that becomes a parable for how we are all called to be God's hands, reaching out to others in need.*

A Presence

AS A JUNIOR doctor on night duty in a London hospital I called on eighty-one-year-old Mrs. Twigg. This spry, courageous woman had been battling cancer of the throat, but even with a raspy, hoarse voice she remained witty and cheerful. She had asked that we do all we could medically to prolong her life, and one of my professors removed her larynx and the malignant tissue around it.

Mrs. Twigg seemed to be making a good recovery until about two o'clock one morning when I was urgently summoned to her ward. She was sitting on the bed, leaning forward, with blood spilling from her mouth. Wild terror filled her eyes. Immediately I guessed that an artery back in her throat had eroded. I knew no way to stop the bleeding but to thrust my finger into her mouth and press on the pulsing spot. Grasping her jaw with one hand, I explored with my index finger deep inside her slippery throat until I found the artery and pressed it shut.

Nurses cleaned up around her face while Mrs. Twigg recovered her breath and fought back a gagging sensation. Fear slowly drained from her as she began to trust me. After ten minutes had passed and she was breathing normally again, with her head tilted back, I tried to remove my finger to replace it with an instrument. But I could not see far enough back in her throat to guide the instrument, and each time I removed my finger the blood spurted afresh and Mrs. Twigg panicked. Her jaw trembled, her eyes bulged, and she forcefully gripped my arm. Finally, I calmed her by saying I would simply wait, with my finger blocking the blood flow, until a surgeon and anesthetist could be summoned from their homes.

We settled into position. My right arm crooked behind her head, supported her. My left hand nearly disappeared inside her contorted mouth, allowing my index finger to apply pressure at the critical point. I knew from visits to the dentist how fatiguing and painful it must be for tiny Mrs. Twigg to stretch her mouth open wide enough to surround my entire hand. But I could see in her intense blue eyes a resolution to maintain that position for days if necessary. With her face a few inches from mine, I could sense her mortal fear. Even her breath smelled of blood. Her eyes pleaded mutely, "Don't move—don't let go!" She knew, as I did, if we relaxed our awkward posture, she would bleed to death.

We sat like that for nearly two hours. Her imploring eyes never left mine. Twice during the first hour, when muscle cramps painfully seized my hand, I tried to move to see if the bleeding had stopped. It had not, and as Mrs. Twigg felt the rush of warm liquid surge up in her throat she gripped my shoulder anxiously.

I will never know how I lasted that second hour. My muscles cried out in agony. My fingertip grew totally numb. I thought of rock climbers who have held their fallen partners for hours by a single rope. In this case the cramping four-inch length of my finger, so numb I could not even feel it, was the strand restraining life from falling away.

I, a junior doctor in my twenties, and this eighty-one-year-old woman clung to each other superhumanly because we had no choice—her survival demanded it.

The surgeon came. Assistants prepared the operating room, and the anesthetist readied his chemicals. Mrs. Twigg and I, still entwined together in our strange embrace, were wheeled into the surgery room. There, with everyone poised with gleaming tools, I slowly eased my finger away from her throat. I felt no gush of blood. Was it because my finger could no longer feel? Or had the blood finally clotted firmly after two hours of pressure?

I removed my hand from her mouth and still Mrs. Twigg breathed easily. Her hand continued to clutch my shoulder and her eyes stayed on my face. But gradually, almost imperceptibly at first, the corners of her bruised, stretched lips turned slightly up, forming a smile. The clot had held. She could not speak—she had no larynx—but she did not need words to express her gratitude. She knew how my muscles had suffered; I knew the depths of her fear. In those two hours in the slumberous hospital wing, we had become almost one person.

As I recall that night with Mrs. Twigg, it stands almost as a parable of the conflicting strains of human helplessness and divine power within us. In this case, my medical training counted very little. What mattered was my presence and my willingness to respond by reaching out and contacting another human being.

Along with most doctors I know, I often feel inadequate in the face of real suffering. Pain strikes like an earthquake, with crushing suddenness and devastation. A woman feels a small lump in her breast, and her sexual identity begins to crumble. A child is stillborn, and the mother wails in anguish: "Nine months I waited for this! Why do so many mothers abort their babies while I would give my life to have a healthy one?" A young boy is thrown through the windshield of a car, permanently scarring his face. His memory flickers on and off like a faulty switch—doctors, ever cautious, can't offer much hope.

When suffering strikes, those of us standing close by are flattened by the shock. We fight back the lumps in our throats, march resolutely to the hospital for visits, mumble a few cheerful words, perhaps look up articles on what to say to the grieving.

But when I ask patients and their families, "Who helped you in your suffering?" I hear a strange, imprecise answer. The person described rarely has smooth answers and a winsome, effervescent personality. It is someone quiet, understanding, who listens more than talks, who does not judge or even offer much advice. "A sense of presence." "Someone there when I needed him." A hand to hold, an understanding, bewildered hug. A shared lump in the throat.

We want psychological formulas as precise as those techniques I study in my surgery manuals. But the human psyche is too complex for a manual. The best we can offer is to be there, to see and to touch.

. . . Is God's plan to possess the earth through a Body composed of frail humans adequate in light of the sheer enormity of the world's problems? Such a question deserves the full treatment of a book much longer and wiser than this one. I can, however, capture a glimpse of God's style of relating to our planet by reviewing the progressive metaphors He has given us.

All language about God is, of course, symbolic. "Can one hold the ocean in a teacup?" Joy Davidman asked. Words, even thoughts, cannot carry Godness. In the Old Testament, symbols for God most often expressed His "otherness." He appeared as a Spirit, so full of light and glory that one who approached Him was struck dead or returned with an unhuman glow. Moses saw only God's back; Job heard Him from a whirlwind; the Israelites followed his shekinah glory cloud.

Is it any wonder that the Jews, accustomed to such mystery and afraid to say aloud or write the name of god, recoiled at the claims of Jesus Christ? "Anyone who has seen me has seen the Father," Jesus said (John 14.9), words that grated harshly on Jewish ears. He had, after all, spent nine fetal months inside a young girl and had grown up in a humble neighborhood. In Chesterton's words, "God who had been only a circumference was seen as a center; and a center is infinitely small." Visibly at least, He seemed too much like any other human. Their suspicions were confirmed when He succumbed to death. How could God be contained inside the flesh and blood of humanity? How could God die? Many still wonder, long after a resurrection that convinced and ignited his followers.

But Jesus departed, leaving no body on earth to exhibit the Spirit of God to an unbelieving world—except the faltering, bumbling community of followers who had largely forsaken Him at His death. *We* are what Jesus left on earth. He did not leave a book or a doctrinal statement or a system of thought; He left a visible community to embody Him and represent Him to the world. The seminal metaphor, Body of Christ, hinted at by Christ and fully expanded by Paul could only arise *after* Jesus Christ had left the earth.

The apostle Paul's great, decisive words about the body of Christ were addressed to congregations in Corinth and Asia Minor that, in the next breath, he assailed for human frailty. Note that Paul, a master of simile and metaphor, did not say the people of God are "like the Body of Christ." In every place he said we *are* the body of Christ. The Spirit has come and dwelt among us, and the world knows an invisible God mainly by our representation, our "enfleshment," of Him.

"The Church is nothing but a section of humanity in which Christ has really taken form," said Bonhoeffer. Too often we shrink from both clauses of that summary. Dismayed we blast ourselves for continuing to manifest our flawed humanity. Disheartened, we in practice, if not in faith, deny that Christ really has taken form in us.

Three dominant symbols—God as a glory cloud, as a Man subject to death, and as a spirit melding together His new Body—show a progression of intimacy, from fear to shared humanity to shared essence. God is present in us, uniting us genetically to Himself and to each other.

Where is God in the world? What is He like? We can no longer point to the Holy of Holies or to a carpenter in Nazareth. *We* form God's presence in the world through the indwelling of His Spirit. It is a heavy burden.

After World War II German students volunteered to help rebuild a cathedral in England, one of the many casualties of the Luftwaffe bombings. As the work progressed, debate broke out on how to best restore a large statue of Jesus with His arms outstretched and bearing the familiar inscription, "Come unto Me." Careful patching could repair all damage to the statue except for Christ's hands, which had been destroyed by bomb fragments. Should they attempt the delicate task of reshaping those hands?

Finally the workers reached a decision that still stands today. The statue of Jesus has no hands, and the inscription now reads, "Christ has no hands but ours."

I show you a mystery: "In him you too are being built together to become a dwelling in which God lives by his Spirit" (Ephesians 2.22).

JOHN POLKINGHORNE

John Polkinghorne (1930–), British physicist and Anglican theologian, is best known for his work in synthesizing seemingly disparate fields: faith and science. In his roles as Fellow at Queens College, Cambridge, Fellow of the Royal Society, and Honorary Curate at the Parish of the Good Shepherd, Cambridge, he is committed to elucidating how the two views of reality relate to each other.

In a chapter of his book Faith in the Living God: A Dialogue, *highlighted here, Polkinghorne opens with a revealing quote by Anselm:* fides quaerens intelletum *(faith seeking understanding). Reaching out to both the novice and the most ardent thinker, he writes in a highly accessible style. Polkinghorne looks at identifiable "stumbling blocks" that science-minded people wrestle with from religion—words and ideas like "faith," "God," "Creator," and "metaphysical." He also grapples with the synthesis of faith and science by using the metaphor of a window to discuss contrasting ideas like cosmic order, religious experience, moral evil, and physical evil.*

Faith in God the Creator

ALL THREE SIGNIFICANT words of the title can trip up a scientist. We shall consider these *skandala* (stones of stumbling) in turn.

FAITH

"Faith" can readily conjure up the image of blind belief in really rather incredible propositions that are presented for unquestioning acceptance on the sole basis of an unquestionable authority. This misconception is perhaps the biggest barrier that has to be surmounted by a scientist with an inclination to look into religious matters. Naturally, such a person does not wish to commit intellectual suicide, but all too easily they can suppose that this is what is being asked of them. The idea that faith might be concerned with the search for understanding (as Anselm said in the Middle Ages) will often be a novel concept for scientists. This misconception about the nature of faith has arisen for a number of reasons.

One is simply the failure to recognize that religious believers have motivations for their beliefs. The whole discipline of apologetics is concerned with seeking to articulate these motivations in a way that will be helpful to an enquirer. This activity is not just the sugar-coating of a bitter fideistic pill that has to be swallowed whole, but it is a genuine attempt to express the reasonable origins of religious faith. I have written books seeking to explain and defend my scientific beliefs in quantum theory and in the role of quarks and gluons as the constituents of nuclear matter,[1] and I have also written books seeking to explain and defend my own Christian belief.[2] Although the material is very different in these two sets of writings, the underlying strategy is the same. In each case, one has to tell a complex story of interlocking experience and interpretation that has developed within a truth-seeking community, not without the struggles, perplexities, and setbacks that are common to human intellectual endeavor. At the same time, one has to convey concepts that are radically different from those of everyday common sense. No one can understand quantum theory who is unwilling to accept the necessity of revisionary thinking. It would be unreasonable to expect that enquiry into the divine would prove free from comparable intellectual surprise.

But, the enquiring scientist might say, is not the material in fact so different in these two exercises that one is seen to be a rational enquiry, while the other amounts, in the end, to no more than dependence on irrational assertion? The issue of the nature of revelation is then put onto the agenda, raising the question of what it is that religious people are appealing to when they make use of "revelation" as the basis of their motivation to believe. It might seem that we have returned to an appeal to unchallengeable authority, for many of those who stumble at the world revelation do so because they believe that it refers to infallible propositions utter *ex cathedra Dei*. Certainly, a concise statement like the Nicene Creed does seem to have an air of categorical assertiveness about it. But so also do the particle data tables that high-energy physicists carry around in their pockets. Both are distillations of the essence of complex interactions between experience and interpretation. In the case of scientific knowledge, the experiments are experiences, that is to say, carefully contrived occasions on which some particular aspect of natural process will be most perspicuously discernible. Because experiments are the results of human manipulation, they represent experience that is repeatable, giving it, at least in principle, a universal accessibility. For the Christian believer, in addition to his or her individual religious experience, the prime motivations for faith are the foundational events of the tradition in which God's will and nature are believed to have been more clearly discerned, through the history of Israel and in the person of Jesus Christ. These events were graciously given by God and so they are unique and they have to be accepted or rejected in their unavoidable uniqueness. Those sciences that have a historical dimension are not totally unfamiliar with the givenness of the unique. Evolutionary biology has only one history of terrestrial life on which to base its insights; cosmology only one universe to study.

There is certainly a significant degree of difference at this point between scientific belief and religious belief, but an appeal to the unique is by no means to be understood as an irrational move. Justifying that claim requires some account of the nature of rational thought. I believe that its essence lies in a seeking to conform our thinking to the nature of the object of our thought. Behind that claim there obviously lies a realist stance in relation to human epistemological and ontological abilities; in other words, a trust that what we know is a reliable guide to what is actually the case. I do not believe that we are lost in a Kantian fog, out of which loom the phenomenal shadows of inaccessible noumena, so that we know only appearance and not things as they are. Here, at least, scientists are unlikely to find much difficulty, for they are almost all, consciously or unconsciously, realists about their encounter with the physical world. I have sought elsewhere to defend a critical realism in both science and theology,[3] and I shall not pursue the general point further on this occasion. Realism is, however, fundamental to the exercise on which we are engaged. Just as I do not accept a pragmatist account of science that would see its primary concern as the achievement of technological success, so I do not accept an account of religious faith that regards it as primarily furnishing a technique for living. Just as I do not accept a social constructivist account of science (while not failing to acknowledge the role played by the community in the enterprise of science), so I do not accept an account of religious faith that regards it primarily as a cultural binding force in society. I believe that both science and religion are concerned with knowing and responding to the way things actually are, though neither of them has access to simple, direct, and unproblematic knowledge of the unseen realities of which they seek to speak, nor absolute certainty about the validity of the insights they attain. Critical realism is the attempt to find a middle way between the heroic optimism of the failed modernist search for certain truth, and the intellectual pessimism that so often leads postmodernism into a slough of relativistic despond.

Even within science itself, we can see that rationality in the sense we have been discussing does not take a single universal form. The diversity of reality prevents this from being so. The quantum world has an entirely different character from that of the everyday world of Newtonian physics. Not only is the quantum world cloudy, so that Heisenberg's uncertainty principles denies us exhaustively clear knowledge of its process, but also its relationships are such that a special quantum logic applies to them,[4] different from the classical logic of Aristotle and everyday life. Quantum entities have to be known on their own terms and in accordance with their idiosyncratic rationality. It would scarcely be surprising if similar considerations applied to knowledge of the divine.

Failure to acknowledge this point, together with a simplistic notion that science deals in plain "facts" (despite it being clear that there are no interesting scientific facts that are not already interpreted facts[5]), has often led scientists to a narrow and unsatisfactory identification of the reasonable with what is thinkable within the limited protocols of scientific argument. Many popular books about science are garnished with a broad-brush kind of intellectual history in which the rise of the sun of science is portrayed as dispelling the irrational mists of an age of faith. The idea that thinkers like Augustine or Aquinas were deficient in reason—or in an interest in the science of their time, for that matter—is a very curious belief. Of course, they were people of their age, with the opportunities and limitations that implied, just as were the precursors of modern science, such as Roger Bacon and Nicholas Oresme, usually given a more sympathetic treatment. One of the benefits that scientific reason acquires from the impersonal repeatability of experiment is that its understanding is cumulative in character. At the beginning of the twenty-first century, an ordinary scientist knows and understands a great deal that was hidden even from the geniuses in 1900. Scientists, in consequence, live in the intellectual present. Theology, together with all other forms of human rational enquiry operating at the level of the personal, has always to engage in dialogue across the centuries in order to avoid the distortions and limitations that would be imposed on its deep and many-faceted encounter with reality by a purely contemporary perspective. Theologians have to live within a historical tradition.

God

The second word at which a scientist might stumble is "God." Two contrasting pitfalls lie in the way. One is the concept of the invisible Magician who from time to time tinkers with the natural process of the universe in a capricious way. Needless to say, such a notion is *theologically* incredible. The God who is worthy of worship must be consistent and faithful. "Shall not the Judge of all the earth do right?" (Genesis 18.25). The Ordainer of the laws of nature will not be an arbitrary interferer with them. A surprising number of scientists, however, seem to suppose that it is just such a magical deity in whom they are being invited to believe. In a recent debate, the Nobel Prize winner and staunch atheist Steven Weinberg said that there could be evidence for a God. As an example he suggested the sudden appearance of a flaming sword that decapitated him, the unbeliever. I replied that were so bizarre and unfortunate an incident to happen, it would cause me the greatest theological difficulty, because of its capricious and irrational character.

It would be disingenuous, however, not to recognize that the Old Testament sometimes seems to portray God as acting in just that kind of way (for example, Exodus 4.24—6), and that some of the tragic happenings of human life might also seem to suggest a God of this trickster character. It is the task of theology, through exegesis and theodicy, to wrestle with these perplexities and to seek to resolve them. It is not possible to pursue these important issues in detail here, nor to claim that were this to be done the apparent problems would easily be solved. The Bible cannot be treated as uniformly inspired and authoritative in all its utterance. Principles of interpretation have to be worked out that acknowledge that its human writings contain both eternal truths and also many matters that are the deposits of historical and cultural particularity and limitation. The long tale of human misery and suffering has also to be treated with the most profound seriousness. It is precisely as it struggles with these difficult issues that theology manifests itself as being a truth-seeking and rational form of human enquiry.

An alternative error about the nature of God would be to use the word simply as a cipher for the rational order of the universe. This seems to have been what Einstein did. His general writings contain a number of often quoted aphorisms about the divine, but he explained more than once that he did not believe in a personal God, but thought of himself as a follower of Spinoza, whose characteristic phrase was *deus sive natura,* equating God and nature. This kind of usage is quite common in contemporary popular books about science. The cynical will say that, following the astounding success of Stephen Hawking's *A Brief History of Time,* with its recurrent and somewhat inconsistent invocation of the Mind of God, authors have come to believe that such a tactic is good for sales. Others might see here a certain wistful but wary concern with the possibility of a deeper level of meaning than that to which science, by itself, can give access. The very persistence with which the question of God continues to exercise many minds, even those of avowed atheists, could be interpreted as evidence for a suppressed but continuing *sensus Dei.* No doubt there is some truth in both these interpretations. Theologically, however, this concept of God is far too thin to be satisfactory. It does not do much work and so many may be tempted to think that they might just as well take the order of the universe as being a brute fact in itself. It is the purpose of what follows to explore whether there are reasonable grounds for belief in a creator God that can support an altogether richer concept of the divine.

Creator

Our final stone of stumbling is the word "creator" itself. No theological misconception is more widespread in the scientific community, or more of a hindrance to a fruitful engagement between science and theology, than that the role of the creator is simply to start things off. One classic expression of this error is Hawking's celebrated and naïve observation that if the universe had no datable beginning (as his speculative cosmological theory supposes), then there would be nothing left for a creator to do.[6] Of course, the doctrine of creation is concerned not with temporal beginning, but with ontological origin. People seem to divide into two classes according to how they regard the question "Why is there something rather that nothing?" For some it raises a deep and important issue; for others it is an unintelligible or uninteresting enquiry. It is the former who are seized of the question of the existence of a creator.

The implication of what has been said so far is that the nature of faith is that it is a commitment and response to the real. When faith seeks understanding (to use again Anselm's celebrated definition of theological task), it is concerned with the exploration of the nature of reality. Whether that quest is fittingly seen as being exploration into God the creator will depend critically upon the scope and character of what is considered to make up reality. A leaden reductionist physicalism will be too earthbound to allow the possibility of a glance heavenwards. Science's own success in its own domain must not be allowed to impose upon us the assumption that there alone is to be found all that is worthy of rational enquiry. Absolutely no one, whatever their official beliefs, actually lives their lives as if this were so, for human personality is richer than so desiccated an account could ever encompass. The reality to which faith seeks to respond must be generously and adequately construed, so that it accommodates not only what we might write about in the abstraction of our studies, but also that by which we live in the profound complexity of our active engagement with the way things are.

Of central importance will be how the human encounter with value is to be understood. What is the nature of our ethical intuitions? Is the statement that torturing children is wrong some sort of veiled strategy for evolutionary effectiveness (it might be more useful to put them to work as slaves), or a socially constructed attitude (a convention of our society), or a fact about the way things are (so that there is genuine moral knowledge, which, in its own way, is as much about reality as scientific knowledge is about its particular aspect of reality)? A similar question may be asked about our aesthetic experiences. Do they derive from a veiled recognition of situations favorable to survival, or are they simply biochemical consequences of the emission of certain neurotransmitters in the brain, or are they indispensible and irreducible insights into the nature of a world that is charged with intrinsic beauty? To be honest, one must also add, what is the status of experiences of ugliness and terror? Are they signs of a hostile or indifferent reality, or the consequences of a fallen world marred by a disastrous ancestral act, or signals of the presence of a malevolent or ambiguous deity, or what?

Three things may be said in answer to these questions. The first is that they certainly refer to realms of experience that are culturally influenced in their character. The moral corruption of certain societies (Hitler and Stalin), the tales that the anthropologists bring back, the recurrent aesthetic crises in which a generation initially rejects the artistic developments of its own pioneers, all make that clear enough. Science itself, being the activity of a community, is not unfamiliar with this kind of effect. Without accepting all that Thomas Kuhn had to say about revolutionary periods in science,[7] one can agree that often a new paradigm triumphs partly because of the death of its older opponents. (Poincaré and Lorentz, great men though they were, never fully came to terms with the interpretation that the young Einstein had given of the equations that they had correctly formulated, but whose real import they had not fully comprehended.) Yet, the presence of cultural tricks of perspective, whether in ethics, art, or science, does not imply that nothing of reality is discernible from that point of view. It simply encourages us to a degree of caution in its assessment.

The second point to make is that though science is often regarded as being officially "value free" (so that the editors of *The Physical Review* would not pass an argument simply alleging that this is the way that things ought to be), nevertheless, within the community of practicing scientists, the acknowledgement of value plays an important role.[8] This is not simply because of the honesty and generosity that are required in any truth-seeking community, but also because, in their informal and heuristic discussions, scientists are often guided to discoveries through following principles of value, such as economy and elegance and the search for beautiful equations. This is a point to which we shall return.

A third, and most important, point is that how the status of value is regarded is fundamental to any metaphysical enterprise, such as the exploration of faith in God the creator. Many scientists—Jacques Monod[9] and Steven Weinberg[10] would be particularly distinguished examples—have a humane respect for the kind of personally perceived values that we have been discussing, but they also believe them simply to be expression of individually or communally constructed attitudes. For such people, our ethical stances and aesthetic experiences are internal to the world of human culture, constituting a little island of self-generated meaning from which we heroically defy the ocean of cosmic hostility and meaninglessness that laps about us. We are simply what we choose to make of ourselves. "The ancient covenant is in pieces; man at last knows that he is alone in the unfeeling immensity of the universe, out of which he emerged by chance."[11] There is a certain stoic nobility in this attitude, but I believe it to be fundamentally mistaken. Instead I believe that our ethical intuitions and aesthetic delights are windows through which we truly look onto a rich realm of created reality, within which the creator has set us and which extends far beyond the world of human-generated thoughts and attitudes.

Perspectives on Reality

Of course, as we approach these windows, we shall often find that some of them are dirty and their glass distorting. If there is real moral knowledge, as I believe there to be, we are not in perfect possession of it. The corruptions of moral judgment that are present in individual lives and within the varied histories of society make that only too clear. A degree of corrective can be found within the moral tradition of a community, but communities are not themselves immune from serious ethical distortion. Two observations may be made. One is the sad fact that terrible deeds are often done for ostensibly "good" reasons (for example the error of attempting forced religious conversions). Though we can see retrospectively the dreadful mistakes that were made in this way, there was some kind of appeal to morality, though a hideously corrupted kind. The second observation is of the existence of a kind of ethical immuno-suppressive system, whereby there is a counter-reaction within a community to the presence of moral infection (the Franciscans at the time of the

Crusades; the Confessing Church in Nazi Germany). Similarly, we must acknowledge that the power of the arts can be used both for human flourishing and for human degradation.

To explore and defend the claim that reality is value-laden is fundamental to the exploration and defense of faith in God the creator. The belief that this enquiry motivates is much more than a vague sense of being at home in the universe. It will achieve its credibility through its detailed content and the richness and comprehensiveness of its explanatory scope.

The quest on which we are embarked is metaphysical in its character. Here is another word at which the scientist may stumble. Metaphysics is concerned with the attainment of a world view, but if that view is rightly to deserve the noble epithet "metaphysical" it will have to strive for the integration of many domains of human knowledge, respecting their proper insights, and even their seeming differences and clashes, while seeking a true synthesis of the whole.

In the vocabulary of the scientific community, "metaphysical" often carries as pejorative a tone as does its companion work "theological." Yet the way in which the writers of popular books on science delight in practicing the metaphysical art (as when an author slides from science to scientism by pretending that the only questions to ask or answer are scientific) makes it clear that it is as natural to have a metaphysics as it is to speak prose. The point to strive for is adequacy to the complexity of reality, eschewing a trivial synthesis obtained through Procrustean truncation.

In this task, it is important to recognize that science constrains metascience but it does not determine it. The point is easily illustrated from within physics. Causality is a metaphysical issue. Is quantum theory indeterministic? Neils Bohr says "Yes"; David Bohm says "No".[12] Their conflicting interpretations have identical empirical consequences but radically different accounts of the nature of reality. Unaided science cannot adjudicate between them. Criteria for metaphysical choice include economy, elegance, and wide scope. In the case of the Bohr/Bohm controversy, it is the feeling that Bohm's clever ideas have about them an unattractive air of contrivance that is one of the main reasons why almost all physicists who think seriously about the matter have sided with Bohr.

In terms of the metaphor of windows onto reality the crucial metaphysical issue of scope can be expressed in terms of the number of different windows through which we look, and whose perspectives we seek to combine in forming our understanding of the multidimensional landscape that we encounter. Reductionist scientism is a one-window view, whose flat portrayal neglects all that is of value and significance in our personal lives. The obverse metaphysical stance is one whose windows are only those that open into the interior human self. René Descartes' appeal to the certainty of the thinking ego, as the basis on which to build reliable knowledge, had this character. This heroic bid for clear and certain ideas has proved a failure. We have to recognize that there is an irreducible degree of precariousness involved in the metaphysical enterprise. There is no Archimedean point from which we can survey reality with complete neutrality; no window that does not impose its own perspective. No one has access to knock-down knowledge.

I shall be arguing for a monotheistic metaphysics, but I do not pretend for a moment that my atheist friends are simply stupid not to see it my way. However, I do believe that Christian monotheism explains more than atheism, that it provides the most satisfactory reconciliation of the views from the widest range of windows to which we have access. We have to use all the resources for inspecting reality that are available to us, for the only way to reduce the chance of perspectival error is to make use of as multi-ocular a vision as possible. The transcendental method of Immanuel Kant was another great metaphysical attempt to be sparing the use of windows. The fact that we now know that Euclidean geometry is not an *a priori* category but a serviceable empirical approximation encourages us to make full use of those scientific windows that look out on the physical world and that Kant was not inclined to employ.

We must also recognize that from time to time people of genius enlarge our view by opening a new window, or cleaning one that had become obscured, so that we gain better access to the metaphysical landscape. The insights of Freud, Jung, and other depth psychologists may be the subject of controversy and contention, but they have made us aware of the existence of unconscious depths and motivations within the human self which must be taken into account in forming an adequate picture of the nature of the personal, since that picture has to go beyond the thoughts and feelings of which we are immediately aware.

In my view, the strategy to be pursued is one that takes with all due seriousness all the perspectives that are available to us in our encounter with reality. I wish now briefly to draw attention to a number of metaphysical windows whose views bear upon the question of belief in God the creator.

Window onto Reality: Light and Darkness

(1) *Cosmic order.* The window of fundamental physical science discloses a universe whose rational transparency makes science possible and whose rational beauty rewards the scientific enquirer with a profound sense of wonder.[13] In short, the cosmos is shot through with signs of mind and it is an attractive, though not inevitable, thought that it is indeed the mind of the creator that is partially disclosed in this way. While we have already rejected the notion of God as functioning solely as a cipher for cosmic order, nevertheless the fact of that order can properly form part of a cumulative case for theistic belief.

(2) *Cosmic fruitfulness.* The much-discussed insights of the Anthropic Principle[14] make it clear that the early universe was already pregnant with the possibility of carbon-based life billions of years before its actual emergence, in that the forces of nature, as we experience them, are "finely tuned" to have just that character and those intrinsic strengths that alone would enable the possibility of the long and delicately balanced chain of circumstances, both terrestrial and astrophysical, that have led to life on earth. The slightest change in the detailed constitution of these forces would have rendered the universe boring and sterile in its history.

Further insights into cosmic fruitfulness may be emerging from the discoveries of the infant science of complexity theory. At present heavily dependent upon the study of computer models, this new discipline shows that complex systems are capable of spontaneously generating astonishing degrees of holistic order in their overall behavior. Stuart Kauffman has suggested that phenomena of this kind may have played a significant role in the evolution of life, in addition to the effects of natural selection.[15] If this is the case, many of the basic structures that comparative anatomists note in the forms of living beings may be ahistorical necessities, rather than the deposit of historical contingency, as conventional neo-Darwinism supposes.

These scientific insights sit comfortably with the theistic understanding that the purpose of the creator lies behind the unfolding history of the universe, without, of course, constituting a conclusive proof that this is so. In particular, theology need feel no anxiety as science reveals more of the structure-generating power of the laws of nature, whether realized through the shuffling explorations of natural selection or through the autopoietic properties of complex systems. The creator's will is as much expressed through the laws of nature that God ordains as it would be through any other form of divine action. This understanding helps to relieve any tension that exegetes might have felt between Genesis 1.24 ("And God said, 'Let the earth bring forth living creatures . . .'") and Genesis 1.25 ("And God made the beasts of the earth . . .").

(3) *The dawning of consciousness.* Perhaps the most surprising and significant event of cosmic history, post–Big Bang, of which we are aware, has been the coming-to-be of self-consciousness here on Earth. In ourselves the universe has becomes aware of itself. As Pascal said, human beings are thinking *reeds* (acknowledging our frailty and insignificance of scale in relation to the vast universe around us), but we are *thinking* reeds, and so greater than all the stars, for we know them and ourselves and they know nothing. The monotheism of the Abrahamic faiths (on this point Judaism, Christianity, and Islam are at one) does not treat this remarkable occurrence as fortuitous—a happy accident—but sees it as a very important clue to the meaning of cosmic process, a striking sign of the deep significance of the personal.

(4) *Religious experience.* At all times and in all places there have been those who testify to encounters with a transcendent reality that we may call the sacred. Often, such people have constituted a majority. It is beyond the scope of this chapter to consider in detail how one should evaluate this testimony, impressive as it is in its weight, and as perplexing as it is in the cognitive clashes that there seem to be between the accounts that the different faith traditions give of their experience and of the insight that testimony conveys.[16] The theist will see behind this kaleidoscopic variety a meeting with the Reality of the divine presence. Two points may briefly be made. In

addition to the experiences of the great religious leaders and prophets, and the experience of the mystical adepts, there is the witness of the ordinary believers, those whom the Christian tradition calls the holy common people of God. Their faith is not sustained by experiences of striking and unusual character but by the diligent practice of their religion in the place of worship, in the home and in daily public life. An account of God the creator must encompass the totality of religious experience and avoid the spiritual elitism that led William James, in *The Varieties of Religious Experience*,[17] to place perhaps too great an emphasis on the religious "pattern setters." The second point is to note that there is widespread witness to the self-authenticating character of this encounter with the sacred. Of course, people can be deluded, but the feeling of spiritual necessity, the "Here I am, I can do no other" is fundamental to the religious life.

(5) *Moral evil.* Human history and individual introspection both show that there is something awry with humanity. Paul spoke for us all when he said "I do not understand my own actions. For I do not do what I want, but I do the very thing I hate" (Romans 7.15). No metaphysical account would be adequate that did not consider seriously the existence of moral evil, the chosen cruelties and shabby compromises of humankind. Christian theism calls this moral slantedness "sin" and diagnoses it as due to the human exercise of God's gift of free will to produce a self-chosen isolation from the life of the creator. Christianity's understanding of human fulfillment is that it does not consist in "doing it my way" but in the embrace of a life lived in communion with God. We have become alienated from the divine life and need to find a way of return. If this is so, the concept of God the creator has to be expanded to include the concept of God the redeemer, who reconciles us and enables our entry into a new kind of life. That spiritual experience will be one of the concerns of my next chapter, but it is important to recognize that Christian theism only attains a "thickness" of insight sufficient to make it fully persuasive when it is considered in its Trinitarian fullness.

(6) *Physical evil.* We have already noted the serious challenge to theistic belief that is represented by the widespread incidence of disease and disaster, sometimes leading to impressive responses of spiritual fortitude, but often appearing to crush people under burdens

too heavy to be borne. This problem is one of great profundity and there is no simple "one-line" answer that a theist can give. There is, however, one small insight that combining science with the doctrine of creation can offer, and which is of some mild help. Science describes an evolving universe, whether it is recounting the history of the stars or the history of terrestrial life. Theologically, an evolutionary world can be understood as a creation allowed by its creator "to make itself." God could no doubt have produced a ready-made world with a snap of the divine fingers, but the God of love does not act in so summary a fashion. Rather, the creator has endowed creation with an intrinsic fruitfulness that it can then explore and realize in its own way. One may see this creaturely self-making as constituting a great good, but it has a necessary cost. The same biochemical processes that have driven evolution by allowing some cells to mutate and so produce new forms of life must, necessarily, in a non-magic universe, allow other cells to mutate and become malignant. One cannot have the one without the other. In other words, the presence of cancer in our world is not a sign of divine callousness or incompetence. It is the necessary cost of a world allowed to make itself. The more science understands the process of the universe, the more it appears to be an interlocking "package deal," with the "good" and the "bad" inextricably intertwined. In this sense, the existence of physical evil is not gratuitous, something that God could have remedied by taking a bit more trouble. Of course, many perplexities remain, but there is some modest help for theism here.

(7) *Futility*. Science tell us, most reliably, that the universe is going to die, through either collapse or decay, over a timespan of tens of billions of years, just as surely as we are going to die over a timespan of tens of years. Both realizations put in question what could be the ultimate purpose of the creator of a world of such transience. Notoriously, when Weinberg thought about the certainty of cosmic futility, he said that the more he understood the universe, the more it seemed pointless to him.[18] The challenge this poses to theism is a serious one. It makes it clear that a mere evolutionary optimism—the feeling that present process will lead to ultimate fulfillment—is an illusion. If there is a hope for true fulfillment, either for ourselves or for the whole of creation, it lies on the other side of death. Of course, Christianity believes that there is such a destiny *post mortem*, not

only for human individuals but also, in some mysterious way, for the whole created order (Colossians 1.15–20). Once again we see how the metaphysical quest for total meaningfulness, if pursued in the direction of Christian theism, leads to a satisfactory response only if its theological base is appropriately rich and Trinitarian.

These windows have looked out onto a variety of landscapes, some sunny and some somber. The beauty of the cosmic order contrasts with the messy and painful scene presented by the existence of physical evil. The fruitfulness of cosmic history to date contrasts with the certainty of eventual cosmic futility. The remarkable emergence of human consciousness has produced at the same time the human capacity for moral evil.

Despite the perplexities expressed in these contrasts, faith in the creator holds to the belief that the universe does make total sense. That faith is grounded in the conviction of the deep meaningfulness of cosmic history and the ultimate hopefulness of cosmic destiny. Such a truly all-embracing belief cannot be an absolute certainty—any more than its denial could be—but it is a motivated understanding of what we know about the richness of reality. It is a belief that countless Christian believers, including the present writer, have been prepared to embrace and to base their lives upon.

Our present discussion has been framed in terms of the metaphor of windows onto reality. Like all metaphors, it has its limitations, for it conjured up the image of a tranquil cognitive gaze directed at a passive reality. But God is not there just to be the answer to our intellectual curiosity. Faith in God affects our lives in ways that have no parallels in scientific understanding. I believe most firmly in quarks and gluons as the constituents of matter, but that belief leaves the greater part of me unaffected. Faith in God the creator does not merely make sense of the cosmos but it calls on me to accept my finite status as a creature and to respond in worshipful obedience to the divine majesty and divine will of the maker of heaven and earth.

Miracles, Longing, and Mysticism

C. S. LEWIS

Unquestionably the most well-known atheist turned Christian writer of the twentieth century, Clive Staples "Jack" Lewis (1898–1963) loved to use imagination and intellect to stimulate discussions on topics like forgiveness, good and evil, the meaning of life, and the supernatural. He was a recognized Oxford scholar specializing in the late Middle Ages, but his more public literary career included subjects as vast and varied as science, theology, history, and philosophy, and included audiences from academics to children. His Chronicles of Narnia *series continues to delight children and adults, and is rich with symbolism of the battle between good and evil. During World War II and the bombing of London, Lewis was a regular feature on BBC radio speaking on the topic of religion. His most widely known work,* Mere Christianity, *is a published compilation of those radio broadcasts.*

Lewis wrote prolifically and with deep insight on virtually all of the issues that reside at the intersection of faith and reason. So it is challenging to identify just one excerpt for this collection. His views on miracles, however, which he further expanded into an entire book by that name, are captured here in a brief but profound essay.

Miracles

I HAVE KNOWN only one person in my life who claimed to have seen a ghost. It was a woman; and the interesting thing is that she disbelieved in the immortality of the soul before seeing the ghost and still disbelieves after having seen it. She thinks it was a hallucination. In other words, seeing is not believing. This is the first thing to get clear in talking about miracles. Whatever experiences we may have, we shall not regard them as miraculous if we already hold a philosophy which excludes the supernatural. Any event which is claimed as a miracle is, in the last resort, an experience received from the senses; and the senses are not infallible. We can always say we have been the victims of an illusion; if we disbelieve in the supernatural this is what we always shall say. Hence, whether miracles have really ceased or not, they would certainly appear to cease in Western Europe as materialism became the popular creed. For let us make no mistake. If the end of the world appeared in all the literal trappings of the Apocalypse,[1] if the modern materialist saw with his own eyes the heavens rolled up[2] and the great white throne appearing,[3] if he had the sensation of being himself hurled into the Lake of Fire,[4] he would continue forever, in that lake itself, to regard his experience as an illusion and to find the explanation of it in psychoanalysis, or cerebral pathology. Experience by itself proves nothing. If a man doubts whether he is dreaming or waking, no experiment can solve his doubt, since every experiment may itself be part of the dream. Experience proves this, or that, or nothing, according to the preconceptions we bring to it.

This fact, that the interpretation of experiences depends on preconceptions, is often used as an argument against miracles. It is said that our ancestors, taking the supernatural for granted and greedy of wonders, read the miraculous into events that were really not miracles. And in a sense I grant it. That is to say, I think that just as our preconceptions would prevent us from apprehending miracles if they really occurred, so their preconceptions would lead them to imagine miracles even if they did not occur. In the same way, the doting man will think his wife faithful when she is not and the suspicious man will not think her faithful when she is: the question of her actual fidelity remains, meanwhile, to be settled, if at all, on other grounds. But there is one thing often said about our ancestors which we must *not* say. We must not say "They believed in miracles because they did not know the Laws of Nature." This is nonsense. When St. Joseph discovered that his bride was pregnant, he was "minded to put her away."[5] He knew enough biology for that. Otherwise, of course he would not have regarded pregnancy as a proof of infidelity. When he accepted the Christian explanation, he regarded it as a miracle precisely because he knew enough of the Laws of Nature to know that this was a suspension of them. When the disciples saw

Christ walking on the water they were frightened:[6] they would not have been frightened unless they had known the laws of Nature and known that this was an exception. If a man had no conception of a regular order in Nature, then of course he could not notice departures from that order: just as a dunce who does not understand the normal meter of a poem is also unconscious of the poet's variations from it. Nothing is wonderful except the abnormal and nothing is abnormal until we have grasped the norm. Complete ignorance of the laws of Nature would preclude the perception of the miraculous just as rigidly as complete disbelief in the supernatural precludes it, perhaps even more so. For while the materialist would have at least to explain miracles away, the man wholly ignorant of Nature would simply not notice them.

The experience of a miracle in fact requires two conditions. First we must believe in a normal stability of nature, which means we must recognize that the data offered by our senses recur in regular patterns. Secondly, we must believe in some reality beyond Nature. When both beliefs are held, and not till then, we can approach with an open mind the various reports which claim that this super- or extra-natural reality has sometimes invaded and disturbed the sensuous content of space and time which makes our "natural" world. The belief in such a supernatural reality itself can neither be proved nor disproved by experience. The arguments for its existence are metaphysical, and to me conclusive. They turn on the fact that even to think and act in the natural world we have to assume something beyond it and even assume that we partly belong to that something. In order to think we must claim for our own reasoning a validity which is not credible if our own thought is merely a function of our brain, and our brains a by-product of irrational physical processes. In order to act, above the level of mere impulse, we must claim a similar validity for our judgments of good and evil. In both cases we get the same disquieting result. The concept of nature itself is one we have reached only tacitly by claiming a sort of *super*-natural status for ourselves.

If we frankly accept this position and then turn to the evidence, we find, of course, that accounts of the supernatural meet us on every side. History is full of them—often in the same documents which we accept wherever they do not report miracles. Respectable missionaries report them not infrequently. The whole Church of Rome claims their continued occurrence. Intimate conversation elicits from almost every acquaintance at least one episode in his life which is what he would call "queer" or "rum." No doubt most stories of miracles are unreliable; but then, as anyone can see by reading the papers, so are most stories of all events. Each story must be taken on its merits: what one must not do is to rule out the supernatural as the one impossible explanation. Thus you may disbelieve in the Mons Angels[7] because you cannot find a sufficient number of sensible people who say they saw them. But if you found a sufficient number, it would, in my view, be unreasonable to explain this by collective hallucination. For we know enough of psychology to know that spontaneous unanimity in hallucination is very improbable, and we do not know enough of the supernatural to know that a manifestation of angels is equally improbable. The supernatural theory is the less improbable of the two. When the Old Testament says that Sennacherib's invasion was stopped by angels,[8] and Herodotus says it was stopped by a lot of mice who came and ate up all the bowstrings of his army,[9] an open-minded man will be on the side of the angels. Unless you start by begging the question, there is nothing intrinsically unlikely in the existence of angels or in the action ascribed to them. But mice just don't do these things.

A great deal of skepticism now current about the miracles of our Lord does not, however, come from disbelief of all reality beyond nature. It comes from two ideas which are respectable but I think mistaken. In the first place, modern people have an almost aesthetic dislike of miracles. Admitting that God can, they doubt if He would. To violate the laws He Himself has imposed on His creation seems to them arbitrary, clumsy, a theatrical device only fit to impress savages—a solecism against the grammar of the universe. In the second place, many people confuse the laws of nature with the laws of thought and imagine that their reversal or suspension would be a contradiction in terms—as if the resurrection of the dead were the same sort of thing as two and two making five.

I have only recently found the answer to the first objection. I found it first in George MacDonald and then later in St. Athanasius. This is what St. Athanasius says in his little book *On the Incarnation*: "Our Lord took a body like to ours and lived as a man in order that those who had refused to recognize Him in His superintendence and captaincy of the whole universe might come to recognize from the works He did here below in the body that what dwelled in this body was the Word of God." This accords exactly with Christ's own account of His miracles: "The Son can do nothing of Himself, but what He seeth the Father do."[10] The doctrine, as I understand it, is something like this:

There is an activity of God displayed throughout creation, a wholesale activity let us say which men refuse to recognize. The miracles done by God incarnate, living as a man in Palestine, perform the very same things as this wholesale activity, but at a different speed and on a smaller scale. One of their chief purposes is that men, having seen a thing done by personal power on the small scale, may recognize, when they see the same thing done on the large scale, that the power behind it is also personal—is indeed the very same person who lived among us two thousand years ago. The miracles in fact are a retelling in small letters of the very same story which is written across the whole world in letters too large for some of us to see. Of that larger script part is already visible, part is still unsolved. In other words, some of the miracles do locally what God has already done universally: others do locally what He has not yet done, but will do. In that sense, and from our human point of view, some are reminders and others prophecies.

God creates the vine and teaches it to draw up water by its roots and, with the aid of the sun, to turn that water into a juice which will ferment and take on certain qualities. Thus every year, from Noah's time till ours, God turns water into wine. That, men fail to see. Either like the Pagans they refer the process to some finite spirit, Bacchus or Dionysus: or else, like the moderns, they attribute real and ultimate causality to the chemical and other material phenomena which are all that our senses can discover in it. But when Christ at Cana makes water into wine, the mask is off.[11] The miracle has only half its effect if it only convinces us that Christ is God: it will have its full effect if whenever we see a vineyard or drink a glass of wine we remember that here works He who sat at the wedding party in Cana. Every year God makes a little corn into much corn: the seed is sown and there is an increase, and men, according to the fashion of their age, say "It is Ceres, it is Adonis, it is the Corn-King," or else

"It is the laws of Nature." The close-up, the translation, of this annual wonder is the feeding of the five thousand.[12] Bread is not made there of nothing. Bread is not made of stones, as the Devil once suggested to Our Lord in vain.[13] A little bread is made into much bread. The Son will do nothing but what He sees the Father do. There is, so to speak, a family *style*. The miracles of healing fall into the same pattern. This is sometimes obscured for us by the somewhat magical view we tend to take of ordinary medicine. The doctors themselves do not take this view. The magic is not in the medicine but in the patient's body. What the doctor does is to stimulate Nature's functions in the body, or to remove hindrances. In a sense, though we speak for convenience of healing a cut, every cut heals itself; no dressing will make skin grow over a cut on a corpse. That same mysterious energy which we call gravitational when it steers the planets and biochemical when it heals a body is the efficient cause of all recoveries, and if God exists, that energy, directly or indirectly, is His. All who are cured are cured by Him, the healer within. But once He did it visibly, a Man meeting a man. Where He does not work within in this mode, the organism dies. Hence Christ's one miracle of destruction is also in harmony with God's wholesale activity. His bodily hand held out in symbolic wrath blasted a single fig tree;[14] but no tree died that year in Palestine, or any year, or in any land, or even ever will, save because He has done something, or (more likely) ceased to do something, to it.

When He fed the thousands he multiplied fish as well as bread. Look in every bay and almost every river. This swarming, pulsating fecundity shows He is still at work. The ancients had a god called Genius—the god of animal and human fertility, the presiding spirit of gynecology, embryology, or the marriage bed—the "genial bed" as they called it after its god Genius.[15] As the miracles of wine and bread and healing showed who Bacchus really was, who Ceres, who Apollo, and that all were one, so this miraculous multiplication of fish reveals the real Genius. And with that we stand at the threshold of the miracle which for some reason most offends modern ears. I can understand the man who denies the miraculous altogether; but what is one to make of the people who admit some miracles but deny the Virgin Birth? Is it that for all their lip service to the laws of Nature there is only one law of Nature that they really believe?

Or is it that they see in this miracle a slur upon sexual intercourse which is rapidly becoming the one thing venerated in a world without veneration? No miracle is in fact more significant. What happens in ordinary generation? What is a father's function in the act of begetting? A microscopic particle of matter from his body fertilizes the female: and with that microscopic particle passes, it may be, the color of his hair and his great grandfather's hanging lip, and the human form in all its complexity of bones, liver, sinews, heart, and limbs, and pre-human form which the embryo will recapitulate in the womb. Behind every spermatozoon lies the whole history of the universe: locked within it is no small part of the world's future. That is God's normal way of making a man—a process that takes centuries, beginning with the creation of matter itself, and narrowing to one second and one particle at the moment of begetting. And once again men will mistake the sense impressions which this creative act throws off for the act itself or else refer it to some infinite being such as Genius. Once, therefore, God does it directly, instantaneously; without a spermatozoon, without the millenniums of organic history behind the spermatozoon. There was of course another reason. This time He was creating not simply a man, but the man who was to be Himself: the only true Man. The process which leads to the spermatozoon has carried down with it through the centuries much undesirable silt; the life which reaches us by that normal route is tainted. To avoid that taint, to give humanity a fresh start, He once short-circuited the process. There is a vulgar anti-God paper which some anonymous donor sends me every week. In it recently I saw the taunt that we Christians believe in a God who committed adultery with the wife of a Jewish carpenter. The answer to that is that if you describe the action of God in fertilizing Mary as "adultery" then, in that sense, God would have committed adultery with every woman who ever had a baby. For what He did once without a human father, He does always even when He uses a human father as His instrument. For the human father in ordinary generation is only a carrier, sometimes an unwilling carrier, always the last in a long line of carriers, of life that comes from the supreme life. Thus the filth that our poor, muddled, sincere, resentful enemies fling at the Holy One, either does not stick, or, sticking, turns into glory.

So much for the miracles which do small and quick what we have already seen in the large letters of God's universal activity. But before I go on to the second class—those which foreshadow parts of the universal activity we have not yet seen—I must guard against a misunderstanding. Do not imagine I am trying to make the miracle less miraculous. I am not arguing that they are more probable because they are less unlike natural events: I am trying to answer those who think them arbitrary, theatrical, unworthy of God, meaningless interruptions of universal order. They remain in my view wholly miraculous. To do instantly with dead and baked corn what ordinarily happens slowly with live seed is just as great a miracle as to make bread of stones. Just as great, but a different *kind* of miracle. That is the point. When I open Ovid,[16] or Grimm,[17] I find the sort of miracles which really would be arbitrary. Trees talk, houses turn into trees, magic rings raise tables richly spread with food in lonely places, ships become goddesses, and men are changed into snakes or birds or bears. It is fun to read about: the least suspicion that it had really happened would turn that fun into nightmare. You find no miracles of that kind in the Gospels. Such things, if they could be, would prove that some alien power was invading Nature; they would not in the least prove that it was the same power which had made Nature and rules her every day. But the true miracles express not simply a god, but God: that which is outside Nature, not as a foreigner, but as her sovereign. They announce not merely that a King has visited our town, but that it is *the* King, *our* King.

The second class of miracles, on this view, foretell what God has not yet done, but will do, universally. He raised one man (the man who was Himself) from the dead because He will one day raise all men from the dead. Perhaps not only men, for there are hints in the New Testament that all creation will eventually be rescued from decay, restored to shape, and subserve the splendor of re-made humanity.[18] The Transfiguration[19] and the walking on the water[20] are glimpses of the beauty and the effortless power over all matter which will belong to men when they are really waked by God. Now resurrection certainly involves "reversal" of natural process in the sense that it involves a series of changes moving in the opposite direction to those we see. At death, matter which has been organic falls back gradually into the inorganic, to be finally scattered and used perhaps in other organisms. Resurrection would be the reverse process. It would not of course mean the restoration to each personality of those very atoms, numerically the same, which had made its first or "natural" body. There would not be enough to go round, for one thing; and for another, the unity of the body even in this life was consistent with a slow but perplexed change of its actual ingredients. But it certainly does mean matter of some kind rushing towards organism as now we see it rushing away. It means, in fact, playing backwards a film we have already seen played forwards. In that sense it is a reversal of Nature. But, of course, it is a further question whether reversal in this sense is necessarily contradiction. Do we know that the film cannot be played backwards?

Well, in one sense, it is precisely the teaching of modern physics that the film never works backwards. For modern physics, as you have heard before, the universe is "running down." Disorganization and chance is continually increasing. There will come a time, not infinitely remote, when it will be wholly run down or wholly disorganized, and science knows of no possible return from that state. There must have been a time, not infinitely remote, in the past when it was wound up, though science knows of no winding-up process. The point is that for our ancestors the universe was a picture: for modern physics it is a story. If the universe is a picture these things either appear in that picture or not; and if they don't, since it is an infinite picture, one may suspect that they are contrary to the nature of things. But a story is a different matter; specially if it is an incomplete story. And the story told by modern physics might be told briefly in the words "Humpty Dumpty was falling." That is, it proclaims itself an incomplete story. There must have been a time before he fell, when he was sitting on the wall; there must be a time after he had reached the ground. It is quite true that science knows of no horses and men who can put him together again once he has reached the ground and broken. But then she also knows of no means by which he could originally have been put on the wall. You wouldn't expect her to. All science rests on observation: all our observations are taken *during* Humpty Dumpty's fall, because we were born after he lost his seat on the wall and shall be extinct long before he reaches the ground. But to assume from observations taken while the clock is running down that the unimaginable winding-up which must have preceded this process cannot occur when the process is over is the merest dogmatism. From the very nature of the case the laws of degradation and disorganization which we find in matter at present cannot be the ultimate and eternal nature of things. If they were, there would have been nothing to degrade and disorganize. Humpty Dumpty can't fall off a wall that never existed.

Obviously, an event that lies outside the falling or disintegrating process which we know as Nature is not imaginable. If anything is clear from the records of Our Lord's appearances after His resurrection, it is that the risen body was very different from the body that died and that it lives under conditions quite unlike those of natural life. It is frequently not recognized by those who see it[21]: and it is not related to space in the same way as our bodies. The sudden appearances and disappearances[22] suggest the ghost of popular tradition: yet He emphatically insists that He is not merely a spirit and takes steps to demonstrate that the risen body can still perform animal operations, such as eating.[23] What makes all this baffling to us is our assumption that to pass beyond what we call Nature—beyond the three dimensions and the five highly specialized and limited senses—is immediately to be in a world of pure negative spirituality, a world where space of any sort and sense of any sort has no function. I know no grounds for believing this. To explain even an atom Schrödinger[24] wants seven dimensions: and give us new senses and we should find a new Nature. There may be Natures piled upon Natures, each supernatural to the one beneath it, before we come to the abyss of pure spirit; and to be in that abyss, at the right hand of the Father, may not mean being absent from any of these Natures—may mean a yet more dynamic presence on all levels. That is why I think it very rash to assume that the story of the Ascension is mere allegory. I know it sounds like the work of people who imagined an absolute up and down and a local heaven in the sky. But to say this is after all to say "Assuming that the story is fake, we could thus explain how it arose." Without that assumption we find ourselves "moving about in worlds unrealized"[25] with no probability—or improbability—to guide us. For if the story is true then a being still in some mode, though not our mode, corporeal, withdrew at His own will from the Nature presented by our three dimensions and five senses, not necessarily into the non-sensuous and undimensioned but possibly into, or through, a world or worlds of super-sense and super-space. And

He might choose to do it gradually. Who on earth knows what the spectators might see? If they say they saw a momentary movement along the vertical plane—then an indistinct mass—then nothing—who is to pronounce this improbable?

My time is nearly up and I must be very brief with the second class of people whom I promised to deal with: those who mistake the laws of Nature for laws of thought and, therefore, think that any departure from them is a self-contradiction, like a square circle or two and two making five. To think this is to imagine that the normal processes of Nature are transparent to the intellect, that we can say why she behaves as she does. For, of course, if we cannot see why a thing is so, then we cannot see any reason why it should not be otherwise. But in fact the actual course of Nature is wholly inexplicable. I don't mean that science has not yet explained it, but may do so some day. I mean that the very nature of explanation makes it impossible that we should even explain why matter has the properties it has. For explanation, by its very nature, deals with a world of "ifs and ands." Every explanation takes the form "Since A, therefore B" or "If C, then D." In order to explain any event you have to assume the universe as a going concern, a machine working in a particular way. Since this particular way of working is the basis of all explanation, it can never be itself explained. We can see no reason why it should not have worked a different way.

To say this is not only to remove the suspicion that miracle is self-contradictory, but also to realize how deeply right St. Athanasius was when he found an essential likeness between the miracles of Our Lord and the general order of Nature. Both are a full stop for the explaining intellect. If the "natural" means that which can be fitted into a class, that which obeys a norm, that which can be paralleled, that which can be explained by reference to other events, then Nature herself as a whole is *not* natural. If a miracle means that which must simply be accepted, the unanswerable actuality which gives no account of itself but simply *is,* then the universe is one great miracle. To direct us to that great miracle is one main object of the earthly acts of Christ: that are, as He himself said, Signs.[26] They serve to remind us that the explanations of particular events which we derive *from* the given, the unexplained, the almost willful character of the actual universe, are not explanations of that character. These

Signs do not take us away from reality; they recall us to it—recall us from our dream world of "ifs and ands" to the stunning actuality of everything that is real. They are focal points at which more reality becomes visible than we ordinarily see at once. I have spoken of how He made miraculous bread and wine and of how, when the Virgin conceived, He had shown Himself the true Genius whom men had ignorantly worshipped long before. It goes deeper than that. Bread and wine were to have an even more sacred significance for Christians and the act of generations was to be the chosen symbol among all mystics for the union of the soul with God. These things are no accidents. With Him there are no accidents. When He created the vegetable world He knew already what dreams the annual death and resurrection of the corn would cause to stir in pious Pagan minds, He knew already that He Himself must so die and live again and in what sense, including and far transcending the old religion of the Corn King. He would say "This is my Body."[27] *Common* bread, miraculous bread, sacramental bread—these three are distinct, but not to be separated. Divine reality is like a fugue. All His acts are different, but they all rhyme or echo to one another. It is this that makes Christianity so difficult to talk about. Fix your mind on any one story or any one doctrine and it becomes at once a magnet to which truth and glory come rushing from all levels of being. Our featureless pantheistic unities and glib rationalist distinctions are alike defeated by the seamless yet ever-varying texture of reality, the liveness, the elusiveness, the intertwined harmonies of the multidimensional fertility of God. But if this is the difficulty, it is also one of the firm grounds of our belief. To think that this was a fable, a product of our own brains as they are a product of matter, would be to believe that this vast symphonic splendor had come out of something much smaller and emptier than itself. It is not so. We are nearer to the truth in the vision seen by Julian of Norwich, when Christ appeared to her holding in His hand a little thing like a hazel nut and saying, "This is all that is created."[28] And it seemed to her so small and weak that she wondered how it could hold together at all.[29]

ALISTER MCGRATH

A vigorous academic leader, a prolific writer, and a gifted thinker all characterize one of Britain's foremost scholars at the start of the twenty-first century. Once a self-proclaimed atheist, Alister McGrath (1953–) is now a committed believer. With his background in both science and theology, McGrath has developed ideas about faith and reason that often bring him into public debate with those of opposing views, such as popular scientific atheist and Oxford zoologist Richard Dawkins. McGrath's principal interest is to encourage his audience to use their intellect, reason, and imagination to consider the personal implications of the existence of a loving God.

His dossier is rich with scholastic accolades and appointments. Currently he's professor of theology, ministry and education, and chair of the Center for Theology, Religion and Culture, King's College, London. In the academy, McGrath spends the majority of his time researching the intersection of science and faith. In 2009 he presented the prestigious Gifford Lectures at the University of Aberdeen.

In the portion chosen here, taken from a book entitled Glimpsing the Face of God: The Search for Meaning in the Universe, *McGrath explores the concept of human longing. He compares the search for the Divine to trying to solve the puzzles of life, seeking out clues that point to something—or, perhaps, Someone.*

Trying to Make Sense of Things

WE LONG TO make sense of things and often gain a sense of deep satisfaction when we are able to resolve the puzzles of life. One of the favorite activities of the Anglo-Saxons was setting riddles to while away the long northern nights. More recently, the huge popular fascination with works of detective fiction points to the continuing interest in unraveling mysteries. Writers such as Sir Arthur Conan

Doyle, Agatha Christie, Erle Stanley Gardner, and Dorothy L. Sayers built their reputations on being able to hold their readers' interest as countless mysterious murder cases were solved before their eyes.

The essence of a good mystery novel is a series of clues. The mystery to be solved is virtually invariably a murder. Perhaps a body has been discovered in the library of an English country house or in a London club. The mystery writers set us alongside their fictional detectives as they try to make sense of what happened by uncovering clues. So what are these clues? Basically, a clue is "a fact or idea that serves as a guide, or suggests a line of enquiry, in a problem or investigation." In other words, it is an observation that sets off a way of thinking about a problem.

In *The Adventure of the Stockbroker's Clerk,* Sir Arthur Conan Doyle introduces us to the great fictional detective Sherlock Holmes's ability to build up an overall picture of events based on small clues. He begins by relating how Holmes deduced that his colleague Dr. Watson had been ill. As usual, the narrator of the passage is Watson himself; the opening speaker is Holmes:

> "I perceive that you have been unwell lately. Summer colds are always a little trying."
>
> "I was confined to the house by a severe chill for three days last week. I thought, however, that I had cast off every trace of it."
>
> "So you have. You look remarkably robust."
>
> "How, then, did you know of it?"
>
> "My dear fellow, you know my methods."
>
> "You deduced it, then?"
>
> "Certainly."
>
> "And from what?"
>
> "From your slippers."
>
> I glanced down at the new patent-leathers which I was wearing. "How on earth—" I began, but Holmes answered my question before it was asked.
>
> "Your slippers are new," he said. "You could not have had them more than a few weeks. The soles which you are at this moment presenting to me are slightly scorched. For a moment I thought they might have got wet and been burned in the dry-

ing. But near the instep there is a small circular wafer of paper with the shopman's hieroglyphics upon it. Damp would of course have removed this. You had, then, been sitting with your feet outstretched to the fire, which a man would hardly do even in so wet a June as this if he were in his full health." Like all Holmes's reasoning the thing seemed simplicity itself when it was once explained. He read the thought upon my features, and his smile had a tinge of bitterness.

"I am afraid that I rather give myself away when I explain," said he. "Results without causes are much more impressive."

It is, of course, easy to overlook clues. Something may take place which appears to be insignificant at the time and yet assumes a much greater significance later, as its full meaning gradually becomes apparent. Conan Doyle's story *Silver Blaze,* which tells of how Sherlock Holmes investigates an attack on a valuable racehorse, is a case in point. The watchdog did not bark during the night in which the racehorse was wounded. Yet the full significance of this fact only became evident at a later stage in Holmes's investigation. The fact was observed but its significance only became apparent later, when Holmes pointed out that it could only mean that the dog knew the intruder.

Important though they are, clues are not, however, decisive. Taken individually, a clue can do little more than suggest. It cannot prove. Yet clues can accumulate, pointing in a certain and definite direction. At times, they even point in different directions. Many of the more celebrated mystery novels of Agatha Christie rely on building up a series of clues that point in a number of directions, leaving the reader wondering how the mystery may be solved. At other times, the clues allow multiple solutions to mysteries. We then have to deal with the question of which of a number of possible solutions is the most probable.

In her famous mystery novel *The Unpleasantness at the Bellona Club,* set in London's high society during the 1920s, Dorothy L. Sayers opens the chapter describing Lord Peter Wimsey's breakthrough in the mystery surrounding the puzzling death of General Fentiman with the following words:

"What put you on to this poison business" [Detective Inspector Parker] asked.

> "Aristotle, chiefly," replied Wimsey. "He says, you know, that one should always prefer the probable impossible to the improbable possible. It was possible, of course, that the General should have died off in that neat way at the most confusing moment. But how much nicer and more probable that the whole thing had been stage-managed."

Wimsey here had to make a judgment concerning which of a number of possible solutions to the mystery of General Fentiman's death was the most likely.

We face similar problems in trying to make sense of the universe and our place within it. We are surrounded by clues, some of which seem to point to one explanation and others in a very different direction. Some suggest that there is indeed a supreme being who created the universe and endowed it with purpose. Others seem to call this into question.

So what sort of clues are we talking about? One clue is provided by the natural sciences, especially physics and cosmology. Here, we find a remarkable degree of ordering within the universe, which can be expressed concisely and elegantly in mathematical forms. The fact that so much of the deep structure of the universe can be represented mathematically points of something remarkable about both the universe itself and to the ability of the human mind to understand it. It is almost as if the human mind has been designed to grasp the patterns and structures of the cosmos.

Albert Einstein appreciated this point. In 1907, Einstein began to develop a new approach that he believed would explain a discrepancy that had been observed in the behavior of the planet Mercury. This planet moved in a way which did not correspond with the predictions of classical astronomy, based on the ideas of Isaac Newton. In November 1915, Einstein finally discovered the theory of general relativity, which could be expressed beautifully in mathematical terms. But it was more than just a beautiful theory—it precisely accounted for the discrepancy in Mercury's movements. It was clear to Einstein that something deeply significant about the universe had been expressed in that theory. Was this not a clue to the universe reflecting the mind of God?

A second clue is provided by what is sometimes called the "fine-tuning" of the universe. The structure of the universe is determined by a series of "fundamental constants" that shape its contours and development. Had these been different, the universe would have taken a very different form—and life, as we know it, could not have emerged. The fabric of the universe seems to have been designed to establish the possibility of life. Perhaps this is entirely accidental. After all, our universe has to take some shape and form. Why not this one? Yet many pause for thought at this point. Could this really be accidental? Is it a pure coincidence that the laws of nature are such that life is possible? Might this not be an important clue to the nature and destiny of humanity?

Another clue is provided by the deep human longing for significance. It seems that nothing in this world really possesses the capacity to satisfy us. There is an emptiness within human nature, which cries out for fulfillment and meaning. Yet nothing created and transient seems able to meet this need. For Blaise Pascal, the only thing that could fill this abyss within human nature was a personal encounter with God. We find a similar theme in Augustine of Hippo, who penned the following prayer to God: "You have made us for yourself, and our heart is restless until it finds its rest in you."

Another prayer to make the same point is due to Anselm of Canterbury, one of the greatest thinkers of the Middle Ages: "Lord, give me what you have made me want; I praise and thank you for the desire that you have inspired; perfect what you have begun, and grant me what you have made me long for." For these writers, the deep human sense of longing has its origins in God, and can only find its fulfillment in God. God is the name of the one we have been looking for all our lives, without knowing it.

But other clues seem to point in another direction. For many, the presence of pain and suffering in the world seems to suggest that there cannot be a God. How, it may be asked, could a loving God allow such suffering to take place? This might not be a problem if God were not to be loving and to care for creation. Yet Christianity insists that God is properly described as "loving." This important and profound belief would seem to be called into question by the pain of the world.

This process of gathering clues could be continued indefinitely. Yet the point that emerges is clear. Some aspects of the world seem to point to a divine creator; others seem to point away from him. The picture is not clear. The same problem, of course, emerges from the endless debate over whether the existence of God can be proved or disproved. Atheists and believers alike find it impossible to clinch their case through argument. At best, they can show that their position is plausible. But decisive proof of any kind is lacking.

Some refuse to recognize the ambiguity of the situation. There has never been any shortage of people who will tell us that the evidence is totally persuasive, and that—unless we are complete fools—we will accept that there is no meaning in life, and no God behind this world. Some argue that atheism is the only logically and scientifically respectable worldview. Yet this overlooks the inconvenient fact that the truth claims of atheism simply cannot be proved. How do we know that there is no God? The simple fact of the matter is that atheism is a faith, which draws conclusions that go beyond the available evidence.

Boris Pasternak, the noted Russian writer and thinker who penned the novel *Dr. Zhivago,* is an eloquent witness to this perhaps surprising point. Although initially highly enthusiastic about the Russian Revolution, he became disaffected with it because of the impact its harsh atheistic philosophy had upon people. He wrote these words in expressing his disillusionment: "I am an atheist who has lost his faith." Others will tell us with equal confidence that the evidence we see in nature is unequivocally in favor of the existence of some kind of God. It's all so simple. Only a fool would disagree.

It is hardly surprising that many are attracted to simple solutions to complex problems. Yet these rightly cause suspicion. We have become cynical of solutions that are too neat and claim to explain everything. We are as weary as we are wary of too-confident answers to difficult questions. The world we experience is just too messy and fuzzy to fit completely into the orderly systems that some crave and others fear. We have to learn to live in an untidy world in which we are not certain of everything—a world in which there are unanswered questions. Some panic at this thought. How can we live when we cannot be confident of anything? The only certainty of our age seems to be that there is no certainty at all. Yet even this confident assertion contradicts itself—like the statement that Bertrand Russell recalled seeing written on a college blackboard: "All statements written on this blackboard are false."

The reality of the situation is that there are few things that can be known with absolute certainty—and these generally take the form of tautologies. In other words, they are true by definition. For example, we can accept the truth of the following statement without any hesitation whatsoever:

The whole is greater than the part.

Once the meaning of the words "whole" and "part" has been grasped, the truth of the statement can be accepted immediately. Yet it can be argued without any difficulty that this statement is merely true by definition. It is true because of the relationship of the words "whole" and "part." It adds nothing to our knowledge, merely restating what is already established.

A more subtle example is provided by the following statement, which may take a little longer to appreciate:

It is impossible for a man to marry his widow's sister.

At first sight, this might seem like an old-fashioned moralist taking a strong line on the ethics of marriage. On closer examination, however, it is nothing of the sort. The statement has nothing to do with ethics, or social acceptability. It has to do with the sheer practicality of death, which brings all human activity to an abrupt end. A man cannot marry his widow's sister precisely because a "widow" is defined as "a woman who has lost her husband by death."

We have to learn to live with the fact that we cannot be certain of many of the most important things about life. We can be certain that 2 + 2 = 4; but that is hardly going to give us a reason to live and die, or cause our hearts to beat a little faster with excitement. Yet with the greater questions of life, we have to learn to live with a degree of uncertainty. Tennyson captures this dilemma perfectly in his poem "The Ancient Sage":

For nothing worthy proving can be proven,
nor yet disproven: wherefore thou be wise,
cleave ever to the sunnier side of doubt.

For Tennyson, anything that was worth believing could not be proved with certainty. It involved a leap of faith—a recognition that the clues to the meaning of the universe do not provide an invincible case for a meaningless cosmos or one brought into being by a caring and loving God. Perhaps we can give up and walk away from the big questions that are raised. Yet in the end, this does not really satisfy us. Might not we be missing out on something important—and even exciting?

THOMAS MERTON

A contemplative Catholic priest, yet also a man with intense social awareness, Thomas Merton (1915–1968) plumbed the depths of human experience through his writings. As a prolific author during the first half of the twentieth century, he produced more than seventy books. His writings on mysticism continue to inspire and renew interest in spiritual exploration today. Merton was also a vocal proponent of interfaith dialogue and understanding and was considered a political activist, devoting special passion to issues of social justice.

Taken from The Ascent to Truth, *this excerpt from Merton's writings defines the nature of deep spiritual contemplation, and how this experience interacts with the intellect, the truths from science and philosophy, and the will.*

Mysticism in Man's Life

My purpose here is to define the nature of the contemplative experience, to show something of the necessary interior ascesis that leads up to it, and to give a brief sketch of mature contemplation. When faith opens out into a deep spiritual understanding and advances beyond the range of concepts into a darkness that can only be enlightened by the fire of love, a man truly begins to know God in the only way that can satisfy his soul.

Concepts tell us the truth about God, but their light is so far from being perfect that the man who is fully content with conceptual knowledge of God, and does not burn to possess Him by love, has never really known Him. But if the contemplative experience of God goes beyond concepts, is it purely subjective? Does it imply a complete rejection of scientific truth? Does it evade the reach of every authority? Is the mystic a kind of religious genius who lives in an atmosphere entirely his own and whose inspiration is nobody else's business? Perhaps the reason why William James admitted the validity of mystical experience was precisely because it could be fitted into the context of his pragmatism by an absolutely affirmative answer to these questions.

The contemplative life demands detachment from the senses, but it is not therefore a complete rejection of sense experience. It rises above the level of reasoning; yet reason plays an essential part in the interior ascesis without which we cannot safely travel the path of mysticism. Mystical prayer rises above the natural operation of the intelligence, yet it is always essentially intelligent. Ultimately, the highest function of the human spirit is the work of the supernaturally transformed intelligence, in the beatific vision of God. Nevertheless, the will plays an integral part in all contemplation since there is, in fact, no contemplation without love. Love is both the starting point of contemplation and its fruition.

Furthermore, contemplation presupposes ascetic action. By this interrelation of the work of intelligence, will, and the rest of our being, contemplation immolates our entire self to God. God is the principal agent in this sublime work. Contemplation is His gift, and He is free to dispose of it as He sees fit. It can never, strictly speaking, be merited by any generosity of ours. However, in actual fact, God usually grants this gift to those who are most generous in emptying themselves of every attachment to satisfactions that fall outside the periphery of pure faith.

Finally, mystical contemplation comes to us, like every other grace, through Christ. Contemplation is the fullness of the Christ-life in the soul, and it consists above all in the supernatural penetration of the mysteries of Christ. This work is performed in us by the Holy Ghost substantially present in our soul by grace, along with the other two Divine Persons. The highest peak of contemplation is a mystical union with God in which the soul and its faculties are said to be "transformed" in God, and enter into a full conscious participation in the hidden life of the Trinity of Persons in Unity of Nature.

My chief preoccupation is not to describe or account for the highest levels of mystical experience, but only to settle certain fundamental questions which refer more properly to the ascetical preparation for graces of mystical prayer. The chief of these questions concerns the relations of the intellect and will in contemplation.

The reason I have insisted on this is that we stand in very great danger of a wave of false mysticism. When the world is in greatest confusion, visionaries become oracles. Panic, like every other passion, blinds the intelligence of man, and he is glad of an excuse to take refuge from everything that bewilders him by giving it a "supernatural" interpretation. Therefore it must be made quite clear that traditional Christian mysticism, although it is certainly not intellectualistic in the same sense as the mystical philosophy of Plato and his followers, is nevertheless neither antirational nor anti-intellectualistic.

There is absolutely no enmity between Christian mysticism, on the one hand, and the physical science, natural philosophy, metaphysics, and dogmatic theology on the other. Contemplation is suprarational, without in the least despising the light of reason. The modern popes have insisted on the fundamental harmony between "acquired" or speculative wisdom and the "infused" wisdom which is a gift of the Holy Ghost and is true contemplation. Pope Pius XI, in holding up Saint Thomas Aquinas as a model for priests and theologians, pointed out that the sanctity of the Angelic Doctor consisted above all in the marvelous union of speculative science and infused contemplation which combined to feed the pure flame of his perfect love for God, in such a way that the whole theology of Saint Thomas has but one end: to bring us to intimate union with God.[1]

Pius XII, in his encyclical *Humani Generis,* insisted on the perfect conformity that exists between theological science and the "connatural" knowledge of God by love in mystical contemplation, while at the same time reproving loose philosophical statements which confused the action of the intelligence and the will in the speculative knowledge of divine things.

All this reminds us that the intelligence has a vitally important part to play in Christian sanctity, and that no one can pretend to love God while rejecting all desire to know Him better and to study His perfections in the truths He has revealed to us about Himself. Nevertheless, love remains the very essence of Christian perfection and sanctity, since it unites us to God directly and without medium even in this life. Love also, which is the fruit of our vision of Him in heaven, will be our purest joy in heaven because by it we will be able not merely to receive of His infinite bounty but also repay Him out of the treasury of His own unbounded perfections.

The traditional teaching of the Church, which has been so strongly emphasized by the encyclicals of recent popes and which is the very heart of the *Summa Theologica,* refuses to divide man against himself. The sanity of Catholic theology will never permit the ascetic to wander off into bypaths of angelism or Gnosticism. The church does not seek to sanctify men by destroying their humanity, but by elevating it, with all its faculties and gifts, to the supreme perfection which the Greek Fathers called "deification." At the same time, the Church does not leave man under any illusions about himself. She clearly shows him the powerlessness of his natural faculties to achieve Divine Union by their own efforts.

There are, then, two extremes to be avoided. On the one hand, false mysticism ascribes to human nature the power and the right to acquire supernatural illuminations by the effort of our own intelligence. On the other hand, false mysticism darkens the intelligence altogether in a formal rejection of truth in order to seek Divine Union in an ecstasy of blind love which takes no account of the intelligence, and which accepts deification as a gift so pure that no effort is required on the part of the one who receives it.

But what is the true nature of mystical contemplation? It is first of all a supernatural experience of God as He is in Himself. This experience is a free gift of God in a more special sense than are all the other graces required for our sanctification, although it forms part of the normal supernatural organism by which we are sanctified. Essentially, mystical experience is a vivid, conscious participation of our soul and of its faculties in the life, knowledge, and love of God Himself. This participation is ontologically possible only because sanctifying grace is imparted to us as a new "being" superadded to our nature and giving it the power to elicit acts which are entirely beyond its own capacity.

More particularly, however, the mystical experience is directly caused by special inspiration of the Holy Ghost substantially present within the soul itself and already obscurely identified with it by grace. The effect of these inspirations is to enable the soul to "see" and appreciate, in a manner totally new and unexpected, the full reality of the truths contained in hitherto "untasted" conceptual statements about God. But above all, this experience gives us a deep penetration into the truth of our identification with God by grace. Contemplative experience in the strict sense of the word is always an experience of God Who is apprehended not as an abstraction, not as a distant alien Being, but as intimately and immediately present to the soul in His infinite Reality and Essence.

Love and Forgiveness as Pointers to God

DIETRICH BONHOEFFER

Dietrich Bonhoeffer (1906–1945), a young, passionate, candid German theologian and pastor, came of age during the rise of Nazism in Germany. Educated in both Berlin and New York City, he was deeply disturbed by the rising political situation in his country, especially the attempt of the State to eradicate God altogether from public life, and to lead by human power alone. His deeply rooted Christian faith led him to steadfast convictions about basic human values, including truth, justice, decency, and goodness. Bonhoeffer not only publicly refuted Nazism by helping to found the Confessional Church, but also worked actively within the resistance movement. These activities led to his imprisonment and eventual death by hanging in 1945.

His most well-known and popular book is The Cost of Discipleship. *This is a serious and compelling call to self-examination and authenticity through unreserved devotion to one another and to God. In the selection chosen here, Bonhoeffer points the reader to faith in God through the extraordinary exhortation of Jesus to love one's enemies. Underlying his commitment to justice and social activism was a deep love and faith in a God whom he entrusted his future to—whether in life or in death.*

The Enemy—The "Extraordinary"

Ye have heard that it was said, Thou shalt love thy neighbor, and hate thine enemy: but I say unto you, Love your enemies, and pray for them that persecute you; that ye may be sons of your Father which is in heaven: for he maketh his sun to rise on the evil and the good, and sendeth rain on the just and the unjust. For if ye love them that love you, what reward have ye? do not even the publicans the same? And if ye salute your brethren only, what do ye more than others? do not even the Gentiles the same? Ye therefore shall be perfect, as your heavenly Father is perfect.

(Matthew 5.43–48)

HERE, FOR THE first time in the Sermon on the Mount, we meet the word which sums up the whole of its message, the word "love." Love is defined in uncompromising terms as the love of our enemies. Had Jesus only told us to love our brethren, we might have misunderstood what he meant by love, but now he leaves us in no doubt whatever as to his meaning.

The enemy was no mere abstraction for the disciples. They knew him only too well. They came across him every day. There were those who cursed them for undermining the faith and transgressing the law. There were those who hated them for leaving all they had to Jesus's sake. There were those who insulted and derided them for their weakness and humility. There were those who persecuted them as prospective dangerous revolutionaries and sought to destroy them. Some of their enemies were numbered among the champions of the popular religion, who resented the exclusive claim of Jesus. These last enjoyed considerable power and reputation. And then there was the enemy which would immediately occur to every Jew, the political enemy in Rome. Over and above all these, the disciples also had to contend with the hostility which invariably falls to the lot of those who refuse to follow the crowd, and which brought them daily mockery, derision, and threats.

It is true that the Old Testament never explicitly bids us hate our enemies. On the contrary, it tells us more than once that we must love them (Ex. 23.4f; Prov. 25.21f; Gen. 45.1ff; I Sam. 24.7; II Kings 6.22, etc.). But Jesus is not talking of ordinary enmity, but of that which exists between the People of God and the world. The wars of Israel were the only "holy wars" in history, for they were the wars of God against the world of idols. It is not this enmity which Jesus condemns, for then he would have condemned the whole history of God's dealing with his people. On the contrary, he affirms the old covenant. He is as concerned as the Old Testament with the defeat of the enemy and the victory of the People of God. No, the real meaning of this saying is that Jesus is again releasing his disciples from the political associations of the old Israel. From now on there can be no more wars of faith. The only way to overcome our enemy is by loving him.

To the natural man, the very notion of loving his enemies is an intolerable offense, and quite beyond his capacity: it cuts right across his ideas of good and evil. More important still, to man under the law, the idea of loving his enemies is clean contrary to the law of God, which requires men to sever all connection with their enemies and to pass judgment on them. Jesus however takes the law of God in his own hands and expounds its true meaning. The will of God, to which the law gives expression, is that men should defeat their enemies by loving them.

In the New Testament our enemies are those who harbor hostility against us, not those against whom we cherish hostility, for Jesus refuses to reckon with such a possibility. The Christian must treat his enemy as a brother, and requite his hostility with love. His behavior must be determined not by the way others treat him, but by the treatment he himself receives from Jesus; it has only one source, and that is the will of Jesus.

By our enemies Jesus means those who are quite intractable and utterly unresponsive to our love, who forgive us nothing when we forgive them all, who requite our love with hatred and our service with derision. "For the love that I had unto them, lo, they now take my contrary part: but I give myself unto prayer" (Ps. 109.4). Love asks nothing in return, but seeks those who need it. And who needs our love more than those who are consumed with hatred and are utterly devoid of love? Who in other words deserves our love more than our enemy? Where is love more glorified than where she dwells in the midst of her enemies?

Christian love draws no distinction between one enemy and another, except that the more bitter our enemy's hatred, the greater his need of love. Be his enmity political or religious, he has nothing to expect from a follower of Jesus but unqualified love. In such love there is no inner discord between private person and official capacity. In both we are disciples of Christ, or we are not Christians at all. Am I asked how this love is to behave? Jesus gives the answer: bless, do good, and pray for your enemies without reserve and without respect of persons.

"*Love your enemies*." The preceding commandment had spoken only of the passive endurance of evil; here Jesus goes further and bids us not only to bear with evil and the evil person patiently, not only to refrain from treating him as he treats us, but actively to engage in heart-felt love towards him. We are to serve our enemy in all things without hypocrisy and with utter sincerity. No sacrifice which a lover would make for his beloved is too great for us to make for our enemy. If out of love for our brother we are willing to sacrifice goods, honor, and life, we must be prepared to do the same for our enemy. We are not to imagine that this is to condone his evil; such a love proceeds from strength rather than weakness, from truth rather than fear, and therefore it cannot be guilty of the hatred of another. And who is to be the object of such a love, if not those whose hearts are stifled with hatred?

"Bless them that persecute you." If our enemy cannot put up with us any longer and takes to cursing us, our immediate reaction must be to lift up our hands and bless him. Our enemies are the blessed of the Lord. Their curse can do us no harm. May their poverty be enriched with all the riches of God, with the blessing of him whom they seek to oppose in vain. We are ready to endure their curses so long as they redound to their blessing.

"Do good to them that hate you." We must love not only in thought and word, but in deed, and there are opportunities of service in every circumstance of daily life. "If thine enemy hunger, feed him; if he thirst, give him to drink" (Rom. 12.20). As brother stands by brother in distress, binding up his wounds and soothing his pain, so let us show our love toward our enemy. There is no deeper distress to be found in the world, no pain more bitter than our enemy's. Nowhere is service more necessary or more blessed than when we serve our enemies. "It is more blessed to give than to receive."

"Pray for them which despitefully use you and persecute you." This is the supreme demand. Through the medium of prayer we go to our enemy, stand by his side, and plead for him to God. Jesus does not promise that when we bless our enemies and do good to them they will not despitefully use and persecute us. They certainly will. But not even that can hurt or overcome us, so long as we pray for them. For if we pray for them, we are taking their distress and poverty, their guilt and perdition upon ourselves, and pleading to God for them. We are doing vicariously for them what they cannot do for themselves. Every insult they utter only serves to bind us more closely to God and them. Their persecution of us only serves to bring them nearer to reconciliation with God and to further the triumphs of love.

How then does love conquer? By asking not how the enemy treats her but only how Jesus treated her. The love for our enemies takes us along the way of the cross and into fellowship with the Crucified. The more we are driven along this road, the more certain is the victory of love over the enemy's hatred. For then it is not the disciple's own love, but the love of Jesus Christ alone, who for the sake of his enemies went to the cross and prayed for them as he hung there. In the face of the cross the disciples realized that they too were his enemies, and that he had overcome them by his love. It is this that opens the disciple's eyes, and enables him to see his enemy as a brother. He knows that he owes his very life to One, who though he was his enemy, treated him as a brother and accepted him, who made him his neighbor, and drew him into fellowship with himself. The disciple can now perceive that even his enemy is the object of God's love, and that he stands like himself beneath the cross of Christ. God asked us nothing about our virtues or our vices, for in his sight even our virtue was ungodliness. God's love sought out his enemies who needed it, and whom he deemed worthy of it. God loves his enemies—that is the glory of his love, as every follow of Jesus knows; through Jesus he has become a partaker in this love. For God allows his sun to shine upon the just and the unjust. But it is not only the earthly sun and the earthly rain: the "Sun of righteousness" and the rain of God's Word which are on the sinner, and reveal the grace of the Heavenly Father. Perfect, all-inclusive love is the act of the Father, it is also the act of the sons of God as it was the act of the only-begotten Son.

"This commandment, that we should love our enemies and forgo revenge, will grow even more urgent in the holy struggle which lies before us and in which we partly have already been engaged for years. In it love and hate engage in mortal combat. It is the urgent duty of every Christian soul to prepare itself for it. The time is coming when the confession of the living God will incur not only the hatred and the fury of the world, for on the whole it has come to that already, but complete ostracism from 'human society,' as they call it. The Christians will be hounded from place to place, subjected to physical assault, maltreatment, and death of every kind. We are approaching an age of widespread persecution. Therein lies the true significance of all the movement and conflicts of our age. Our adversaries seek to root out the Christian Church and the Christian

faith because they cannot live side by side with us, because they see in every word we utter and every deed we do, even when they are not specifically directed against them, a condemnation of their own words and deeds. They are not far wrong. They suspect too that we are indifferent to their condemnation. Indeed they must admit that it is utterly futile to condemn us. We do not reciprocate their hatred and contention, although they would like it better if we did, and so sink to their own level. And how is the battle to be fought? Soon the time will come when we shall pray, not as isolated individuals, but as a corporate body, a congregation, a Church: we shall pray in multitudes (albeit relatively small multitudes) and among the thousands and thousands of apostates we shall loudly praise and confess the Lord who was crucified and is risen and shall come again. And what prayer, what confession, what hymn of praise will it be? It will be the prayer of earnest love for these very sons of perdition who stand around and gaze at us with eyes aflame with hatred, and who have perhaps already raised their hands to kill us. It will be a prayer for the peace of these erring, devastated, and bewildered souls, a prayer for the same love and peace which we ourselves enjoy, a prayer which will penetrate to the depths of their souls and rend their hearts more grievously than anything they can do to us. Yes, the Church which is really waiting for its Lord, and which discerns the signs of the times of decision, must fling itself with its utmost power and with the panoply of its holy life into this prayer of love."[1]

What is undivided love? Love which shows no special favor to those who love us in return. When we love those who love us, our brethren, our nation, our friends, yes, and even our own congregation, we are no better than the heathen and the publicans. Such love is ordinary and natural, and not distinctively Christian. We can love our kith and kin, our fellow-countrymen and our friends, whether we are Christians or not, and there is no need for Jesus to teach us that. But he takes that kind of love for granted, and in contrast asserts that we must love our enemies. Thus he shows us what *he* means by love, and the attitude we must display towards it.

How then do the disciples differ from the heathen? What does it really mean to be a Christian? Here we meet the word which controls the whole chapter, and sums up all we have heard so far. What makes the Christian different from other men is the "peculiar," the περισσόν, the "extraordinary," the "unusual," that which is not "a matter of course." This is the quality whereby the better righteousness exceeds the righteousness of the scribes and Pharisees. It is "the more," the "beyond-all-that." The natural is τὸ αὐτὸ (one and the same) for heathen and Christian, the distinctive quality of the Christian life begins with the περισσόν. It is this quality which first enables us to see the natural in its true light. Where it is lacking, the peculiar graces of Christianity are absent. It cannot occur within the sphere of natural possibilities, but only when they are transcended. The περισσὸν never merges into the τὸ αὐτὸ. That was the fatal mistake of the false Protestant ethic which diluted Christian love into patriotism, loyalty to friends and industriousness, which in short, perverted the better righteousness into *justitia civilis*. Not in such terms as these does Jesus speak. For him the hallmark of the Christian is the "extraordinary." The Christian cannot live at the world's level, because he must always remember the περισσόν.

What is the precise nature of the περισσόν? It is the life described in the beatitudes, the life of the followers of Jesus, the light which lights the world, the city set on the hill, the way of self-renunciation, of utter love, of absolute purity, truthfulness, and meekness. It is unreserved love for our enemies, for the unloving and the unloved, love for our religious, political, and personal adversaries. In every case it is the love which was fulfilled in the cross of Christ. What is the περισσόν? It is the love of Jesus Christ himself, who went patiently and obediently to the cross—it is in fact the cross itself. The cross is the differential in Christian religion, the power which enables the Christian to transcend the world and to win the victory. The *passio* in the love of the Crucified is the supreme expression of the "extraordinary" quality of the Christian life.

The "extraordinary" quality is undoubtedly identical with the light which shines before men and for which they glorify the Father which is in heaven. It cannot be hidden under a bushel, it must be seen of men. The community of the followers of Jesus, the community of the better righteousness, is the visible community: it has left the world and society, and counted everything but loss for the cross of Christ.

And how does this quality work out in practice? The "extraordinary"—and this is the supreme scandal—is something which the followers of Jesus *do*. It must be *done* like the better righteousness, and done so that all men can see it. It is not strict Puritanism, not some eccentric pattern of Christian living, but simple, unreflecting obedience to the will of Christ. If we make the "extraordinary" our standard, we shall be led into the *passio* of Christ, and in that its peculiar quality will be displayed. This activity itself is ceaseless suffering. In it the disciple endures the suffering of Christ. If this is not so, then *this* is not the activity of which Jesus speaks.

Hence the περισσόν is the fulfillment of the law, the keeping of the commandments. In Christ crucified and in his people the "extraordinary" becomes reality.

These men are the perfect, the men in whom the undivided love of the Heavenly Father is perfected. It was that love which gave the Son to die for us upon the cross, and it is by suffering in the fellowship of this cross that the followers of Jesus are perfected. The perfect are none other than the blessed of the Beatitudes.

VIKTOR FRANKL

Finding meaning in the worst of circumstances was the hallmark of Viktor Frankl's (1905–1997) life. As an Austrian Jew, he was a prisoner in four Nazi concentration camps, including Auschwitz, during the Holocaust. Even while experiencing the most hellish existence and cruel injustice, he held onto the belief that there is meaning in life, even spiritual meaning, when everything around indicates otherwise.

Best known internationally as a neurologist and psychologist, he is credited with creating a new existential therapy known as logotherapy. At the core, logotherapy teaches that a person's dominant human drive is meaning, not pleasure. And although this drive may bring tension and suffering, it is not without purpose because each of us chooses how to deal with it. Frankl's method is chronicled in his internationally known book entitled Man's Search for Meaning.

Besides receiving twenty-nine honorary degrees from universities around the world, Frankl was the first non-American to receive the prestigious Oskar Pfister Prize by the American Psychiatric Association. Even in his twilight years he continued to exemplify the value of a meaningful life. Thus, in his late sixties he achieved his pilot's license, and remained a teaching professor in Vienna until he was eighty-five years old.

The Will to Meaning

MAN'S SEARCH FOR meaning is the primary motivation in his life and not a "secondary rationalization" of instinctual drives. This meaning is unique and specific in that it must and can be fulfilled by him alone; only then does it achieve a significance which will satisfy his own *will* to meaning. There are some authors who contend that meanings and values are "nothing but defense mechanisms, reaction formations, and sublimations." But as for myself, I would not be willing to live merely for the sake of my "defense mechanisms," nor would I be ready to die merely for the sake of my "reaction formations." Man, however, is able to live and even to die for the sake of his ideals and values!

A public-opinion poll was conducted a few years ago in France. The results showed that 89 percent of the people polled admitted that man needs "something" for the sake of which to live. Moreover, 61 percent conceded that there was something, or someone, in their own lives for whose sake they were even ready to die. I repeated this poll at my hospital department in Vienna among both the patients and the personnel, and the outcome was practically the same as among the thousands of people screened in France; the difference was only 2 percent.

Another statistical survey, of 7,948 students at forty-eight colleges, was conducted by social scientists from Johns Hopkins University. Their preliminary report is part of a two-year study sponsored by the National Institute of Mental Health. Asked what they considered "very important" to them now, 16 percent of the students checked "making a lot of money"; 78 percent said their first goal was "finding a purpose and meaning to my life."

Of course, there may be some cases in which an individual's concern with values is really a camouflage of hidden inner conflicts; but, if so, they represent the exceptions from the rule rather than the rule itself. In these cases we have actually to deal with pseudovalues, and as such they have to be unmasked. Unmasking, however, should stop as soon as one is confronted with what is authentic and genuine in man, e.g., man's desire for a life that is as meaningful as possible. If it does not stop then, the only thing that the "unmasking psychologist" really unmasks is his own "hidden motive"—namely, his unconscious need to debase and depreciate what is genuine, what is genuinely human, in man.

Noö-Dynamics

To be sure, man's search for meaning may arouse inner tension rather than inner equilibrium. However, precisely such tension is an indispensable prerequisite of mental health. There is nothing in the world, I venture to say, that would so effectively help one to survive even the worst conditions as the knowledge that there is a meaning in one's life. There is much wisdom in the words of Nietzsche: "He who has a *why* to live for can bear almost any *how*." I can see in these words a motto which holds true for any psychotherapy. In the Nazi concentration camps, one could have witnessed that those who knew that there was a task waiting for them to fulfill were most apt to survive. The same conclusion has since been reached by other authors of books on concentration camps, and also by psychiatric investigations into Japanese, North Korean, and North Vietnamese prisoner-of-war camps.

As for myself, when I was taken to the concentration camp of Auschwitz, a manuscript of mine ready for publication was confiscated.[1] Certainly, my deep desire to write this manuscript anew helped me to survive the rigors of the camps I was in. For instance, when in a camp in Bavaria I fell ill with typhus fever, I jotted down on little scraps of paper many notes intended to enable me to rewrite the manuscript, should I live to the day of liberation. I am sure that this reconstruction of my lost manuscript in the dark barracks of a Bavarian concentration camp assisted me in overcoming the danger of cardiovascular collapse.

Thus it can be seen that mental health is based on a certain degree of tension, the tension between what one has already achieved and what one still ought to accomplish, or the gap between what one is and what one should become. Such a tension is inherent in the human being and therefore is indispensable to mental well-being. We should not, then, be hesitant about challenging man with a potential meaning for him to fulfill. It is only thus that we evoke his will to meaning from its state of latency. I consider it a dangerous misconception of mental hygiene to assume that what man needs in the first place is equilibrium or, as it is called in biology, "homeostasis," i.e., a tensionless state. What man actually needs is not a tensionless state but rather the striving and struggling for a worthwhile goal, a freely chosen task. What he needs is not the discharge of tension at any cost but the call of a potential meaning waiting to be fulfilled by him. What man needs is not homeostasis but what I call "noödynamics," i.e., the existential dynamics in a polar field of tension where one pole is represented by a meaning that is to be fulfilled and the other pole by the man who has to fulfill it. And one should not think that this holds true only for normal conditions; in neurotic individuals, it is even more valid. If architects want to strengthen a decrepit arch, they *increase* the load which is laid upon it, for thereby the parts are joined more firmly together. So if therapists wish to foster their patients' mental health, they should not be afraid to create a sound amount of tension through a reorientation toward the meaning of one's life.

Having shown the beneficial impact of meaning orientation, I turn to the detrimental influence of that feeling of which so many patients complain today, namely, the feeling of the total and ultimate meaninglessness of their lives. They lack the awareness of a meaning worth living for. They are haunted by the experience of their inner emptiness, a void within themselves; they are caught in that situation which I have called the "existential vacuum."

The Existential Vacuum

The existential vacuum is a widespread phenomenon of the twentieth century. This is understandable; it may be due to a twofold loss which man has had to undergo since he became a truly human being. At the beginning of human history, man lost some of the basic animal instincts in which an animal's behavior is imbedded and by which it is secured. Such security, like Paradise, is closed to man forever; man has to make choices. In addition to this, however, man has suffered another loss in his more recent development inasmuch as the traditions which buttressed his behavior are now rapidly diminishing. No instinct tells him what he has to do, and no tradition tells him what he ought to do; sometimes he does not even know what he wishes to do. Instead, he either wishes to do what other people do (conformism) or he does what other people wish him to do (totalitarianism).

A statistical survey recently revealed that among my European students, 25 percent showed a more or less marked degree of existential vacuum. Among my American students it was not 25 but 60 percent.

The existential vacuum manifests itself mainly in a state of boredom. Now we can understand Schopenhauer when he said that mankind was apparently doomed to vacillate eternally between the two extremes of distress and boredom. In actual fact, boredom is now causing, and certainly bringing to psychiatrists, more problems to solve than distress. And these problems are growing increasingly crucial, for progressive automation will probably lead to an enormous increase in the leisure hours available to the average worker. The pity of it is that many of these will not know what to do with all their newly acquired free time.

Let us consider, for instance, "Sunday neurosis," that kind of depression which afflicts people who become aware of the lack of content in their lives when the rush of the busy week is over and the void within themselves becomes manifest. Not a few cases of suicide can be traced back to this existential vacuum. Such widespread phenomena as depression, aggression, and addiction are not understandable unless we recognize the existential vacuum underlying them. This is also true of the crises of pensioners and aging people.

Moreover, there are various masks and guises under which the existential vacuum appears. Sometimes the frustrated will to meaning is vicariously compensated for by a will to power, including the most primitive form of the will to power, the will to money. In other cases, the place of frustrated will to meaning is taken by the will to pleasure. That is why existential frustration often eventuates in sexual compensation. We can observe in such cases that the sexual libido becomes rampant in the existential vacuum.

An analogous event occurs in neurotic cases. There are certain types of feedback mechanisms and vicious-circle formations which I will touch upon later. One can observe again and again, however, that this symptomatology has invaded an existential vacuum wherein it then continues to flourish. In such patients, what we have to deal with is not a noögenic neurosis. However, we will never succeed in having the patient overcome his condition if we have not supplemented the psychotherapeutic treatment with logotherapy. For by filling the existential vacuum, the patient will be prevented from suffering further relapses. Therefore, logotherapy is indicated not only in noögenic cases, as pointed out above, but also in psychogenic cases, and sometimes even the somatogenic (pseudo-) neuroses. Viewed in this light, a statement once made by Magda B. Arnold is justified: "Every therapy must in some way, no matter how restricted, also be logotherapy."[2]

Let us now consider what we can do if a patient asks what the meaning of his life is.

The Meaning of Life

I doubt whether a doctor can answer this question in general terms. For the meaning of life differs from man to man, from day to day and from hour to hour. What matters, therefore, is not the meaning of life in general but rather the specific meaning of a person's life at a given moment. To put the question in general terms would be comparable to the question posed to a chess champion: "Tell me, Master, what is the best move in the world?" There simply is no such thing as the best or even a good move apart from a particular situation in a game and the particular personality of one's opponent. The same holds for human existence. One should not search for an abstract meaning of life. Everyone has his own specific vocation or mission in life to carry out a concrete assignment which demands fulfillment. Therein he cannot be replaced, nor can his life be repeated. Thus, everyone's task is as unique as is his specific opportunity to implement it.

As each situation in life represents a challenge to man and presents a problem for him to solve, the question of the meaning of life may actually be reversed. Ultimately, man should not ask what the meaning of his life is, but rather he must recognize that it is *he* who is asked. In a word, each man is questioned by life; and he can only answer to life by *answering for* his own life; to life he can only respond by being responsible.

The Meaning of Love

Love is the only way to grasp another human being in the innermost core of his personality. No one can become fully aware of the very essence of another human being unless he loves him. By his love he is enabled to see the essential traits and features in the beloved person; and even more, he sees that which is potential in him, which is not yet actualized but yet ought to be actualized. Furthermore, by his love, the loving person enables the beloved person to actualize these potentialities. By making him aware of what he can be and of what he should become, he makes these potentialities come true.

The Meaning of Suffering

We must never forget that we may also find meaning in life even when confronted with a hopeless situation, when facing a fate that cannot be changed. For what then matters is to bear witness to the uniquely human potential at its best, which is to transform a personal tragedy into a triumph, to turn one's predicament into a human achievement. When we are no longer able to change a situation—just think of an incurable disease such as inoperable cancer—we are challenged to change ourselves.

Let me cite a clear-cut example: Once, an elderly general practitioner consulted me because of his severe depression. He could not overcome the loss of his wife who had died two years before and whom he had loved above all else. Now, how could I help him? What should I tell him? Well, I refrained from telling him anything but instead confronted him with the question. "What would have happened, Doctor, if you had died first, and your wife would have had to survive you?" "Oh," he said, "for her this would have been terrible; how she would have suffered!" Whereupon I replied, "You see, Doctor, such a suffering has been spared her, and it was you who have spared her this suffering—to be sure, at the price that now you have to survive and mourn her." He said no word but shook my hand and calmly left my office. In some way, suffering ceases to be suffering at the moment it finds a meaning, such as the meaning of a sacrifice.

Of course, this was no therapy in the proper sense since, first, his despair was no disease; and second, I could not change his fate; I could not revive his wife. But in that moment I did succeed in changing his *attitude* toward his unalterable fate inasmuch as from that time on he could at least see a meaning in his suffering. It is one of the basic tenets of logotherapy that man's main concern is not to gain pleasure or to avoid pain but rather to see a meaning in his life. That is why man is even ready to suffer, on the condition, to be sure, that his suffering has a meaning.

But let me make it perfectly clear that in no way is suffering *necessary* to find meaning. I only insist that meaning is possible even in spite of suffering—provided, certainly, that the suffering is unavoidable. If it *were* avoidable, however, the meaningful thing to do would be to remove its cause, be it psychological, biological, or political. To suffer unnecessarily is masochistic rather than heroic.

There are situations in which one is cut off from the opportunity to do one's work or to enjoy one's life; but what never can be ruled out is the unavoidability of suffering. In accepting this challenge to suffer bravely, life has a meaning up to the last moment, and it retains this meaning literally to the end. In other words, life's meaning is an unconditional one, for it even includes the potential meaning of unavoidable suffering.

Let me recall that which was perhaps the deepest experience I had in the concentration camp. The odds of surviving the camp were no more than one in twenty-eight, as can easily be verified by exact statistics. It did not even seem possible, let alone probable, that the manuscript of my first book, which I had hidden in my coat when I arrived at Auschwitz, would ever be rescued. Thus, I had to undergo and to overcome the loss of my mental child. And now it seemed as if nothing and no one would survive me; neither a physical nor a mental child of my own! So I found myself confronted with the question whether under such circumstances my life was ultimately void of any meaning.

Not yet did I notice that an answer to this question with which I was wrestling so passionately was already in store for me, and that soon thereafter this answer would be given to me. This was the case when I had to surrender my clothes and in turn inherited the worn-out rags of an inmate who had already been sent to the gas chamber immediately after his arrival at the Auschwitz railway station. Instead of the many pages of my manuscript, I found in a pocket of the newly acquired coat one single page torn out of a Hebrew prayer book, containing the most important Jewish prayer, *Shema Yisrael*. How should I have interpreted such a "coincidence" other than as a challenge to *live* my thoughts instead of merely putting them on paper?

A bit later, I remember, it seemed to me that I would die in the near future. In this critical situation, however, my concern was different from that of most of my comrades. Their question was, "Will we survive the camp? For, if not, all this suffering has no meaning." The question which beset me was, "Has all this suffering, this dying around us, a meaning? For, if not, then ultimately there is no meaning to survival; for a life whose meaning depends upon such a happenstance—as whether one escapes or not—ultimately would not be worth living at all."

MOTHER TERESA

Considered by many as the twentieth century's most beloved woman, Albanian Mother Teresa (1910–1997), a Roman Catholic nun, was most known for her work among outcasts in India. In 1950, she founded the Missionaries of Charity in Calcutta. For over forty-five years she reached out and loved the orphaned, the sick, and the dying. As a humanitarian, she believed every single human life has value. Time and again she reached beyond the borders of a degrading caste system, and advocated for the poorest of the poor. For that she was awarded the Nobel Peace Prize in 1979.

She exemplified the way a person can intertwine their faith and intellect by how she lived out her personal belief in a loving, omniscient God. Time and again, through operating missions, orphanages, hospices, schools, soup kitchens, and counseling centers she demonstrated the vast and incomparable love and mercy of God. In the following compendium of some of her brief reflections, she illuminates several subjects that defined her life: love, surrender, compassion, family, and suffering.

A Gift for God

FAITH IS LACKING because there is so much selfishness and so much gain only for self. But faith, to be true, has to be a giving love. Love and faith go together. They complete each other.

Suffering is increasing in the world today. People are hungry for something more beautiful, for something greater than people round about can give. There is a great hunger for God in the world today. Everywhere there is much suffering, but there is also great hunger for God and love for each other.

There is no great difference in reality between one country and another, because it is always people you meet everywhere. They may look different or be dressed differently, they may have a different education or position; but they are all the same. They are all people to be loved; they are all hungry for love.

Some weeks back I heard there was a family who had not eaten for some days—a Hindu family—so I took some rice and I went to the family. Before I knew where I was, the mother of the family had divided the rice into two and she took the other half to the next-door neighbors, who happened to be a Muslim family. Then I asked her: "How much will all of you have to share? There are ten of you with that bit of rice." The mother replied: "They have not eaten either." This is greatness.

Let us not be satisfied with just giving money. Money is not enough, money can be got, but they need your hearts to love them. So, spread love everywhere you go: first of all in your home. Give love to your children, to your wife or husband, to a next-door neighbor.[1]

~

Total surrender consists in giving ourselves completely to God. Why must we give our selves fully to God? Because God has given himself to us. If God, who owes nothing to us, is ready to impart to us no less than himself, shall we answer him with just a fraction of ourselves? To give ourselves fully to God is a means of receiving God himself. I live for God and give up my own self and in this way induce God to live for me. Therefore, to possess God, we must allow him to possess our souls. How poor we would be if God had not given us the power of giving ourselves to him. How rich we are now. How easy it is to conquer God! We give ourselves to God; then God is ours and there can be nothing more ours than God. The money with which God repays our surrender is himself.[2]

~

One cannot say, "Love God, not your neighbor." St. John calls liars those who pretend to love God but do not love their neighbor. How can we love God whom we do not see if we do not love our fellow human being whom we do see? Whom we can touch? With whom we live? It is important to realize that love, to be genuine, must bring some suffering with it.

Jesus too suffered in order to love us. He still suffers. To be sure that we might remember his great love he became our bread of life to satisfy our hunger for his love, our hunger for God, because it was for this love that we were created. We were created to love and to be loved, and he became man to enable us to love him as he loves us. He has become one with the hungry, the naked, the homeless, the sick, the persecuted, the lonely, the abandoned ones; and he tells us: "You made me like this." He hungers for our love, and this is the hunger that afflicts our poor people. This is the hunger that every one of us ought to seek out. It might even be found in our own homes.[3]

In England and other places, in Calcutta, in Melbourne, in New York, we find lonely people who are known by the number of their room. Why are we not there? Do we really know that there are some people, maybe next door to us? Maybe there is a blind man who would be happy if you would read the newspaper for him—he has plenty of other things, he is nearly drowned in them, but there is not that touch and he needs your touch. Some time back a very rich man came to our place, and he said to me: "Please, either you or somebody, come to my house. I am nearly half-blind and my wife is nearly mental; our children have all gone abroad, and we are dying of loneliness, we are longing for the loving sound of a human voice."

One day I visited a house where our sisters shelter the aged. This is one of the nicest houses in England, filled with beautiful and precious things, yet there was not one smile on the faces of these people. All of them were looking toward the door.

I asked the sister in charge, "Why are they like that? Why can't you see a smile on their faces?" (I am accustomed to seeing smiles on people's faces. I think a smile generates a smile, just as love generates love.)

The sister answered, "The same thing happens every day. They are always waiting for someone to come and visit them. Loneliness eats them up, and day after day they do not stop looking. Nobody comes."

Abandonment is an awful poverty. There are poor people everywhere, but the deepest poverty is not being loved.

The poor we seek may live near us or far away. They can be materially or spiritually poor. They may be hungry for bread or hungry for friendship. They may need clothing, or they may need the sense of wealth that God's love for them represents. They may need the shelter of a house made of bricks and cement or the shelter of having a place in our hearts.[4]

The same loving hand that has created you has created me. If he is your Father, he must be my Father also. We all belong to the same family. Hindus, Muslims, and all people are our brothers and sisters. They too are the children of God.[5]

Voices from the East

MAHATMA GANDHI

Revered as a nonviolent liberator who worked to free the Indian people from the unfair treatment of British colonizers, Mahatma Gandhi (1869–1948) rose to distinction by opposing injustice and promoting peace. He embraced both of these principles, even though suffering and death were a constant personal threat.

As a young lawyer traveling in South Africa, a singular experience changed the course of Gandhi's life. While riding a train across the country he encountered a grossly unjust situation—he was asked to leave the first-class car and eventually thrown off the train because of the color of his skin. The experience became a watershed moment for him. He determined never to allow an indignity like this to happen again, either for himself or for others.

As a devout Hindu, religion was central in Gandhi's life. More than just tradition or an outward practice, he believed that faith was "a heart grasp." The chosen selection by him addresses this topic, as well as how to treat an enemy, truth, the importance of not being afraid, and reasons not to steal. A final piece is a brief essay on reasons to believe in God.

Ideals for the Ashram of Soul-Force

NO WORK DONE by any man, however great, will really prosper unless it has a distinct religious backing. But what is Religion? I for one would answer: "Not the Religion you will get after reading all the scriptures of the world. Religion is not really what is grasped by the brain, but a heart grasp."

Religion is a thing not alien to us. It has to be evolved out of us. It is always within us: with some, consciously so; with others, quite unconsciously. But it is always there. And whether we wake up this religious instinct in us through outside assistance or by inward growth, no matter how it is done, it has got to be done, if we want to do anything in the right manner, or to achieve anything that is going to persist.

Our Scriptures have laid down certain rules as maxims of human life. They tell us that without living according to these maxims we are incapable of having a reasonable perception of Religion. Believing in these implicitly, I have deemed it necessary to seek the association of those who think with me in founding this Institution. The following are the rules that have been drawn up and have to be observed by everyone who seeks to be a member.

The first and foremost is

The Vow of Truth

Not simply as we ordinarily understand it, not truth which merely answers the saying, "Honesty is the best policy," implying that if it is not the best policy we may depart from it. Here Truth as it is conceived means that we may have to rule our life by this law of Truth at any cost; and in order to satisfy the definition I have drawn upon the celebrated illustration of the life of Prahlad.[1] For the sake of Truth he dared to oppose his own father; and he defended himself, not by paying his father back in his own coin. Rather, in defense of Truth as he knew it, he was prepared to die without caring to return the blows that he had received from his father, or from those who were charged with his father's instructions. Not only that, he would not in any way even parry the blows; on the contrary, with a smile on his lips, he underwent the innumerable tortures to which he was subjected, with the result that at last Truth rose triumphant. Not that he suffered the tortures because he knew that some day or other in his very lifetime he would be able to demonstrate the infallibility of the Law of Truth. That fact was there; but if he had died in the midst of tortures he would still have adhered to Truth. That is the Truth which I would like to follow. In our Ashram we make it a rule that we must say "No" when we mean No, regardless of consequences.

Then we come to the

Doctrine of Ahimsā

Literally speaking, Ahimsā means "non-killing." But to me it has a world of meaning, and takes me into realms much higher, infinitely higher. It really means that you may not offend anybody; you may not harbor an uncharitable thought, even in connection with one who may consider himself to be your enemy. To one who follows this doctrine there is no room for an enemy. But there may be people who consider themselves to be his enemies. So it is held that we may not harbor an evil thought even in connection with such persons. If we return blow for blow we depart from the doctrine of Ahimsā. But I go farther. If we resent a friend's action, or the so-called enemy's action, we still fall short of this doctrine. But when I say we should not resent, I do not say that we should acquiesce: by the word "resenting" I mean wishing that some harm should be done to the enemy; or that he should be put out of the way, not even by any action of ours, but by the action of somebody else, or, say, by divine agency. If we harbor even this thought we depart from this doctrine of Non-Violence. Those who join the Ashram have literally to accept that meaning.

This does not mean that we practice that doctrine in its entirety. Far from it. It is an ideal which we have to reach, and it is an ideal to be reached even at this very moment, if we are capable of doing so. But it is not a proposition in geometry; it is not even like solving difficult problems in higher mathematics—it is infinitely more difficult. Many of us have burnt the midnight oil in solving those problems. But if you want to follow out this doctrine you will have to do much more than burn the midnight oil. You will have to pass many a sleepless night, and go through many a mental torture, before you can even be within measurable distance of this goal. It is the goal, and nothing less than that, which you and I have to reach, if we want to understand what a religious life means.

A man who believes in the efficacy of this doctrine finds in the ultimate stage, when he is about to reach the goal, the whole world at his feet. If you express your love—Ahimsā—in such a manner that it impresses itself indelibly upon your so-called enemy, he must return that love. Under this rule there is no room for organized assassinations, or for murders openly committed, or for any violence for the sake of your country or even for guarding the honor of precious ones that may be under your charge. After all, that would be a poor defense of their honor. This doctrine tells us that we may guard the honor of those under our charge by delivering our own lives into the hands of the man who would commit the sacrilege. And that requires far greater courage than delivering of blows. If you do not retaliate, but stand your ground between your charge and the opponent, simply receiving the blows without retaliating, what happens? I give you my promise that the whole of his violence will be expended on you, and your friend will be left unscathed. Under this plan of life there is no conception of patriotism that justifies such wars as you witness to-day in Europe.

Then again there is

The Vow of Non-Thieving

I suggest that we are thieves in a way. If I take anything that I do not need for my own immediate use and keep it, I thieve it from somebody else. It is the fundamental law of Nature, without exception, that Nature produces enough for our wants from day to day; and if only everybody took enough for himself and nothing more, there would be no pauperism in this world, there would be no man dying of starvation. I am no Socialist, and I do not want to dispossess those who have got possessions; but I do say that personally those of us who want to see light out of darkness have to follow this rule. I do not want to dispossess anybody; I should then be departing from the rule of Non-Violence. If somebody else possesses more than I do, let him. But so far as my own life has to be regulated I dare not possess anything which I do not want. In India we have got many millions of people who have to be satisfied with one meal a day, and that meal consisting of a *chapatti*[2] containing no fat in it and a pinch of salt. You and I have no right to anything that we really have until these many millions are clothed and fed. You and I, who ought to know better, must adjust our wants, and even undergo voluntary privation in order that they may be nursed, fed, and clothed.

Then there is the "Vow of Non-Possession," which follows as a matter of course, and needs no further explanation at this point, where only a brief summary of various difficulties and their answer is being given.

Then I go to

The Vow of Fearlessness

I found, through my wanderings in India, that my country is seized with a paralyzing fear. We may not open our lips in public:

we may only talk about our opinions secretly. We may do anything we like within the four walls of our house; but those things are not for public consumption.

If we had taken a vow of silence I would have nothing to say. I suggest to you that there is only One whom we have to fear, that is God. When we fear God, then we shall fear no man, however high-placed he may be; and if you want to follow the vow of Truth, then fearlessness is absolutely necessary. Before we can aspire to guide the destinies of India we shall have to adopt this habit of fearlessness.

On God

There is an indefinable mysterious Power that pervades everything. I feel it, though I do not see it. It is this unseen Power which makes itself felt and yet defies all proof, because it is so unlike all that I perceive through my senses. It transcends the senses. But it is possible to reason out the existence of God to a limited extent.

Even in ordinary affairs we know that people do not know who rules or why and how he rules; and yet they know that there is a power that certainly rules. In my tour last year in Mysore I met many poor villagers, and I found upon inquiry that they did not know who ruled Mysore; they simply said some god ruled it. If the knowledge of these poor people was so limited about their ruler, I who am infinitely lesser in respect to God than they to their ruler need not be surprised if I do not realize the presence of God, the King of kings.

Nevertheless I do feel, as the poor villagers felt about Mysore, that there is orderliness in the universe; there is an unalterable Law governing everything and every being that exists or lives. It is not a blind law; for no blind law can govern the conduct of living beings; and thanks to the marvelous researches of Sir J. C. Bose, it can now be proved that even matter is life.

That Law, then, which governs all life is God. Law and the Law-Giver are one. I may not deny the Law or the Law-Giver because I know so little about It or Him. Just as my denial or ignorance of the existence of an earthly power will avail me nothing, even so my denial of God and His law will not liberate me from its operation; whereas humble and mute acceptance of divine authority makes life's journey easier even as the acceptance of earthly rule makes life under it easier.

I do dimly perceive that whilst everything around me is ever-changing, ever-dying, there is underlying all that change a Living Power that is changeless, that holds all together, that creates, dissolves, and re-creates. That informing Power or Spirit is God; and since nothing else that I see merely through the senses can or will persist, He alone is.

And is this power benevolent or malevolent? I see it as purely benevolent. For I can see that in the midst of death life persists; in the midst of untruth, truth persists; in the midst of darkness, light persists. Hence I gather that God is Life, Truth, Light. He is Love. He is the supreme Good.

But He is no God who merely satisfies the intellect, if He ever does. God, to be God, must rule the heart and transform it. He must express Himself in every smallest act of His votary. This can only be done through a definite realization more real than the five senses can ever produce. Sense perceptions can be, and often are, false and deceptive, however real they may appear to us. Where there is a realization outside the senses it is infallible. It is proved, not by extraneous evidence, but in the transformed conduct and character of those who have felt the real presence of God within.

Such testimony is to be found in the experiences of an unbroken line of prophets and sages in all countries and climes. To reject this evidence is to deny oneself.

This realization is preceded by an immovable faith. He who would in his own person test the fact of God's presence can do so by a living faith; and since faith itself cannot be proved by extraneous evidence, the safest course is to believe in the moral government of the world, and therefore in the supremacy of the moral law, the law of Truth and Love. Exercise of faith will be the safest where there is a clear determination summarily to reject all that is contrary to Truth and Love.

I confess that I have no argument to convince through reason. Faith transcends reason. All I can advise is not to attempt the impossible. I cannot account for the existence of evil by any rational method. To want to do so is to be co-equal with God. I am therefore humble enough to recognize evil as such; and I call God long-suffering and patient precisely because He permits evil in the world. I know that He has no evil in Himself; and yet if there is evil He is the author of it and yet untouched by it.

I know, too, that I shall never know God if I do not wrestle with and against evil, even at the cost of life itself. I am fortified in the belief by my own humble and limited experience. The purer I try to become the nearer to God I feel myself to be. How much more should I be near to Him when my faith is not a mere apology, as it is to-day, but has become as immovable as the Himalayas and as white as the snows on their peaks?

THE DALAI LAMA
(TENZIN GYATSO)

As both the temporal and spiritual Buddhist leader of the Tibetan people, Tenzin Gyatso (1935–) is the fourteenth Dalai Lama. Along with other notable awards, he has received both the Congressional Gold Medal and the Nobel Peace Prize.

The Dalai Lama has achieved international recognition as a spiritual leader and human rights activist. Because of this he often speaks on subjects like suffering. But in more recent days he has joined the public discussion in the area of science and faith. In this excerpt from his latest book, The Universe in a Single Atom: The Convergence of Science and Spirituality, *the Dalai Lama explores the importance of spirituality and the supernatural within the realms of science, Buddhism, critical investigation, and reality.*

Reflection

I HAVE SPENT many years reflecting on the remarkable advances of science. Within the short space of my own lifetime, the impact of science and technology on humanity has been tremendous. Although my own interest in science began with curiosity about a world, foreign to me at that time, governed by technology, it was not very long before the colossal significance of science for humanity as a whole dawned on me—especially after I came into exile in 1959. There is almost no area of human life today that is not touched by the effects of science and technology. Yet are we clear about the place of science in the totality of human life—what exactly it should do and by what it should be governed? This last point is critical because unless the direction of science is guided by a consciously ethical motivation, especially compassion, its effects may fail to bring benefit. They may indeed cause great harm.

Seeing the tremendous importance of science and recognizing its inevitable dominance in the modern world fundamentally changed my attitude to it from curiosity to a kind of urgent engagement. In Buddhism the highest spiritual ideal is to cultivate compassion for all sentient beings and to work for their welfare to the greatest possible extent. From my earliest childhood I have been conditioned to cherish this ideal and attempt to fulfill it in my every action. So I wanted to understand science because it gave me a new area to explore in my personal quest to understand the nature of reality. I also wanted to learn about it because I recognized in it a compelling way to communicate insights gleaned from my own spiritual tradition. So, for me, the need to engage with this powerful force in our world has become a kind of spiritual injunction as well. The central question—central for the survival and well-being of our world—is how we can make the wonderful developments of science into something that offers altruistic and compassionate service for the needs of humanity and the other sentient beings with whom we share this earth.

Do ethics have a place in science? I believe they do. First of all, like any instrument, science can be put to good use or bad. It is the state of mind of the person wielding the instrument that determines to what end it will be put. Second, scientific discoveries affect the way we understand the world and our place in it. This has consequences for our behavior. For example, the mechanistic understanding of the world led to the Industrial Revolution, in which the exploitation of nature became the standard practice. There is, however, a general assumption that ethics are relevant to only the application of science, not the actual pursuit of science. In this model the scientist as an individual and the community of scientists in general occupy a morally neutral position, with no responsibility for the fruits of what they have discovered. But many important scientific discoveries, and particularly the technological innovations they lead to, create new conditions and open up new possibilities which give rise to new ethical and spiritual challenges. We cannot simply absolve the scientific enterprise and individual scientists from responsibility for contributing to the emergence of a new reality.

Perhaps the most important point is to ensure that science never becomes divorced from the basic human feeling of empathy with our fellow beings. Just as one's fingers can function only in relation to the palm, so scientists must remain aware of their connection to society at large. Science is vitally important, but it is only one finger of the hand of humanity, and its greatest potential can be actualized only so long as we are careful to remember this. Otherwise, we risk losing our sense of priorities. Humanity may end up serving the interests of scientific progress rather than the other way around. Science and technology are powerful tools, but we must decide how best to use them. What matters above all is the motivation that governs the use of science and technology, in which ideally heart and mind are united.

For me, science is first and foremost an empirical discipline that provides humanity with a powerful access to understanding the nature of the physical and living world. It is essentially a mode of inquiry that gives us fantastically detailed knowledge of the empirical world and the underlying laws of nature, which we infer from the empirical data. Science proceeds by means of a very specific method that involves measurement, quantification, and inter-subjective verification through repeatable experiments. This, at least, is the nature of scientific method as it exists within the current paradigm. Within this model, many aspects of human existence, including values, creativity, and spirituality, as well as deeper metaphysical questions, lie outside the scope of scientific inquiry.

Though there are areas of life and knowledge outside the domain of science, I have noticed that many people hold an assumption that the scientific view of the world should be the basis for all knowledge and all that is knowable. This is scientific materialism. Although I am not aware of a school of thought that explicitly propounds this notion, it seems to be a common unexamined presupposition. This view upholds a belief in an objective world, independent of the contingency of its observers. It assumes that the data being analyzed within an experiment are independent of the preconceptions, perceptions, and experience of the scientist analyzing them.

Underlying this view is the assumption that, in the final analysis, matter, as it can be described by physics and as it is governed by the laws of physics, is all there is. Accordingly, this view would uphold that psychology can be reduced to biology, biology to chemistry, and chemistry to physics. My concern here is not so much to argue against this reductionist position (although I myself do not share it) but to draw attention to a vitally important point: that these ideas do not constitute scientific knowledge; rather they represent a philosophical, in fact a metaphysical, position. The view that all aspects of reality can be reduced to matter and its various particles is, to my mind, as much a metaphysical position as the view that an organizing intelligence created and controls reality.

One of the principal problems with a radical scientific materialism is the narrowness of vision that results and the potential for nihilism that might ensue. Nihilism, materialism, and reductionism are above all problems from a philosophical and especially a human perspective, since they can potentially impoverish the way we see ourselves. For example, whether we see ourselves as random biological creatures or as special beings endowed with the dimension of consciousness and moral capacity will make an impact on how we feel about ourselves and treat others. In this view many dimensions of the full reality of what it is to be human—art, ethics, spirituality, goodness, beauty, and above all, consciousness—either are reduced to the chemical reactions of firing neurons or are seen as a matter of purely imaginary constructs. The danger then is that human beings may be reduced to nothing more than biological machines, the products of pure chance in the random combination of genes, with no purpose other than the biological imperative of reproduction.

It is difficult to see how questions such as the meaning of life or good and evil can be accommodated within such a worldview. The problem is not with the empirical data of science but with the contention that these data alone constitute the legitimate ground for developing a comprehensive worldview or an adequate means for responding to the world's problems. There is more to human existence and to reality itself than current science can ever give us access to.

By the same token, spirituality must be tempered by the insights and discoveries of science. If as spiritual practitioners we ignore the discoveries of science, our practice is also impoverished, as this mind-set can lead to fundamentalism. This is one of the reasons I encourage my Buddhist colleagues to undertake the study of science, so that its insights can be integrated into the Buddhist worldview.

Looking back over my seventy years of life, I see that my personal encounter with science began in an almost entirely prescientific world where the technological seemed miraculous. I suppose my fascination for science still rests in an innocent amazement at the wonders of what it can achieve. From these beginnings my journey into science has led me into issues of great complexity, such as science's impact on our understanding of the world, its power to transform human lives and the very earth we live on, and the awesome moral dilemmas which its new findings have posed. Yet one cannot and should not forget the wonder and the beauty of what has been made possible.

The insights of science have enriched many aspects of my own Buddhist worldview. Einstein's theory of relativity, with its vivid thought experiments, has given an empirically tested texture to my grasp of Nagarjuna's theory of the relativity of time. The extraordinarily detailed picture of the behavior of subatomic particles at the minutest levels imaginable brings home the Buddha's teaching on the dynamically transient nature of all things. The discovery of the genome all of us share throws into sharp relief the Buddhist view of the fundamental equality of all human beings.

What is the place of science in the totality of human endeavor? It has investigated everything from the smallest amoeba to the complex neurobiological system of human beings, from the creation of the universe and the emergence of life on earth to the very nature of matter and energy. Science has been spectacular in exploring reality. It has not only revolutionized our knowledge but opened new avenues of knowing. It has begun to make inroads into the complex question of consciousness—the key characteristic that makes us sentient. The question is whether science can provide a comprehensive understanding of the entire spectrum of reality and human existence.

From the Buddhist perspective, a full human understanding must not only offer a coherent account of reality, our means of apprehending it, and the place of consciousness but also include a clear awareness of how we should act. In the current paradigm of science, only knowledge derived through a strictly empirical method underpinned by observation, inference, and experimental verification can be considered valid. This method involves the use of quantification and measurement, repeatability, and confirmation by others. Many aspects of reality as well as some key elements of human existence, such as the ability to distinguish between good and evil, spirituality, artistic creativity—some of the things we most value about human beings—inevitably fall outside the scope of the method. Scientific knowledge, as it stands today, is not complete. Recognizing this fact, and clearly recognizing the limits of scientific knowledge, I believe, is essential. Only by such recognition can we genuinely appreciate the need to integrate science within the totality of human knowledge. Otherwise our conception of the world, including our own existence, will be limited to the facts adduced by science, leading to a deeply reductionist, materialistic, even nihilistic worldview.

My difficulty is not with reductionism as such. Indeed, many of our great advances have been made by applying the reductionist approach that characterizes so much scientific experimentation and analysis. The problem arises when reductionism, which is essentially a method, is turned into a metaphysical standpoint. Understandably this reflects a common tendency to conflate the means with the end, especially when a specific method is highly effective. In a powerful image, a Buddhist text reminds us that when someone points his finger at the moon, we should direct our gaze not at the tip of the finger but at the moon to which it is pointing.

Scientists have a special responsibility, a moral responsibility, in ensuring that science serves the interests of humanity in the best possible way. What they do in their specific disciplines has the power to affect the lives of all of us. For whatever historical reasons, scientists have come to enjoy a much higher level of public trust than other professionals. It is true, however, that this trust is no longer an absolute faith. There have been too many tragedies related either directly or indirectly to science and technology for the trust in science to remain unconditional. In my own lifetime, we need only think of Hiroshima, Chernobyl, Three Mile Island, or Bhopal in terms of nuclear or chemical disasters, and of the degradation of the environment—including the depletion of the ozone layer—among ecological crises.

My plea is that we bring our spirituality, the full richness and simple wholesomeness of our basic human values, to bear upon the course of science and the direction of technology in human society. In essence, science and spirituality, though differing in their approaches, share the same end, which is the betterment of humanity. At its best, science is motivated by a quest for understanding to help lead us to greater flourishing and happiness. In Buddhist language, this kind of science can be described as wisdom grounded in and tempered by compassion. Similarly, spirituality is a human journey into our internal resources, with the aim of understanding who we are in the deepest sense and of discovering how to live according to the highest possible idea. This too is the union of wisdom and compassion.

Since the emergence of modern science, humanity has lived through an engagement between spirituality and science as two important sources of knowledge and well-being. Sometimes the relationship has been a close one—a kind of friendship—while at other times it has been frosty, with many finding the two to be incompatible. Today, in the first decade of the twenty-first century, science and spirituality have the potential to be closer than ever, and to embark upon a collaborative endeavor that has far-reaching potential to help humanity meet the challenges before us. We are all in this together. May each of us, as a member of the human family, respond to the moral obligation to make this collaboration possible. This is my heartfelt plea.

The Irrationality of Atheism

G. K. CHESTERTON

Is human thought valid? G. K. Chesterton (1874–1936), one of Britain's most influential thinkers and prolific writers in the early decades of the twentieth century, explores this question along with many others. As a journalist and social critic, he was known to probe the edges of ideas and question the issues he was most passionate about.

This is certainly true in Orthodoxy, *from which the selection is taken. Employing a winsome, down-to-earth style—one that doesn't take himself too seriously—Chesterton looks into his own religious explanations for faith, set on a backdrop of an analytical and expressive intellect. He expounds on the collaboration of faith and reason like this, "It is idle to talk always of the alternative of reason and faith. Reason is itself a matter of faith. It is an act of faith to assert that our thoughts have any relation to reality at all."*

The Suicide of Thought

THE PHRASES OF the street are not only forcible but subtle: for a figure of speech can often get into a crack too small for a definition. Phrases like "put out" or "off color" might have been coined by Mr. Henry James in an agony of verbal precision. And there is no more subtle truth than that of the everyday phrase about a man having "his heart in the right place." It involves the idea of normal proportion; not only does a certain function exist, but it is rightly related to other functions. Indeed, the negation of this phrase would describe with peculiar accuracy the somewhat morbid mercy and perverse tenderness of the most representative moderns. If, for instance, I had to describe with fairness the character of Mr. Bernard Shaw, I could not express myself more exactly than by saying that he has a heroically large and generous heart; but not a heart in the right place. And this is so of the typical society of our time.

The modern world is not evil; in some ways the modern world is far too good. It is full of wild and wasted virtues. When a religious scheme is shattered (as Christianity was shattered at the Reformation), it is not merely the vices that are let loose. The vices are, indeed, let loose, and they wander and do damage. But the virtues are let loose also; and the virtues wander more wildly, and the virtues do more terrible damage. The modern world is full of the old Christian virtues gone mad. The virtues have gone mad because they have been isolated from each other and are wandering alone. Thus some scientists care for truth; and their truth is pitiless. Thus some humanitarians only care for pity; and their pity (I am sorry to say) is often untruthful. For example, Mr. Blatchford attacks Christianity because he is mad on one Christian virtue: the merely mystical and almost irrational virtue of charity. He has a strange idea that he will make it easier to forgive sins by saying that there are no sins to forgive. Mr. Blatchford is not only an early Christian, he is the only early Christian who ought really to have been eaten by lions. For in his case the pagan accusation is really true: his mercy would mean mere anarchy. He really is the enemy of the human race—because he is so human. As the other extreme, we may take the acrid realist, who has deliberately killed in himself all human pleasure in happy tales or in the healing of the heart. Torquemada tortured people physically for the sake of moral truth. Zola tortured people morally for the sake of physical truth. But in Torquemada's time there was at least a system that could to some extent make righteousness and peace kiss each other. Now they do not even bow. But a much stronger case than these two of truth and pity can be found in the remarkable case of the dislocation of humility.

It is only with one aspect of humility that we are here concerned. Humility was largely meant as a restraint upon the arrogance and infinity of the appetite of man. He was always outstripping his mercies with his own newly invented needs. His very power of enjoyment destroyed half his joys. By asking for pleasure he lost the chief pleasure; for the chief pleasure is surprise. Hence it became evident that if a man would make his world large, he must be always making himself small. Even the haughty visions, the tall cities, and the toppling pinnacles are the creations of humility. Giants that tread down forests like grass are the creations of humility. Towers that vanish upwards above the loneliest star are the creations of humility.

For towers are not tall unless we look up at them: and giants are not giants unless they are larger than we. All this gigantesque imagination, which is, perhaps, the mightiest of the pleasures of man, is at bottom entirely humble. It is impossible without humility to enjoy anything—even pride.

But what we suffer from to-day is humility in the wrong place. Modesty has moved from the organ of ambition. Modesty has settled upon the organ of conviction; where it was never meant to be. A man was meant to be doubtful about himself, but undoubting about the truth; this has been exactly reversed. Nowadays the part of a man that a man does assert is exactly the part he ought not to assert—himself. The part he doubts is exactly the part he ought not to doubt—the Divine Reason. Huxley preached a humility content to learn from Nature. But the new skeptic is so humble that he doubts if he can even learn. Thus we should be wrong if we had said hastily that there is no humility typical of our time. The truth is that there is a real humility typical of our time; but it so happens that it is practically a more poisonous humility than the wildest prostrations of the ascetic. The old humility was a spur that prevented a man from stopping; not a nail in his boot that prevented him from going on. For the old humility made a man doubtful about his efforts, which might make him work harder. But the new humility makes a man doubtful about his aims, which will make him stop working altogether.

At any street corner we may meet a man who utters the frantic and blasphemous statement that he may be wrong. Every day one comes across somebody who says that of course his view may not be the right one. Of course his view must be the right one, or it is not his view. We are on the road to producing a race of men too mentally modest to believe in the multiplication table. We are in danger of seeing philosophers who doubt the law of gravity as being a mere fancy of their own. Scoffers of old time were too proud to be convinced; but these are too humble to be convinced. The meek do inherit the earth; but the modern skeptics are too meek even to claim their inheritance. It is exactly this intellectual helplessness which is our second problem.

The last chapter has been concerned only with a fact of observation: that what peril or morbidity there is for man comes rather from his reason than his imagination. It was not meant to attack the authority of reason; rather it is the ultimate purpose to defend it. For it needs defense. The whole modern world is at war with reason; and the tower already reels.

The sages, it is often said, can see no answer to the riddle of religion. But the trouble with our sages is not that they cannot see the answer; it is that they cannot even see the riddle. They are like children so stupid as to notice nothing paradoxical in the playful assertion that a door is not a door. The modern latitudinarians speak, for instance, about authority in religion not only as if there were no reason in it, but as if there had never been any reason for it. Apart from seeing its philosophical basis, they cannot even see its historical cause. Religious authority has often, doubtless, been oppressive or unreasonable; just as every legal system (and especially our present one) has been callous and full of a cruel apathy. It is rational to attack the police; nay, it is glorious. But the modern critics of religious authority are like men who should attack the police without ever having heard of burglars. For there is a great and possible peril to the human mind: a peril as practical as burglary. Against it religious authority was reared, rightly or wrongly, as a barrier. And against it something certainly must be reared as a barrier, if our race is to avoid ruin.

That peril is that the human intellect is free to destroy itself. Just as one generation could prevent the very existence of the next generation, by all entering a monastery or jumping into the sea, so one set of thinkers can in some degree prevent further thinking by teaching the next generation that there is no validity in any human thought. It is idle to talk always of the alternative of reason and faith. Reason is itself a matter of faith. It is an act of faith to assert that our thoughts have any relation to reality at all. If you are merely a skeptic, you must sooner or later ask yourself the question, "Why should *anything* go right; even observation and deduction? Why should not good logic be as misleading as bad logic? They are both movements in the brain of a bewildered ape?" The young skeptic says, "I have a right to think for myself." But the old skeptic, the complete skeptic, says, "I have no right to think for myself. I have no right to think at all."

There is a thought that stops thought. That is the only thought that ought to be stopped. That is the ultimate evil against which all religious authority was aimed. It only appears at the end of decadent ages like our own: and already Mr. H. G. Wells has raised its ruinous banner; he has written a delicate piece of skepticism called "Doubts of the Instrument." In this he questions the brain itself, and endeavors to remove all reality from all his own assertions, past, present, and to come. But it was against this remote ruin that all the military systems in religion were originally ranked and ruled. The creeds and the crusades, the hierarchies and the horrible persecutions were not organized, as is ignorantly said, for the suppression of reason. They were organized for the difficult defense of reason. Man, by a blind instinct, knew that if once things were wildly questioned, reason could be questioned first. The authority of priests to absolve, the authority of popes to define the authority, even of the inquisitors to terrify: these were all only dark defenses erected round one central authority, more undemonstrable, more supernatural than all—the authority of a man to think. We know now that this is so; we have no excuse for not knowing it. For we can hear skepticism crashing through the old ring of authorities, and at the same moment we can see reason swaying upon her throne. In so far as religion is gone, reason is going. For they are both of the same primary and authoritative kind. They are both methods of proof which cannot themselves be proved. And in the act of destroying the idea of Divine authority we have largely destroyed the idea of that human authority by which we do a long-division sum. With a long and sustained tug we have attempted to pull the mitre off pontifical man; and his head has come off with it.

Lest this should be called loose assertion, it is perhaps desirable, though dull, to run rapidly through the chief modern fashions of thought which have this effect of stopping thought itself. Materialism and the view of everything as a personal illusion have some such effect; for if the mind is mechanical, thought cannot be very exciting, and if the cosmos is unreal, there is nothing to think about. But in these cases the effect is indirect and doubtful. In some cases it is direct and clear; notably in the case of what is generally called evolution.

Evolution is a good example of that modern intelligence which, if it destroys anything, destroys itself. Evolution is either an innocent scientific description of how certain earthly things came about; or, if it is anything more than this, it is an attack upon thought itself. If evolution destroys anything, it does not destroy religion but rationalism. If evolution simply means that a positive thing called an ape turned very slowly into a positive thing called a man, then it

is stingless for the most orthodox; for a personal God might just as well do things slowly as quickly, especially if, like the Christian God, he were outside time. But if it means something more, it means that there is no such thing as an ape to change, and no such thing as a man for him to change into. It means that there is no such thing as a thing. At best, there is only one thing, and that is the flux of everything and anything. This is an attack not upon the faith, but upon the mind; you cannot think if there are no things to think about. You cannot think if you are not separate from the subject of thought. Descartes said, "I think; therefore I am." The philosophic evolutionist reverses and negatives the epigram. He says, "I am not; therefore I cannot think."

Then there is the opposite attack on thought: that urged by Mr. H. G. Wells when he insists that every separate thing is "unique," and there are no categories at all. This also is merely destructive. Thinking means connecting things, and stops if they cannot be connected. It need hardly be said that this skepticism forbidding thought necessarily forbids speech; a man cannot open his mouth without contradicting it. Thus when Mr. Wells says (as he did somewhere), "All chairs are quite different," he utters not merely a misstatement, but a contradiction in terms. If all chairs were quite different, you could not call them "all chairs."

Akin to these is the false theory of progress, which maintains that we alter the test instead of trying to pass the test. We often hear it said, for instance, "What is right in one age is wrong in another." This is quite reasonable, if it means that there is a fixed aim, and that certain methods attain at certain times and not at other times. If women, say, desire to be elegant, it may be that they are improved at one time by growing fatter and at another time by growing thinner. But you cannot say that they are improved by ceasing to wish to be elegant and beginning to wish to be oblong. If the standard changes, how can there be improvement, which implies a standard? Nietzsche started a nonsensical idea that men had once sought as good what we now call evil; if it were so, we could not talk of surpassing them or even falling short of them. How can you overtake Jones if you walk in the other direction? You cannot discuss whether one people has succeeded more in being miserable than another succeeded in being happy. It would be like discussing whether Milton was more puritanical than a pig is fat.

It is true that a man (a silly man) might make change itself his object or ideal. But as an ideal, change itself becomes unchangeable. If the change-worshipper wishes to estimate his own progress, he must be sternly loyal to the ideal of change; he must not begin to flirt gaily with the ideal of monotony. Progress itself cannot be progress. It is worth remark, in passing, that when Tennyson, in a wild and rather weak manner, welcomed the idea of infinite alteration in society, he instinctively took a metaphor which suggests an imprisoned tedium. He wrote—

> Let the great world spin for ever down the ringing grooves of change.

He thought of change itself as an unchangeable groove; and so it is. Change is about the narrowest and hardest groove that a man can get into.

The main point here, however, is that this idea of a fundamental alteration in the standard is one of the things that make thought about the past or future simply impossible. The theory of a complete change of standards in human history does not merely deprive us of the pleasure of honoring our fathers; it deprives us even of the more modern and aristocratic pleasure of despising him.

This bald summary of the thought-destroying forces of our time would not be complete without some reference to pragmatism; for though I have here used and should everywhere defend the pragmatist method as a preliminary guide to truth, there is an extreme application of it which involves the absence of all truth whatever. My meaning can be put shortly thus. I agree with the pragmatists that apparent objective truth is not the whole matter; that there is an authoritative need to believe the things that are necessary to the human mind. But I say that one of those necessities precisely is a belief in objective truth. The pragmatist tells a man to think what he must think and never mind the Absolute. But precisely one of the things that he must think is the Absolute. This philosophy, indeed, is a kind of verbal paradox. Pragmatism is a matter of human needs; and one of the first of human needs is to be something more than a pragmatist. Extreme pragmatism is just as inhuman as the determinism it so powerfully attacks. The determinist (who, to do him justice, does

not pretend to be a human being) makes nonsense of the human sense of actual choice. The pragmatist, who professes to be specially human, makes nonsense of the human sense of actual fact.

To sum up our contention so far, we may say that the most characteristic current philosophies have not only a touch of mania, but a touch of suicidal mania. The mere questioner has knocked his head against the limits of human thought; and cracked it. This is what makes so futile the warnings of the orthodox and the boasts of the advanced about the dangerous boyhood of free thought. What we are looking at is not the boyhood of free thought; it is the old age and ultimate dissolution of free thought. It is vain for bishops and pious bigwigs to discuss what dreadful things will happen if wild skepticism runs its course. It has run its course. It is vain for eloquent atheists to talk of the great truths that will be revealed if once we see free thought begin. We have seen it end. It has no more questions to ask; it has questioned itself. You cannot call up any wilder vision than a city in which men ask themselves if they have any selves. You cannot fancy a more skeptical world than that in which men doubt if there is a world. It might certainly have reached its bankruptcy more quickly and cleanly if it had not been hampered by the application of indefensible laws of blasphemy or by the absurd pretence that modern England is now Christian. But it would have reached the bankruptcy anyhow. Militant atheists are still unjustly persecuted; but rather because they are an old minority than because they are a new one. Free thought has exhausted its own freedom. It is weary of its own success. If any eager freethinker now hails philosophic freedom as the dawn, he is only like the man in Mark Twain who came out wrapped in blankets to see the sun rise and was just in time to see it set. If any frightened curate still says that it will be awful if the darkness of free thought spread, we can only answer him in the high and powerful words of Mr. Belloc, "Do not, I beseech you, be troubled about the increase of forces already in dissolution. You have mistaken the hour of the night: it is already morning." We have no more questions left to ask. We have looked for questions in the darkest corners and on the wildest peaks. We have found all the questions that can be found. It is time we gave up looking for questions and began looking for answers.

HANS KÜNG

As a distinguished Swiss-Catholic theologian, Hans Küng (1928–) is currently the president of the Foundation for a Global Ethic and professor emeritus at the University of Tübingen. An accomplished writer, he has authored more than fifty books. By his peers he is considered both influential and controversial. In 1962, then Pope John XXIII appointed Küng to serve as a theologian to the Second Vatican Council.

A probing intellectual, Küng wrote a very lengthy treatise on theology entitled On Being a Christian*—720 pages long! In addition to his keen interest in theology, he has also pursued other popular subjects, like critiquing the philosophy of those who have shaped modern thinking. Küng has written a cogent analysis examining Sigmund Freud's religion and philosophy. Primary to Freud's belief about religion is the phrase "wish-fulfillment." In this piece from* Freud and the Problem of God*, Küng tackles Freud's idea head-on and draws some conclusions to stimulate the reader.*

Religion—Merely Wishful Thinking?

Historically and biographically there can be no doubt that Freud was an atheist from his student years. He was an atheist long before he became a psychoanalyst. Consequently Freud's atheism was not grounded in his psychoanalysis, but preceded it. This too is what Freud constantly maintained, that psychoanalysis does not necessarily lead to atheism. It is a method of investigation and healing and can be practiced by both atheists and theists. And for that very reason Freud the atheist defends himself against the charge of extrapolating an atheistic Weltanschauung from a "neutral working tool." Methodological "atheism" must not be turned into ideological atheism; psychoanalysis cannot be made into a total explanation of reality.

Freud *took over from Feuerbach and his successors* the essential arguments for his personal atheism: "All I have done—and this is the only thing that is new in my exposition—is to add some psychological foundation to the criticisms of my great predecessors," says Freud both modestly and rightly.[1] Even Feuerbach had produced a psychological substantiation of atheism: wishes, fantasies, or the power of imagination are responsible for the projection of the idea of God and of the whole religious pseudo- or dream-world. Like Marx's opium theory at an earlier stage, Freud's illusion theory is grounded in Feuerbach's projection theory. What is essentially new is merely Freud's psychoanalytical reinforcement of Feuerbach's theory.

This means, however, that for the critique of Freud's atheism as well the arguments that can be adduced against Feuerbach's (and Marx's) atheism, particularly against the evidence drawn from psychology and philosophy of religion, are valid. And insofar as Feuerbach's (and Marx's) atheism has turned out to be a hypothesis which in the last resort has not been conclusively proved, so too must Freud's atheism now, in the last resort, be seen as a *hypothesis which has not been conclusively proved*.

Of course, Freud has asked about the background of Feuerbach's psychological projection theory and applied the tests of depth psychology to its unconscious assumptions. Hence he was able to give greater depth to this hypothesis in the light of the history of religion and then of psychology of religion. But by this means Freud has no more provided an independent substantiation for the projection theory than Marx did. For Freud had *taken for granted* this projection theory (apparently irrefutably substantiated by his "great predecessors") and then had asked, and tried to show, how it could be explained in the light of the history of religion and the psychology of religion. And it is precisely this assumption which turns out in the last resort to be without foundation.

It is to Freud's immense credit that he worked out how much the unconscious determines the individual human being and the history of mankind, how fundamental are even the earliest childhood years, the first parent-child relationships, and the approach to sexuality for a person's religious attitudes and ideas as well. But we have to see very clearly in connection with Feuerbach, Marx, and Freud that from the indisputable influence of *psychological* (or economic or social) factors on religion and the idea of God no conclusions can be drawn about the existence or nonexistence of God.

We may put this in a more concrete summary form by referring to Freud's main statement on the critique of religion: "Religious ideas are fulfillments of the oldest, strongest, and most urgent wishes of mankind." This is quite true, as the believer in God can also say. And he will admit at the same time:

> Religion, as Marx shows, can certainly be opium, a means of social assuagement and consolation (repression). But it need not be.
>
> Religion, as Freud shows, can certainly be an illusion, the expression of a neurosis and psychological immaturity (regression). But it need not be.

All human believing, hoping, loving—related to a person, a thing, or God—certainly contains an element of projection. But its object need not, for that reason, be a mere projection. Belief in God can certainly be very greatly influenced by the attitude of the child to its father. But this does not mean that God may not exist.

Consequently the problem does not lie in the fact that belief in God can be psychologically explained. It is not a question of a choice for or against psychology. From the psychological standpoint belief in God always exhibits the structure and content of a projection or can be under suspicion of being a mere projection. It is the same with lovers: every lover necessarily projects his own image of her on to the beloved. But does this mean that his beloved does not exist or at any rate does not exist substantially as he sees her and thinks of her? With the aid of his projections can he not even understand her more profoundly than someone who tries as a neutral observer to judge her from outside? The mere fact of projection, therefore, does not decide the existence or nonexistence of the object to which it refers.

It is at this point that the Freudian argument from the abnormal to the normal, from the neurotic to the religious—however well justified—finds its essential limitations. Is religion human *wishful thinking*? And must God for that reason be merely a human wishful structure, an infantile illusion or even a purely neurotic delusion? As we have argued elsewhere against Feuerbach, a real God may certainly correspond to the wish for God. This possibility is one which even Freud did not exclude. And why should wishful thinking be entirely and universally discredited? Is not wishing wholly and entirely human, wishing in small matters or in great, wishing in regard to the goods of this world, in regard to our fellowmen, to the world, and perhaps also in regard to God?

Of course, religious belief would be in a bad way if there were no genuine grounds for it or if no grounds remained after a psychoanalytic treatment of the subject; however devout its appearance, such a faith would be immature, infantile, and perhaps even neurotic. But is a faith bad and its truth dubious simply because—like psychoanalysis itself—it also involves all possible instinctual motivations, lustful inclinations, psycho-dynamic mechanisms, conscious and unconscious desires? Why in fact should I not be permitted to wish? Why should I not be allowed to wish that the sweat, blood, and tears, all the suffering of millennia, may not have been in vain, that definitive happiness may finally be possible for all men—especially the despised and downtrodden? And why should I not on the other hand fell an aversion to being required to be satisfied with rare moments of happiness and—for the rest—to come to terms with "normal unhappiness"? May I not too feel aversion to the idea that the life of the individual and of mankind is ruled only by pitiless laws of nature, by the play of chance and by the survival of the fittest, and that all dying is a dying into nothingness?[2]

It does not follow—as some theologians have mistakenly concluded—from man's profound desire for God and eternal life that God exists and eternal life and happiness are real. But those atheists who think that what follows is the nonexistence of God and the unreality of eternal life are mistaken too. It is true that the wish alone does not contain within itself its fulfillment. It *may* be that nothing corresponds to the oldest, strongest, and most urgent wishes of mankind and that mankind has actually been cherishing illusions for millennia. Just like a child who in its solitude, forsakenness, distress, and need for happiness wishes wholeheartedly, longs, imagines, and fantasizes that it might have a father in some distant Russian camp, cherishes illusions, gives way to self-deception, pursues wish images, unless . . . unless? Unless the father, long assumed to be dead, whom the child knows only from hearsay, had by some chance remained alive and—although no one believed it any longer—still existed. Then—then indeed—the child would actually be right against the many who did not believe in the father's existence. Then there would in fact be a reality corresponding to the child's wishful thinking and one day perhaps it might be seen face-to-face.

Here, then, we have reached the crux of the problem, which is not at all difficult to understand and in the face of which any kind of projection theory, opium theory, or illusion theory momentarily loses its suggestive power. Perhaps this being of our longings and dreams does actually exist. Perhaps this being who promises us eternal bliss does exist. Not only the bliss of the baby at its mother's breast—which, according to Freud, permanently determines a person's unconscious—but a quite different reality in the future which corresponds to the unconscious and conscious aspirations precisely of the mature, adult human being and to which the oldest, strongest, most urgent wishes of mankind are oriented, which can fulfill our longing for infinite happiness. Perhaps. Who knows?

Freud's explanation of the psychological genesis of belief in God did not refute this faith itself. Freud analyzed and deduced these religious ideas psychologically. And this is precisely what theologians and churchmen should never have denied him or Feuerbach the right to do at an earlier stage. For it is possible and also legitimate to give a psychological interpretation of belief in God. But is the psychological aspect itself the whole of religion? It must be observed that Freud has not in fact destroyed and refuted religious ideas in principle and neither atheists nor theologians should ever have read this into Freud's critique of religion. For psychological interpretation alone, from its very nature, cannot penetrate to the absolutely final or first reality: as to what this reality is it remains neutral in principle. From the psychological standpoint—and even the positive force of the argument must not be overestimated—the existence of God must remain an open question.

Freud's atheism, of which he was quite certain long before any of his psychological discoveries, thus turns out to be a pure hypothesis, an unproved postulate, a dogmatic claim. And at bottom Freud was well aware of this. For religious ideas, though incredible, are for him also irrefutable. In principle they might also be true. Even for him, what has to be said of their psychological nature by no means decides their truth content and truth value. We have heard his answer: "We tell ourselves, it would indeed be fine . . . , but . . ."

Faith in Science

For Freud belief in God is replaced by belief in science, "our god logos,"[3] in which he finds the "sure support" which is "lacking" to believers in God.[4] We see how emphatically Freud, fully aware of the inadequacy of man and of his progress, nevertheless confessed his faith: "We believe that it is possible for scientific work to gain some knowledge about the reality of the world . . ."[5] And how emphatically he forswore unbelief: "No, our science is no illusion."[6]

Can faith in science replace faith in God? We cannot explain here what we would have to say about the modern ideal of knowledge, natural science, and the question of God; this position would certainly not be opposed to a critical rationality, but it would definitely be against an ideological rationalism. In any case, we have to draw attention to the fact that, contrary to Freud's prophecy, neither in the West nor in the East has belief in God yet disappeared to make way for science; particularly after the experience of National Socialism and of communism, modern atheism has lost much of its credibility. But for innumerable people throughout the world belief in God has gained a new future, particularly in our time. Both Feuerbach's anthropological atheism and Marx's social-political atheism, as well as Freud's psychoanalytical atheism, are still far from gaining universal acceptance. Freud's thesis, then, of the supersession of religion by science turns out to be an assertion without any apparent foundation: an extrapolation into the future which even today, in retrospect, cannot in any way be verified.

On the other hand, for a long time we have ceased to take every advance in science—as was assumed in Freud's student years—as a contradiction to belief in God. And among natural scientists and psychologists also the question is asked whether the core of belief in God has really been affected by the progress of science up to now and by the corrections which were, to be sure, necessarily involved in it. Is there really an essential contradiction between science and belief in God?

Meanwhile, however, the very progress of science has involved it in a crisis far greater than what Freud—for all his skepticism in regard to progress—anticipated. The indubitable progress of science in all fields leads many today, particularly in industrial nations, to doubt this faith in science, which was held also by Freud—the belief that science, and the technology resulting from it, automatically implies progress and is thus the key to that universal happiness of mankind which, according to Freud, is not provided by religion. On the other hand, it is possible today to point to the ambivalent character of this progress of science and technology, which so easily evades any kind of human control and now spreads a fear of the future often amounting to apocalyptic terror.[7] Freud himself had only a limited confidence in progress. He was not certain of the future of our civilization; he regarded as highly dangerous the force of the death-instinct and excessive accumulation of the potential of aggression. For him the struggle between reason and destruction was far from being decided.[8]

The ideology which maintains that the progress of scientific development leads of itself to a more human outlook has now been shattered anyway. This progress had been in many ways a destructive influence, a rationality bearing irrational feature, a god "logos" which has increasingly turned out to be an idol. Scientists will still rightly insist on a continual concern for science and technology and consequently also for human progress in great things and in small. But even they think that belief in science as a total explanation of reality, as a Weltanschauung, must be abandoned. Technology must no longer be regarded as a substitute religion providing a cure for all evils. The euphoria of progress as an ideology must be abandoned; the illusion that everything can be planned, of total feasibility, must be given up. From this standpoint, for many people and even for many scientists, there arises a question which is the very opposite of the one that faces Freud: might not ethics and religion themselves prove helpful in the quest for a new synthesis between controlled technical progress and a human existence liberated from the pressures of progress? Such a synthesis would comprise not only a more just social structure, more humane working conditions, greater closeness to nature, but also the satisfaction of man's nonmaterial needs, those values that is, which alone make human life worth living, which alone make it truly human.

Nevertheless, it would be wrong in principle to exploit the now widespread skepticism in regard to science and technology for theological advantage. Not every step away from scientific credulity is a step toward theistic piety. Skepticism toward science and technology is far from being a foundation for belief in God.

Theologians must recognize the fact that today there are many people who reject an ideologizing of science as a total explanation of reality, but who are equally skeptical when it comes to belief in God. There are today many people who no longer fight passionately for their atheistic convictions, but they are even less inclined to speak out passionately for a belief in God. Between skepticism and affirmation we now find all too often not indeed a militant atheism, but one that is practical, everyday, and banal.

Justification of Freud's Critique of Religion

But, over and above the general requirement of intellectual honest and critical rationality, it must be said that the *relative justification of Freud's specific critique of religion* can no more be disputed than that of similar attempts on the part of Feuerbach and Marx. What Feuerbach wanted from the philosophical standpoint and Marx from the political-social, Freud sought from the standpoint of depth psychology: emancipation, comprehensive liberation, more humanity on the part of man. It meant in particular opposition to tutelage, domination, oppression by religion, Church, God himself. Was all this entirely wrong? To bring out its concrete meaning, a few points may be mentioned here—which incidentally can be substantiated also from Adler or Jung.

Freud rightly criticizes defective *forms of religion*. Christians should admit in a spirit of self-criticism:

> When religion is completely concentrated on the "wholly Other," contact with reality is inevitably lost. Religious questions thus easily become a form of self-deception and escapism. Religion becomes an infantile commitment, without regard to reality, to a tyrannical superego; God becomes displacement-substitute.
>
> When religion relies solely on wish-fulfillment and not on intrinsic truth, it is reduced to pure satisfaction of need. Such a religion is unquestionably a return to infantile structures, a regression to childish wishing.
>
> When religion is manifested in rigid fidelity to the letter, in a legalistic conscience, in obsessive, pedantic, and petty repetition of certain prayers, formulas, and rituals, religious ideas

come close to delusive fabrications, religious observances to substitute satisfaction resulting from obsessive cultic repetition. Such religious practices, which have become pointless or inadequately motivated, are often defensive and protective measures dictated by fear, guilt feelings, and tormented conscience, against certain—often unconscious—temptations and threatening punishments, just like the private ritual (for example, ablutomania) of the obsessional neurotic.

Freud also rightly criticizes *the churches' misuse of power.* The facts are well known:

> How abundant are the examples of arrogance of power and misuse of power in the history of the churches: intolerance and cruelty toward deviationists, crusades, inquisition, extermination of heretics, obsession with witches, struggle against theological research, oppression of their own theologians—right up to the present time.
>
> How over the centuries the churches have acted like a superego: dominating souls in the name of God, exploiting the dependence and immaturity of poor sinners, requiring submission to the taboos of untested authority, continually repressing sexuality and displaying contempt for women (in the law of celibacy, in excluding women from church ministries). What a heap of *ecclesiogenic neuroses:* neuroses that result from the constraints of the ecclesiastical system, clerical domination, confessional practice, sexual repression, hostility to progress and to science. There is no need to reopen here the *chronique scandaleuse* of Christianity and the churches.[9]

Freud rightly criticizes, finally, the *traditional image of God.* People are still too little aware of some of the ways in which it has been formed.

Often enough a believer's image of God springs, not from original insight and free decision, but from an *image of a vindictive or kind father* imprinted at an early age.

Often enough early childhood experiences with adults who appear as "gods" are *transferred* both positively and negatively *to*

God, so that behind the image of God the image of one's own father becomes visible, even though the latter has long been forgotten or repressed (it is the same with the mother image as reflected in the Mother of God or in Mother Church).

Often enough the vindictive Father-God is deliberately *misused* by parents *as a means of education,* in order to discipline their children, with long-term negative consequences for the religious attitudes of those children as they grow up.

Often enough *religion and sexuality* (the latter frequently repressed by religion) are knit together from the very beginning in such a way that what appear to be religious conflicts are really only fixations on the early experiences of the family-scene.

ALVIN PLANTINGA

Currently the John A. O'Brien Professor of Philosophy at the University of Notre Dame, Alvin Plantinga (1932–) is a distinguished academic, writer, and apologist. Time *magazine, in a 1980 article, characterized him as "America's leading orthodox Protestant philosopher of God," adding that he's a pivotal contributor in a "quiet revolution" which seeks to restore respectability of belief in God among academics. On three separate occasions, Plantinga has achieved the distinction of delivering the prestigious Gifford Lectures at the University of Aberdeen, Scotland.*

Arguably the most influential philosopher of religion in contemporary culture and an active participant in the current debate concerning faith and reason, Plantinga is fond of using logical argument to point out the irrationality of atheism. In the following article, he offers an evocative discussion on naturalism (the belief that "there is no such person as God or anything like God") and evolution. He dissects the popular argument that acceptance of evolution inexorably leads to a wholesale embrace of naturalism and an atheist worldview. Quite the opposite—Plantinga's "evolutionary argument against atheism" leads to the conclusion that pure naturalists must be forced to distrust the conclusions of their own intellect.

Evolution vs. Naturalism

As everyone knows, there has been a recent spate of books attacking Christian belief and religion in general. Some of these books are little more than screeds, long on vituperation but short on reasoning, long on name-calling but short on competence, long on righteous indignation but short on good sense; for the most part they are driven by hatred rather than logic. Of course there are others that are intellectually more respectable—for example Walter Sinnott-Armstrong's contribution to *God? A Debate Between a Christian and an Atheist*[1] and Michael Tooley's contribution to *Knowledge of God*.[2] Nearly all of these books have been written by philosophical naturalists. I believe it's extremely important to see that naturalism itself, despite the smug and arrogant tone of the so-called New Atheists, is in very serious philosophical hot water: one can't sensibly believe it.

Naturalism is the idea that there is no such person as God or anything like God; we might think of it as high-octane atheism or perhaps atheism-plus. It is possible to be an atheist without rising to the lofty heights (or descending to the murky depths) of naturalism. Aristotle, the ancient Stoics, and Hegel (in at least certain stages) could properly claim to be atheists, but they couldn't properly claim to be naturalists: each endorses something (Aristotle's Prime Mover, the Stoics' Nous, Hegel's Absolute) no self-respecting naturalist could tolerate.

These days naturalism is extremely fashionable in the academy; some say it is contemporary academic orthodoxy. Given the vogue for various forms of postmodern anti-realism and relativism, that may be a bit strong. Still, naturalism is certainly widespread, and it is set forth in such recent popular books as Richard Dawkins's *The Blind Watchmaker,* Daniel Dennett's *Darwin's Dangerous Idea,* and many others. Naturalists like to wrap themselves in the mantle of science, as if science in some way supports, endorses, underwrites, implies, or anyway is unusually friendly to naturalism. In particular, they often appeal to the modern theory of evolution as a reason for embracing naturalism; indeed, the subtitle of Dawkins's *Watchmaker* is "Why the Evidence of Evolution Reveals a Universe Without Design." Many seem to think that evolution is one of the pillars in the temple of naturalism (and "temple" is the right word: contemporary naturalism has certainly taken on a religious cast, with a secular priesthood as zealous to stamp out opposing views as any mullah). I propose to argue that naturalism and evolution are in conflict with each other.

I said naturalism is in philosophical hot water; this is true on several counts, but here I want to concentrate on just one—one connected with the thought that evolution supports or endorses or is in some way evidence for naturalism. As I see it, this is a whopping error: evolution and naturalism are not merely uneasy bedfellows; they are more like belligerent combatants. One can't rationally accept both evolution and naturalism; one can't rationally be an evolutionary naturalist. The problem, as several thinkers (C. S. Lewis, for example) have seen, is that naturalism, or evolutionary naturalism, seems to lead to a deep and pervasive skepticism. It leads to the conclusion that our cognitive or belief-producing faculties—memory, perception, logical insight, etc.—are unreliable and cannot be trusted to produce a preponderance of true beliefs over false. Darwin himself had worries along these lines: "With me," says Darwin, "the horrid doubt always arises whether the convictions of man's mind, which has been developed from the mind of the lower animals, are of any value or at all trustworthy. Would any one trust in the convictions of a monkey's mind, if there are any convictions in such a mind?"[3]

Clearly this doubt arises for naturalists or atheists, but not for those who believe in God. That is because if God has created us in his image, then even if he fashioned us by some evolutionary means, he would presumably want us to resemble him in being able to know; but then most of what we believe might be true even if our minds have developed from those of the lower animals. On the other hand, there is a real problem here for the evolutionary naturalist. Richard Dawkins once claimed that evolution made it possible to be an intellectually fulfilled atheist. I believe he is dead wrong: I don't think it's possible at all to be an intellectually fulfilled atheist; but in any event you can't rationally accept both evolution and naturalism.

Why not? How does the argument go?[4] The first thing to see is that naturalists are also always or almost always materialists: they think human beings are material objects, with no immaterial or spiritual soul, or self. We just are our bodies, or perhaps some part of our bodies, such as our nervous systems, or brains, or perhaps part of our brains (the right or left hemisphere, for example), or perhaps some still smaller part. So let's think of naturalism as including materialism.[5] And now let's think about beliefs from a materialist perspective. According to materialists, beliefs, along with the rest of mental life, are caused or determined by neurophysiology, by what goes on in the brain and nervous system. Neurophysiology, furthermore, also causes behavior. According to the usual story, electrical signals proceed via afferent nerves from the sense organs to the brain; there some processing goes on; then electrical impulses go via efferent nerves from the brain to other organs including muscles; in response to these signals, certain muscles contract, thus causing movement and behavior.

Now what evolution tells us (supposing it tells us the truth) is that our behavior (perhaps more exactly the behavior of our ancestors) is adaptive; since the members of our species have survived and reproduced, the behavior of our ancestors was conducive, in their environment, to survival and reproduction. Therefore the neurophysiology that caused that behavior was also adaptive; we can sensibly suppose that it is still adaptive. What evolution tells us, therefore, is that our kind of neurophysiology promotes or causes adaptive behavior, the kind of behavior that issues in survival and reproduction.

Now this same neurophysiology, according to the materialist, also causes belief. But while evolution, natural selection, rewards adaptive behavior (rewards it with survival and reproduction) and penalizes maladaptive behavior, it doesn't, as such, care a fig about true belief. As Francis Crick, the co-discoverer of the genetic code, writes in *The Astonishing Hypothesis*, "Our highly developed brains, after all, were not evolved under the pressure of discovering scientific truth, but only to enable us to be clever enough to survive and leave descendents." Taking up this theme, naturalist philosopher Patricia Churchland declares that the most important thing about the human brain is that it has evolved; hence, she says, its principal function is to enable the organism to move appropriately:

> Boiled down to essentials, a nervous system enables the organism to succeed in the four F's: feeding, fleeing, fighting, and reproducing. The principal chore of nervous systems is to get the body parts where they should be in order that the organism may survive. . . . Improvements in sensorimotor control confer an evolutionary advantage: a fancier style of representing is advantageous *so long as it is geared to the organism's way of life and enhances the organism's chances of survival* [Churchland's emphasis]. Truth, whatever that is, definitely takes the hindmost.[6]

What she means is that natural selection doesn't care about the truth or falsehood of your beliefs; it cares only about adaptive behavior. Your beliefs may all be false, ridiculously false; if your behavior is adaptive, you will survive and reproduce. Consider a frog sitting on a lily pad. A fly passes by; the frog flicks out its tongue to capture it. Perhaps the neurophysiology that causes it to do so also causes beliefs. As far as survival and reproduction is concerned, it won't matter at all what these beliefs are: if that adaptive neurophysiology causes true belief (e.g., those little black things are good to eat), fine. But if it causes false belief (e.g., if I catch the right one, I'll turn into a prince), that's fine too. Indeed, the neurophysiology in question might cause beliefs that have nothing to do with the creature's current circumstances (as in the case of our dreams); that's also fine, as long as the neurophysiology causes adaptive behavior. All that really matters, as far as survival and reproduction is concerned, is that the neurophysiology cause the right kind of behavior; whether it also causes true belief (rather than false belief) is irrelevant.

Next, to avoid interspecies chauvinism, let's not think about ourselves, but instead about a hypothetical population of creatures a lot like us, perhaps living on a distant planet. Like us, these creatures enjoy perception, memory, and reason; they form beliefs on many topics, they reason and change belief, and so on. Let's suppose, furthermore, that naturalistic evolution holds for them; that is, suppose they live in a naturalistic universe and have come to be by way of the processes postulated by contemporary evolutionary theory. What we know about these creatures, then, is that they have survived; their neurophysiology has produced adaptive behavior. But what about the truth of their beliefs? What about the reliability of their belief-producing or cognitive faculties?

What we learn from Crick and Churchland (and what is in any event obvious) is this: the fact that our hypothetical creatures have survived doesn't tell us anything at all about the truth of their beliefs or the reliability of their cognitive faculties. What it tells us is that the neurophysiology that produces those beliefs is adaptive, as is the behavior caused by that neurophysiology. But it simply doesn't matter whether the beliefs also caused by that neurophysiology are true. If they are true, excellent; but if they are false, that's fine too, provided the neurophysiology produces adaptive behavior.

So consider any particular belief on the part of one of those creatures: what is the probability that it is true? Well, what we know is that the belief in question was produced by adaptive neurophysiology, neurophysiology that produces adaptive behavior. But as we've seen, that gives us no reason to think the belief true (and none to think it false). We must suppose, therefore, that the belief in question is about as likely to be false as to be true; the probability of any particular belief's being true is in the neighborhood of 1/2. But then it is massively unlikely that the cognitive faculties of these creatures produce the preponderance of true beliefs over false required by reliability. If I have 1,000 independent beliefs, for example, and the probability of any particular belief's being true is 1/2, then the probability that 3/4 or more of these beliefs are true (certainly a modest enough requirement for reliability) will be less than 10(to the power –58). And even if I am running a modest epistemic establishment of only 100 beliefs, the probability that 3/4 of them are true, given that the probability of any one's being true is 1/2, is very low, something like .000001.[7] So the chances that these creatures' true beliefs substantially outnumber their false beliefs (even in a particular area) are small. The conclusion to be drawn is that it is exceedingly unlikely that their cognitive faculties are reliable.

But of course this same argument will also hold for us. If evolutionary naturalism is true, then the probability that our cognitive faculties are reliable is also very low. And that means that one who accepts evolutionary naturalism has a defeater for the belief that her cognitive faculties are reliable: a reason for giving up that belief, for rejecting it, for no longer holding it. If there isn't a defeater for that defeater—a defeater-defeater, we could say—she can't rationally believe that her cognitive faculties are reliable. No doubt she can't help believing that they are; no doubt she will in fact continue to believe it; but that belief will be irrational. And if she has a defeater for the reliability of her cognitive faculties, she also has a defeater for any belief she takes to be produced by those faculties—which, of course, is all of her beliefs. If she can't trust her cognitive faculties, she has a reason, with respect to each of her beliefs, to give it up. She is therefore enmeshed in a deep and bottomless skepticism. One of her beliefs, however, is her belief in evolutionary naturalism itself; so then she also has a defeater for that belief. Evolutionary naturalism, therefore—the belief in the combination of naturalism and evolution—is self-refuting, self-destructive, shoots itself in the foot. Therefore you can't rationally accept it. For all this argument shows, it may be true; but it is irrational to hold it. So the argument isn't an argument for the falsehood of evolutionary naturalism; it is instead for the conclusion that one cannot rationally believe that proposition. Evolution, therefore, far from supporting naturalism, is incompatible with it, in the sense that you can't rationally believe them both.

What sort of reception has this argument had? As you might expect, naturalists tend to be less than wholly enthusiastic about it, and many objections have been brought against it. In my opinion (which of course some people might claim is biased), none of these objections is successful.[8] Perhaps the most natural and intuitive objection goes as follows. Return to that hypothetical population of a few paragraphs back. Granted, it could be that their behavior is adaptive even though their beliefs are false; but wouldn't it be much more likely that their behavior is adaptive if their beliefs are true? And doesn't that mean that, since their behavior is in fact adaptive, their beliefs are probably true and their cognitive faculties probably reliable?

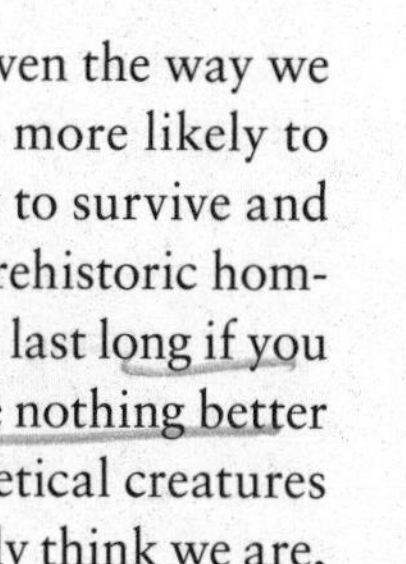

This is indeed a natural objection, in particular given the way we think about our own mental life. Of course you are more likely to achieve your goals, and of course you are more likely to survive and reproduce if your beliefs are mostly true. You are a prehistoric hominid living on the plains of Serengeti; clearly you won't last long if you believe lions are lovable overgrown pussycats who like nothing better than to be petted. So, if we assume that these hypothetical creatures are in the same kind of cognitive situation we ordinarily think we are, then certainly they would have been much more likely to survive if their cognitive faculties were reliable than if they were not.

But of course we can't just assume that they are in the same cognitive situation we think we are in. For example, we assume that our cognitive faculties are reliable. We can't sensibly assume that about this population; after all, the whole point of the argument is to show that if evolutionary naturalism is true, then very likely we and our cognitive faculties are not reliable. So reflect once more on what we know about these creatures. They live in a world in which evolutionary naturalism is true. Therefore, since they have survived and reproduced, their behavior has been adaptive. This means that the neurophysiology that caused or produced that behavior has also been adaptive: it has enabled them to survive and reproduce. But what about their beliefs? These beliefs have been produced or caused by that adaptive neurophysiology; fair enough. But that gives us no reason for supposing those beliefs true. So far as adaptiveness of their behavior goes, it doesn't matter whether those beliefs are true or false.

Suppose the adaptive neurophysiology produces true beliefs: fine; it also produces adaptive behavior, and that's what counts for survival and reproduction. Suppose on the other hand that neurophysiology produces false beliefs: again fine: it produces false beliefs but adaptive behavior. It really doesn't matter what kind of beliefs the neurophysiology produces; what matters is that it cause adaptive behavior; and this it clearly does, no matter what sort of beliefs it also produces. Therefore there is no reason to think that if their behavior is adaptive, then it is likely that their cognitive faculties are reliable.

The obvious conclusion, so it seems to me, is that evolutionary naturalism can't sensibly be accepted. The high priests of evolutionary naturalism loudly proclaim that Christian and even theistic belief is bankrupt and foolish. The fact, however, is that the shoe is on the other foot. It is evolutionary naturalism, not Christian belief, that can't rationally be accepted.

ANTONY FLEW

Once a prominent British proponent of the atheistic worldview, Antony Garrard Newton Flew (1923–) is now a believer in God, having been particularly influenced by the evidence of design in the universe. Among his colleagues in the academy, he is known as a well-established thinker in the evidentialist and analytic schools of thought for the philosophy of religion, and has taught at such distinguished universities as Oxford, Aberdeen, Keele, and Reading in the United Kingdom.

In There Is a God: How the World's Most Notorious Atheist Changed His Mind, *Flew describes his own intellectual journey to conversion and seeks to challenge the reader's preconceptions, focusing specifically on how conclusions are reached about the existence of God. Precisely because of the change in his belief system, Flew's work holds exceptional weight. He not only speaks from his breadth and depth of academic knowledge, but also from his own personal metamorphosis.*

A Pilgrimage of Reason

LET US BEGIN with a parable. Imagine that a satellite phone is washed ashore on a remote island inhabited by a tribe that has never had contact with modern civilization. The natives play with the numbers on the dial pad and hear different voices upon hitting certain sequences. They assume first that it's the device that makes these noises. Some of the cleverer natives, the scientists of the tribe, assemble an exact replica and hit the numbers again. They hear the voices again. The conclusion seems obvious to them. This particular combination of crystals and metals and chemicals produces what seems like human voices, and this means that the voices are simply properties of the device.

But the tribal sage summons the scientists for a discussion. He has thought long and hard on the matter and has reached the following conclusion: the voices coming through the instrument must be coming from people like themselves, people who are living and conscious although speaking in another language. Instead of assuming that the voices are simply properties of the handset, they should investigate the possibility that through some mysterious communication network they are "in touch" with other humans. Perhaps further study along these lines could lead to a greater understanding of the world beyond their island. But the scientists simply laugh at the sage and say: "Look, when we damage the instrument, the voices stop coming. So they're obviously nothing more than sounds produced by a unique combination of lithium and printed circuit boards and light-emitting diodes."

In this parable we see how easy it is to let preconceived theories shape the way we view evidence instead of letting the evidence shape our theories. A Copernician leap may thus be prevented by a thousand Ptolemaic epicycles. (Defenders of Ptolemy's geocentric model of the solar system resisted Copernicus's heliocentric model by using the concept of epicycles to explain away observations of planetary motion that conflicted with their model.) And in this, it seems to me, lies the peculiar danger, the endemic evil, of dogmatic atheism. Take such utterances as "We should not ask for an explanation of how it is that the world exists; it is here and that's all" or "Since we cannot accept a transcendent source of life, we choose to believe the impossible: that life arose spontaneously by chance from matter" or "The laws of physics are 'lawless laws' that arise from the void—end of discussion." They look at first sight like rational arguments that have a special authority because they have a no-nonsense air about them. Of course, this is no more sign that they are either rational or arguments.

Now to make a rational argument that such and such is the case is necessarily to provide reasons to support one's case. Suppose then that we are in doubt what someone who gives vent to an utterance of this sort is arguing, or suppose that, more radically, we are skeptical about whether they are really arguing anything at all, one way of trying to understand their utterance is to attempt to find what evidence, if any, they offer to support the truth of their claims. For if the utterance is indeed rational and an argument, it must indeed provide reasons in its favor from science or philosophy. And anything that would count against the utterance, or which would induce the speaker to withdraw it and to admit that it had been mistaken, must be laid out. But if there is no reason and no evidence offered in its support, then there is no reason or evidence that it is a rational argument.

When the Sage in the parable tells the scientists to investigate all dimensions of the evidence, he was suggesting that a failure to explore what seems prima facie reasonable and promising ipso facto precludes the possibility of a greater understanding of the world beyond the island inhabited by the tribe.

Now it often seems to people who are not atheists as if there is no conceivable piece of evidence that would be admitted by apparently scientific-minded dogmatic atheists to be a sufficient reason for conceding "There might be a God after all." I therefore put to my former fellow-atheists the simple central question: "What would have to occur or to have occurred to constitute for you a reason to at least consider the existence of a superior Mind?"

Laying the Cards on the Table

Moving on now from the parable, it's time for me to lay my cards on the table, to set out my own views and the reasons that support them. I now believe that the universe was brought into existence by an infinite Intelligence. I believe that this universe's intricate laws manifest what scientists have called the Mind of God. I believe that life and reproduction originate in a divine Source.

Why do I believe this, given that I expounded and defended atheism for a half-century? The short answer is this: this is the world picture, as I see it, that has emerged from modern science. Science spotlights three dimensions of nature that point to God. The first is the fact that nature obeys laws. The second is the dimension of life, of intelligently organized and purpose-driven beings, which arose from matter. The third is the very existence of nature. But it is not science alone that has guided me. I have also been helped by a renewed study of the classical philosophical arguments.

My departure from atheism was not occasioned by any new phenomenon or argument. Over the last two decades, my whole framework of thought has been in a state of migration. This was a consequence of my continuing assessment of the evidence of nature. When I finally came to recognize the existence of a God, it was not a paradigm shift, because my paradigm remains, as Plato in his *Republic* scripted his Socrates to insist: "We must follow the argument wherever it leads."

You might ask how I, a philosopher, could speak to issues treated by scientists. The best way to answer this is with another question. Are we engaging in science or philosophy here? When you study the interaction of two physical bodies, for instance, two subatomic particles, you are engaged in science. When you ask how it is that those subatomic particles—or *anything* physical—could exist and why, you are engaged in philosophy. When you draw philosophical conclusions from scientific data, then you are thinking as a philosopher.

Thinking as a Philosopher

So let's apply this insight here. In 2004 I said that the origin of life cannot be explained if you start with matter alone. My critics responded by triumphantly announcing that I had not read a particular paper in a scientific journal or followed a brand-new development relating to abiogenesis (the spontaneous generation of life from nonliving material). In doing so, they missed the whole point. My concern was not with this or that fact of chemistry or genetics, but with the fundamental question of what it means for something to be alive and how this relates to the body of chemical and genetic facts viewed as a whole. To think at this level is to think as a philosopher. And, at the risk of sounding immodest, I must say that this is properly the job of philosophers, not of the scientists as scientists; the competence specific to scientists gives no advantage when it comes to considering this question, just as a star baseball player has no special competence on the dental benefits of a particular toothpaste.

Of course, scientists are just as free to think as philosophers as anyone else. And, of course, not all scientists will agree with my particular interpretation of the facts they generate. But their disagreements will have to stand on their own two philosophical feet. In other words, if they are engaged in philosophical analysis, neither their authority nor their expertise as scientists is of any relevance. This should be easy to see. If they present their views on the economics of science, such as making claims about the number of jobs created by science and technology, they will have to make their case in the court of economic analysis. Likewise, a scientist who speaks as a philosopher will have to furnish a philosophical case. As Albert Einstein himself said, "The man of science is a poor philosopher."[1]

Happily, this is not always the case. The leaders of science over the last hundred years, along with some of today's most influential scientists, have built a philosophically compelling vision of a rational universe that sprang from a divine Mind. As it happens, this is the particular view of the world that I now find to be the soundest philosophical explanation of a multitude of phenomena encountered by scientists and laypersons alike.

Three domains of scientific inquiry have been especially important for me, and I will consider them as we proceed in the light of today's evidence. The first is the question that puzzled and continues to puzzle most reflective scientists: How did the laws of nature come to be? The second is evident to all: How did life as a phenomenon originate from nonlife? And the third is the problem that the philosophers handed over to cosmologists: How did the universe, by which we mean all that is physical, come into existence?

A Recovery of Wisdom

As for my new position on the classical philosophical debates about God, in this area I was persuaded above all by the philosopher David Conway's argument for God's existence in his book *The Recovery of Wisdom: From Here to Antiquity in Quest of Sophia*. Conway is a distinguished British philosopher who is equally at home with classical and modern philosophy.

The God whose existence is defended by Conway and myself is the God of Aristotle. Conway writes:

> In sum, to the Being whom he considered to be the explanation of the world and its broad form. Aristotle ascribed the following attributes: immutability, immateriality, omnipotence, omniscience, oneness or indivisibility, perfect goodness and necessary existence. There is an impressive correspondence between this set of attributes and those traditionally ascribed to God within the Judaeo-Christian tradition. It is one that fully justifies us in viewing Aristotle as having had the same Divine Being in mind as the cause of the world that is the object of worship of these two religions.[2]

As Conway sees it, then, the God of the monotheistic religions has the same attributes as the God of Aristotle.

In his book, Conway attempts to defend what he describes as "the classical conception of philosophy." That conception is "the view that the explanation of the world and its broad form is that it is the creation of a supreme omnipotent and omniscient intelligence, more commonly referred to as God, who created it in order to bring into existence and sustain rational beings."[3] God created the world so as to bring into being a race of rational creatures. Conway believes, and I concur, that it is possible to learn of the existence and nature of this Aristotelian God by the exercise of unaided human reason.

I must stress that my discovery of the Divine has proceeded on a purely natural level, without any reference to supernatural phenomena. It has been an exercise in what is traditionally called natural theology. It has had no connection with any of the revealed religions. Nor do I claim to have had any personal experience of God or any experience that may be called supernatural or miraculous. In short, my discovery of the Divine has been a pilgrimage of reason and not of faith.

Acknowledgments

FIRST OF ALL, I thank Cynthia DiTiberio of HarperOne for suggesting the need for this project, and convincing me to take it on during a brief period between intense intervals of government service in the cause of biomedical research. But I never could have done this by myself. Profound thanks are due to my able colleague and research assistant, Meg Saunders, who spent many hours in the library carefully searching out possible contributions from a long list of potential authors. Her persistence and good judgment turned an almost impossible task into a real learning experience for us both. Thanks also to the Virginia Theological Seminary Library for giving Meg free rein of their remarkable collection. Finally, I would like to acknowledge the thoughtful input about the selection of essays from Alister McGrath and Art Lindsley, both of whom have vast knowledge and experience in the literature of faith and reason. But none of these people should be blamed for the shortcomings of this book; for that, I take full responsibility.

Notes

JOHN LOCKE

1. A *gry* is one-tenth of a line, a line one-tenth of an inch, an inch one-tenth of a philosophical foot, a philosophical foot one-third of a pendulum, whose diadroms, in the latitude of forty-five degrees, are each equal to one second of time, or one-sixtieth of a minute. I have affectedly made use of this measure here, and the parts of it, under a decimal division, with names to them; because I think it would be of general convenience that this should be the common measure in the Commonwealth of Letters.

BLAISE PASCAL

1. By Descartes (1644).
2. By Pico della Mirandola (1486).

JOHN STOTT

1. Quoted by H. J. Blackham in *Humanism* (Harmondsworth: Penguin, 1968), p. 101.
2. 2 Corinthians 10.4–5, Jerusalem Bible.
3. Quoted by *The Times* (London) UN correspondent in New York on December 8, 1959.
4. Psalm 32.9.
5. Psalm 32.9.
6. Psalm 73.22.
7. Proverbs 6.6–11; Isaiah 1.3; Jeremiah 8.7.
8. Ephesians 4.18; Romans 1.18–23; 8.5–8.
9. Isaiah 1.18.
10. Matthew 16.1–4; Luke 12.54–57.
11. Psalm 19.1–4.
12. Romans 1.18–21.
13. James Orr, *The Christian View of God and the World* (Grand Rapids: Eerdmans, 1954), pp. 20–21. First published in 1893.
14. Matthew 11.25.
15. Job 38.3; 40.7.

DAVID ELTON TRUEBLOOD

1. Carl Gustav Jung, *Psychology and Religion* (New Haven: Yale University Press, 1938), p. 113.
2. I am indebted to Cohen and Nagel, *An Introduction to Logic and Scientific Method* (New York/Burlingame: Harcourt Brace World, 1934), for this example.

3. H. W. B. Joseph, *An Introduction to Logic* (Oxford: Clarendon Press), second edition, p. 523.
4. My colleague Professor David L. Webster, chairman of the Department of Physics at Stanford University, provides the following note: "In this sort of verification the repetition of the fallacy must be of the right kind. This may be illustrated by the case of atoms. The first piece of evidence to be discovered for them was the fact that the hypothesis of their existence explained an important law of chemistry, namely the law that in any compound the elements occur in certain fixed proportions. This fact led Dalton, at the opening of the nineteenth century, to state his belief in atoms. The law of fixed proportions was verified anew with the analysis of each new compound, but still for about half the century most scientists remained skeptical about atoms. Their skepticism was the correct attitude for that time, because, if there had been a mistake in the theory that atoms were the cause of the fixed proportions, the mistake would have applied to each new compound as well as to the old ones. This sort of repetition in committing a possible fallacy is useless.

   "On the other hand, near the middle of the century it was found that the hypothesis of the existence of atoms explained also phenomena of a very different sort, namely the changes of pressure of gases, such as the steam in the cylinder of an engine; and soon explanations of other radically different phenomena were added to its list of achievements. If there had been a mistake about the explanation of the fixed proportions in chemistry, that mistake would not have been likely to apply also in the steam engine. The steam engine would have needed a new mistake, independent of the first and pointing also to atoms only by coincidence. Such a coincidence, like doublets in throwing a pair of dice, would have been remarkable, but not extraordinary.

   "As more phenomena pointed to atoms, however, the belief that such mistakes had occurred came to require a coincidence like that of many throws of the dice, all showing the same number. The required coincidence was soon extraordinary and eventually incredible. It is now so very incredible that all reputable scientists find it far easier to believe in atoms, in fact so far easier that they now regard the hypothesis of atom as an established fact.

   "In the intermediate period, however, opinions were divided enough to make a gradual transition, covering about a century, from the time when Dalton stood alone in his belief in atoms to the time when the only unbelievers were a few die-hards generally regarded as eccentric. It would indeed be an interesting study to see what sorts of men believed and what sorts disbelieved when their numbers were nearly alike."

KEITH WARD

1. W. C. Smith, *The Meaning and End of Religion* (New York: Macmillan, 1962), p. 120.
2. Edward Herbert, *De Religione Gentilium* [1663], trans. John Anthony Butler as *Pagan Religion* (Toronto: Dovehouse, 1996), p. 5. A good account is to be found in Peter Byrne, *Natural Religion and the Nature of Religion* (London: Routledge, 1989).
3. See Edward Said, *Orientalism* (Harmondsworth: Penguin, 1985).

ART LINDSLEY

1. C. S. Lewis, *Surprised by Joy: The Shape of My Early Life* (New York: Harcourt Brace, 1984), p. 65.
2. C. S. Lewis, *Mere Christianity* (New York: Touchstone, 1996), pp. 45-46.
3. Lewis, *Mere Christianity,* p. 19.
4. C. S. Lewis, *The Abolition of Man; or, Reflections on Education with Special Reference to the Teaching of English in the Upper Forms of School* (Oxford: Collier, 1947), p. 42.
5. Arthur Allen Leff, "Unspeakable Ethics, Unnatural Law," *Duke Law Journal*, December 1979, pp. 1229–30.
6. Leff, "Unspeakable Ethics, Unnatural Law," p. 1229.
7. Leff, "Unspeakable Ethics, Unnatural Law," p. 1230.
8. Leff, "Unspeakable Ethics, Unnatural Law," p. 1231.
9. Leff, "Unspeakable Ethics, Unnatural Law," p. 1232.
10. Leff, "Unspeakable Ethics, Unnatural Law," p. 1236.
11. Leff, "Unspeakable Ethics, Unnatural Law," p. 1240.
12. Robert Nozick, quoted in Leff, "Unspeakable Ethics, Unnatural Law."
13. Richard Posner, quoted in Leff, "Unspeakable Ethics, Unnatural Law," pp. 1242–43.
14. Posner, quoted in Leff, "Unspeakable Ethics, Unnatural Law," p. 1249.
15. Arthur Koestler, *The Lotus and the Robot* (New York: Harper & Row, 1960), pp. 273–74, quoted in Pat Means, *The Mystical Maze* (San Bernadino, CA: Campus Crusade for Christ, 1976), p. 63.
16. Richard Rorty, "Wild Orchids and Trotsky," in *Wild Orchids and Trotsky: Messages from American Universities,* ed. Mark Edmundson (New York: Penguin, 1993), p. 44.
17. Richard Rorty, "Human Rights, Rationality and Sentimentality," in *The Human Rights Reader*, eds. Walter Laqueur and Barry Rubin (New York: New American Library, 1993), p. 266.
18. James Miller, *The Passion of Michel Foucault* (Cambridge: Harvard University Press, 1993), p. 384.
19. Miller, *The Passion of Michel Foucault.*
20. Acharya Rajneesh, *Beyond and Beyond* (Bombay: Jeevan Jagruti Kendra, 1970), cited in Vishal Mangalwadi, *The World of Gurus* (New Delhi: Nivedit Good Books Distributors, 1987), p. 159.
21. Yun-Men, quoted in Os Guinness, *The East, No Exit* (Downers Grove, IL: InterVarsity Press, 1974), p. 40.
22. Herman Hesse, *Siddhartha,* trans. Hilda Rosner (New York: New Directions, 1951), p. 116.
23. "13 Principles," *Principles of Wiccan Belief,* adopted by Council of American Witches, Spring 1974 Witchmeet, April 11–14, Minneapolis, from *Green Egg,* Box 1542, Ukiah, CA 95482.
24. Erica Jong, *Witches* (New York: Harry N. Abrams, 1981), p. 52, cited in *Christian Research Journal,* summer 1990, p. 26.
25. Starhawk, *The Spiral Dance: A Rebirth of the Ancient Religion of the Great Goddess* (San Francisco: Harper & Row, 1979), pp. 29, 80.
26. Alistair Crowley, cited in Margot Adler, *Drawing Down the Moon: Witches, Druids, Goddess-Worshippers and Other Pagans in America Today* (Boston: Beacon Press, 1979), p. 99.

TIM KELLER

1. Mark Lilla, "Getting Religion: My Long-lost Years as a Teenage Evangelical," in the *New York Times Magazine,* September 18, 2005, pp. 94–95.
2. "If what you want is an argument against Christianity . . . you can easily find some stupid and unsatisfactory Christian and say . . . 'So there's your boasted new man! Give me the old kind.' But if once you have begun to see that Christianity is on other grounds probable, you will know in your heart that this is only evading the issue. What can you ever really know of other people's souls—of their temptations, their opportunities, their struggles? One soul in the whole creation you do know: and it is the only one whose fate is placed in your hands. If there is a God, you are, in a sense, alone with Him. You cannot put Him off with speculations about your next-door neighbors or memories of what you have read in books. What will all that chatter and hearsay count when the anesthetic fog we call 'nature' or 'the real world' fades away and the Divine Presence in which you have always stood becomes palpable, immediate, and unavoidable?" C. S. Lewis, *Mere Christianity* (New York: Macmillan, 1965), p. 168.
3. Christopher Hitchens, *God Is Not Great: How Religion Poisons Everything* (New York: Hachette, 2007), pp. 35–36.
4. Some secular thinkers today insist that every religion has the seeds for oppression within it. This view, however, fails to take into consideration the enormous differences between religious faiths in their views of conversion. Buddhism and Christianity, for example, require a profound inner transformation based on personal decision. Coerced compliance with external rules is seen as spiritually deadly. These faiths, then, are much more likely to seek a society that values religious freedom, so that individuals can learn the truth and give themselves to it freely. Max Weber and others have demonstrated that Christian doctrine, particularly in its Protestant form, provides a basis for individual rights and freedom that is conducive for the growth of both democracy and capitalism. Other philosophies and faiths put much less value on individual freedom of choice. The difference between Christianity and Islam on the meaning of conversion is a case in point. Christian conversion involves coming from only "knowing about" God to "knowing God" personally. Most Muslims would consider it presumptuous to speak of knowing God intimately and personally. A child growing up in a Christian home may nonetheless speak of his or her conversion at age ten or fifteen or twenty. A children growing up in a Muslim home would never speak of being converted to Islam. This difference in understanding means that Christians see little value in putting social pressure on people to convert or to maintain their Christian profession. Islam, however, sees no problem with applying legal and social pressure to keep citizens aligned with Muslim commitments. (Thanks to Don Carson for this insight).
5. Alister McGrath, *The Dawkins Delusion? Atheist Fundamentalism and the Denial of the Divine* (Downers Grove, IL: InterVarsity Press, 2007), p. 81.
6. Merold Westphal, *Suspicion and Faith: The Religious Uses of Modern Atheism* (Grand Rapids, MI: Eerdmans, 1993), chapters 32–34. See page 203: "I would like to . . . accuse Marx of plagiarism. His critique of capi-

talism is, in essence, the biblical concern for widows and orphans, stripped of its theological foundation and applied to the conditions of modernity."

7. Westphal, *Suspicion and Faith,* p. 205.
8. See Proverbs 14.81; 19.17; Matthew 25.31–46. Calvin's remark is from his commentary on Habbakuk 2.6 and is quoted in Westphal, *Suspicion and Faith,* p. 200.
9. C. John Sommerville, *The Decline of the Secular University* (Oxford: Oxford University Press, 2006), p. 63.
10. Sommerville, *The Decline of the Secular University,* pp. 69–70.
11. Sommerville, *The Decline of the Secular University,* p. 70.
12. Rodney Stark, *For the Glory of God: How Monotheism Led to Reformations, Science, Witch-Hunts, and the End of Slavery* (Princeton, NJ: Princeton University Press, 2004), p. 291. See pp. 338–53 for an overview of abolition movements.
13. See Deuteronomy 24.7 and 1 Timothy 1.9–11, which forbids kidnapping. Many people (both inside the Christian church and outside) assume that the Bible supports slavery. For more on this see Chapter 6.
14. See Mark Noll's *The Civil War as a Theological Crisis* (Chapel Hill: University of North Carolina Press, 2006) for an extensive discussion of how Christians debated slavery through different interpretations of the Scripture. Noll's book demonstrates how some church leaders used texts in the Bible regarding slavery to justify the slave trade. But they were blind to the stark differences between African chattel slavery and the bond-service and indentured servanthood treated in the Bible.
15. Stark, *For the Glory of God,* pp. 350ff.
16. David L. Chappell, *A Stone of Hope: Prophetic Religion and the Death of Jim Crow* (Chapel Hill: University of North Carolina Press, 2003).
17. A narrative of the Catholic church's resistance to Communism in the 1970s and 1980s is given in Chapter 17 in "Between Two Crosses," in Charles Colson and Ellen Vaughn, *The Body* (Nashville, TN: Thomas Nelson, 2003).
18. Dietrich Bonhoeffer, *Letters and Papers from Prison: Enlarged Edition,* Eberhard Bethge, ed. (New York: Macmillan, 1971), p. 418.

JOHN POLKINGHORNE

1. J. C. Polkinghorne, *The Quantum World* (New York/Princeton, NJ: Longman/Princeton University Press, 1984); *Rochester Roundabout* (New York: Longman/W. H. Freeman, 1989).
2. J. C. Polkinghorne, *The Way the World Is* (Newton, MA/Grand Rapids: Triangle/Eerdmans, 1983); *Science and Christian Belief/The Faith of a Physicist* (London/Princeton, NJ: SPCK/Princeton University Press, 1994).
3. J. C. Polkinghorne, *Rochester Roundabout,* chapter 21; *Reason and Reality* (London: SPCK/Trinity Press International, 1991), chapters 1 and 2; *Beyond Science* (New York: Cambridge University Press, 1996), chapter 2; *Belief in God in an Age of Science* (New Haven and London: Yale University Press, 1998), chapters 2 and 5.
4. The superposition principle allows the addition of A and not-A to produce a middle term undreamed of by Aristotle; see Polkinghorne, *Quantum World,* chapter 3.

5. See note 1.
6. S. W. Hawking, *A Brief History of Time* (New York: Bantam, 1988), p. 141.
7. T. Kuhn, *The Structure of Scientific Revolutions* (Chicago: Chicago University Press, 1970).
8. Polkinghorne, *Beyond Science,* chapter 8.
9. J. Monod, *Chance and Necessity* (New York: Collins, 1972).
10. S. Weinberg, *Dreams of a Final Theory* (New York: Hutchinson, 1993), chapter 11.
11. Monod, *Chance and Necessity,* p. 167.
12. See, for instance, Polkinghorne, *Quantum World,* chapters 6 and 8.
13. See note 8.
14. See, for instance, J. Leslie, *Universes* (London: Routledge, 1989).
15. S. Kauffman, *At Home in the Universe* (Oxford: Oxford University Press, 1995).
16. See Polkinghorne, *Christian Belief/Faith,* chapter 10.
17. W. James, *The Varieties of Religious Experience* (London: Collins, 1960).
18. S. Weinberg, *The First Three Minutes* (Glasgow: A. Deutsch, 1977), p. 149.

C. S. LEWIS

1. The book of Revelation.
2. The book of Revelation 6.14.
3. The book of Revelation 20.11.
4. The book of Revelation 19.20; 20.10; 20.14–15; 21.8.
5. Matthew 1.19.
6. Matthew 14.26; Mark 6.49; John 6.19.
7. Lewis is referring to the story that angels appeared, protecting British troops in their retreat from Mons, France, on August 26, 1914. A recent summary of the event by Jill Kitson, "Did Angels Appear to British Troops at Mons?" is found in *History Makers,* No. 3 (1969), pp. 132–33.
8. 2 Kings 19.35.
9. Herodotus, Bk. II, Sect. 141.
10. John 5.19.
11. John 2.1–11.
12. Matthew 14.15–21; Mark 6.34–44; Luke 9.12–17; John 6.1–11.
13. Matthew 4.3; Luke 4.3.
14. Matthew 21.19; Mark 11.13–20.
15. For further information on this subject see the chapter on "Genius and Genius" in Lewis's *Studies in Medieval and Renaissance Literature,* ed. Walter Hooper (Cambridge: Cambridge, 1966), pp. 169–74.
16. The reference is to Ovid's (43 BC–AD 18) *Metamorphoses.*
17. The fairy tales of the brothers Jacob Ludwig Carl (1785–1863) and Wilhelm Carl (1786–1859) Grimm.
18. For example, Romans 8.22: "We know that the whole creation groaneth and travaileth in pain together until now."
19. Matthew 17.1–9; Mark 9.2–10.
20. Matthew 14.26; Mark 6.49; John 6.19.
21. Luke 24.13–31, 36–7; John 20.14–16.

22. Mark 16.14; Luke 24.31, 36; John 20.19, 26.
23. Luke 24.42–3; John 21.13.
24. Arthur Schrödinger (1887–1961), the Austrian physicist.
25. This is probably a misquotation of Wordsworth's "Moving about in worlds not realized" from *Intimations of Immortality.*
26. Matthew 12.39; 16.4; 24.24, 30; Mark 13.22; 16.17, 20; Luke 21.11, 25.
27. Matthew 26.26; Mark 14.22; Luke 22.19; I Corinthians 11.24.
28. *Sixteen Revelations of Divine Love,* ed. Roger Hudleston (London: Burns, Oates, & Washbourne, 1927), p. 9.
29. See Letter 3.

THOMAS MERTON

1. *Sancti Thomae huc omnis theologia spectat ut ad intime vivendum in Deo nos adducat.* Pius XI, *Studiorum Ducem,* June 29, 1927.

DIETRICH BONHOEFFER

1. A.F.C. Vilmar, 1880.

VIKTOR FRANKL

1. It was the first version of my first book, the English translation of which was published by Alfred A. Knopf, New York, in 1955, under the title *The Doctor and the Soul: An Introduction to Logotherapy.*
2. Magda B. Arnold and John A. Gasson, *The Human Person* (New York: Ronald Press, 1954), p. 618.

MOTHER TERESA

1. *A Gift for God,* pp. 64–65.
2. *Total Surrender,* pp. 36–37.
3. *Mother Teresa: Her Life, Her Works,* p. 137.
4. *In the Heart of the World,* pp. 65–66.
5. *Words to Love By,* p. 35.

MAHATMA GANDHI

1. The story of the young boy Prahlad, who suffered for the Truth's sake, is one of the most famous in ancient Indian literature. It is well known by every Indian child—just as the story of George Washington is famous in the West.
2. Bread made without yeast—somewhat like a pancake.

HANS KÜNG

1. S. Freud, *Die Zukunft einer Illustion* in *Studienausgabe* 9:169. (*The Future of an Illustion* in *S.E.* 21 [1961]: 35.)
2. Cf. A. Gorres, "Alles spricht dafur, nichts Haltbares dagegen. Kritische Reflexionen eines Analytikers uber den christlichen Glauben" in H. Zahrnt (ed.), *Jesus und Freud. Ein Symposium von Psychoanalytikern und Theologen* (Munich: R. Piper & Co. Verlag, 1972), pp. 36–52.

3. S. Freud, *Die Zukunft einer Illusion* in *Studienausgabe* 9:187. (*The Future of an Illusion* in *S.E.* 21 [1964]: 54.)
4. Freud, *Die Zukunft einer Illusion* 9:188. (*S.E.* 21:54–55.)
5. Freud, *Die Zukunft einer Illusion* 9:188. (*S.E.* 21:54–55.)
6. Freud, *Die Zukunft einer Illusion* 9:198. (*S.E.* 21:56.)
7. G. R. Taylor, *The Doomsday Book* (London: Thames & Hudson, 1970); S. Kirban, *Die geplante Verwirrung* (Wetzlar: Schulte Verlag, 1972); G. Ehrensvard, *Nach uns die Steinzeit. Das Ende des technischen Zeitalters* (Bern: Hallwag, 1972); D. Widener, *Kein Platz fur Menschen. Das programmierte Selbstmord* (Frankfurt: Fischer, 1972); E. E. Snyder, *Todeskandidat Erde. Programmierter Selbstmord durch unkontrollierten Fortschritt* (Munich: Heyne, 1972); M. Lohmann (ed.), *Gefahrdete Zukunft* (Munich: Carl Hanser Verlag, 1973; H. Gruhl, *Ein Planet wird geplundert. Die Schreckensbilanz unserer Politik* (Frankfurt: Fischer, 1976).
8. In this connection cf. S. Freud, *Das Unbehagen in der Kultur* (1930) in *Studienausgabe* 9:191–270. (*Civilisation and Its Discontents* in *S.E.* 21 [1961]: 56–145.)
9. Cf. H. Küng, *Christ sein* (Munich: Piper, 1974); DI: "Die Praxis der Kirche." (*On Being a Christian* [New York: Doubleday, 1976/London, 1977]; D I: "The Practice of the Church.")

ALVIN PLANTINGA

1. Reviewed elsewhere in this issue by Douglas Groothuis, in a piece covering four books dealing with atheism in one fashion or another.
2. Coauthored with Alvin Plantinga in Blackwell's Great Debates in Philosophy series (Blackwell, 2008).
3. Letter to William Graham (Down, July 3, 1881), in *The Life and Letters of Charles Darwin,* ed. Francis Darwin (London: John Murray, 1887), Volume 1, pp. 315–16.
4. Here I'll just give the bare essentials of the argument; for fuller statements, see my *Warranted Christian Belief* (Oxford: Oxford University Press, 2000), chapter 7; or my contribution to *Knowledge of God* (Blackwell, 2008); or *Natural Selection and the Problem of Evil (The Great Debate),* edited by Paul Draper, www.infidels.org/library/modern/paul_draper/evil.html or (best of all) the last couple of chapters of my forthcoming book *Religion and Science: Where the Conflict Really Lies.*
5. If you don't think naturalism does include materialism, then take my argument as for the conclusion that you can't sensibly accept the tripartite conjunction of naturalism, evolution, and materialism.
6. "Epistemology in the Age of Neuroscience," *Journal of Philosophy,* Vol. 84 (October 1987), pp. 548–49.
7. My thanks to Paul Zwier, who performed the calculations.
8. See, for example, *Naturalism Defeated?,* ed. James Beilby (Ithaca: Cornell University Press, 2002), which contains some ten essays by critics of the argument, together with my replies to their objections.

ANTONY FLEW

1. Albert Einstein, *Out of My Later Years* (New York: Philosophical Library, 1950), p. 58.
2. David Conway, *The Rediscovery of Wisdom* (London: Macmillan, 2000), p. 74.
3. Conway, *The Rediscovery of Wisdom*, pp. 2–3.

Credits and Permissions

Every effort has been made to obtain permissions for pieces quoted in this work. If any required acknowledgments have been omitted, or any rights overlooked, it is unintentional. Please notify the publishers of any omission, and it will be rectified in future editions.

N. T. WRIGHT

Simply Christian by N. T. Wright. Copyright © 2006 by N. T. Wright. Reprinted by permission of HarperCollins Publishers. Published in the UK by SPCK.

PLATO

Plato and the Christians, trans. by Adam Fox, © SCM Press 1957. Used by permission.

AUGUSTINE OF HIPPO

Taken from *Classical Readings in Christian Apologetics* by L. Russ Bush. Copyright © 1983 by The Zondervan Corporation. Used by permission of Zondervan.

ANSELM OF CANTERBURY

"That God Truly Exists" (pp. 87–89) from *Anselm of Canterbury: The Major Works Oxford World's Classics* edited by Davies, B. & Evans, G.R. (1998)

BLAISE PASCAL

Pensées by Blaise Pascal, translated with a revised introduction by A. J. Krailsheimer (Penguin Classics 1966, Revised edition 1995). Copyright © A. J. Krailsheimer, 1966, 1995. Reproduced by permission of Penguin Books Ltd.

OS GUINNESS

Os Guinness, *Time for Truth: Living Free in a World of Lies, Hype & Spin,* originally published by Hourglass Books, a division of Baker Publishing Group © 2000.

MADELEINE L'ENGLE

Reprinted from *The Rock That Is Higher.* Copyright © 1993, 2003 by Crosswicks. Used by permission of WaterBrook Press, Colorado Springs, CO. All rights reserved.

DOROTHY L. SAYERS

Reprinted by permission. *Christian Letters to a Post-Christian World: A Selection of Essays,* by Dorothy Sayers, selected and introduced by Roderick Jellema, copyright 1969, Thomas Nelson Inc. Nashville, Tennessee. All rights reserved.

Reprinted "The Persona Dei: the image of truth" by Dorothy Sayers from *Dorothy L. Sayers Spiritual Writings,* selected and introduced by Ann Loades, SPCK, London, England. Permission granted by Ann Loades.

JOHN STOTT

Your Mind Matters by John Stott, published by InterVarsity Press (IVP).

DAVID ELTON TRUEBLOOD

The Knowledge of God by David Elton Trueblood. Copyright © 1939 by Harper & Brothers, Renewed 1967 by D. Elton Trueblood. Reprinted by permission of HarperCollins Publishers.

KEITH WARD

The Case for Religion by Keith Ward, published by Oneworld 2004.

ART LINDSLEY

Taken from *True Truth Defending Absolute Truth in a Relativistic World* by Art Lindsley. Copyright © 2004 by Art Lindsley. Used by permission of InterVarsity Press, P.O. Box, 1400 Downers Grove, IL 60515. www.ivpress.com.

DESMOND TUTU

From *God Has a Dream: A Vision of Hope for Our Time* by Desmond Tutu and Douglas Abrams, copyright © 2004 by Desmond Tutu. Used by permission of Doubleday, a division of Random House, Inc.

ELIE WIESEL

Evil and Exile by Elie Wiesel and Philippe de Saint-Cheron. Copyright © 1990 by Elie Wiesel. Reprinted by permission of Georges Borchardt, Inc., on behalf of the authors.

TIM KELLER

"The Church Is Responsible for So Much Injustice" from *The Reason for God* by Timothy Keller, copyright © 2008 by Timothy Keller. Used by permission of Dutton, a division of Penguin Group (USA) Inc. Published in the UK and used by permission of Hodder and Stoughton Limited.

MARTIN LUTHER KING JR.

Reprinted by arrangement with The Heirs to the Estate of Martin Luther King Jr., c/o Writers House as agent for the proprietor, New York, NY, copyright 1963, Dr. Martin Luther King Jr., copyright renewed 1991, Coretta Scott King.

PAUL BRAND

Taken from *Fearfully and Wonderfully Made* by Philip D. Yancey; Estate of Paul W. Brand. Copyright © 1980 by Paul Brand and Philip Yancey. Used by permission of Zondervan.

JOHN POLKINGHORNE

John Polkinghorne and Michael Welker, *Faith in the Living God: A Dialogue,* © John Polkinghorne and Michael Welker 2001, admin. Augsburg Fortress. Used by permission. Published in the UK by Society for Promoting Christian Knowledge, used by permission of SPCK.

C. S. LEWIS

Miracles by C. S. Lewis, copyright © C. S. Lewis Pte. Ltd. 1947, 1960. Extract reprinted by permission.

ALISTER MCGRATH

Extract taken from *Glimpsing the Face of God* by Alister McGrath, published by Lion. Copyright © 2002 Alister McGrath. Used with permission of Lion Hudson plc.

THOMAS MERTON

Excerpt from "Mysticism in Man's Life" from *The Ascent to Truth* by Thomas Merton, copyright © 1951 by The Abbey of Our Lady of Gethsemani and renewed 1979 by the Trustees of the Merton Legacy Trust, reprinted by permission of Harcourt, Inc. and Curtis Brown, Ltd.

DIETRICH BONHOEFFER

Reprinted with the permission of Scribner, a Division of Simon & Schuster, Inc., from *The Cost of Discipleship* by Dietrich Bonhoeffer (translated from the German by R. H. Fuller, with revisions by Irmgard Booth). Copyright © 1959 by SCM Press Ltd. All rights reserved.

VIKTOR FRANKL

Man's Search for Meaning by Viktor E. Frankl. Copyright © 1959, 1962, 1984, 1992 by Viktor E. Frankl. Reprinted by permission of Beacon

Press, Boston. Published in the UK by Rider. Reprinted by permission of the Random House Group Ltd.

MOTHER TERESA

A Gift for God: Prayers and Meditations by Mother Teresa of Calcutta. Copyright © 1975 by Mother Teresa Missionaries of Charity. Reprinted by permission of HarperCollins Publishers.

Taken from *Mother Teresa: Total Surrender,* copyright 1985, by Mother Teresa and edited by Brother Angelo Devananda Scolozzi. Reprinted with permission of St. Anthony Messenger Press, 28 W. Liberty St., Cincinnati, OH 45202. To order copies call 1–800–488–0488 or visit www.servantbooks.org.

From the book *In the Heart of the World.* Copyright © 1997 New World Library. Reprinted with permission of New World Library, Novato, CA. www.newworldlibrary.com.

From the book *Mother Teresa: Her Life, Her Works* by Lush Gjergji, New City Press, Hyde Park, NY. © 1991

Mother Teresa, *Words to Love By,* Notre Dame, Ind.: Ave Maria Press, 1983.

MAHATMA GANDHI

Mahatma Gandhi Essays and Reflections on His Life and Work, Edited by S. Radhakrishnan, George Allen & Unwin Ltd, London, 1949.

THE DALAI LAMA (TENZIN GYATSO)

From *The Universe in a Single Atom: The Convergence of Science and Spirituality* by His Holiness The Dalai Lama, Copyright © 2005 The Dalai Lama. Used by permission of an imprint of The Doubleday Broadway Publishing, a division of Random House, Inc.

HANS KUNG

Hans Küng, Translated by Edward Quinn, *Freud and the Problem of God,* Yale University Press © 1990.

ALVIN PLANTINGA

Evolution vs. Naturalism: Why They Are Like Oil and Water. Reprinted by permission of Alvin Plantinga.

ANTONY FLEW

There Is a God by Antony Flew and Roy Abraham Varghese. Copyright © 2007 by Antony Flew. Reprinted by permission of HarperCollins Publishers.